Jim Marshall

THE FATHER OF LOUD

THE STORY OF THE MAN BEHIND THE WORLD'S MOST FAMOUS GUITAR AMPLIFIERS

BY RICH MALOOF

San Francisco

Published by Backbeat Books
600 Harrison Street, San Francisco, CA 94107
www.backbeatbooks.com
email: books@musicplayer.com

An imprint of the Music Player Network
Publishers of *Guitar Player, Bass Player, Keyboard,* and other magazines
United Entertainment Media, Inc.
A CMP Information company

Distributed to the book trade in the US and Canada by
Publishers Group West, 1700 Fourth Street, Berkeley, CA 94710

Distributed to the music trade in the US and Canada by
Hal Leonard Publishing, P.O. Box 13819, Milwaukee, WI 53213

Text design by Michael Cutter
Composition by Michael Cutter, Michael Baughan, Nancy Tabor, and Damien Castaneda
Cover design by Richard Leeds – BigWigDesign.com
Cover photos courtesy Marshall Amplification/Korg USA

Library of Congress Control Number: 2003063782

ISBN: 0-87930-803-6

Printed in Canada

04 05 06 07 08 5 4 3 2 1

Table of Contents

Foreword by Slash

Pretty much from the very first moment I got into actually playing guitar, I just knew that the *only* way I was going to get that fat, warm, rock 'n' roll, "*A* chord" sound I wanted was from a Marshall. How did I know that? It was pretty *$#%ing obvious, really. Everyone I thought sounded cool—from Jimi Hendrix to Aerosmith, and everybody in between—all had Marshalls. So for me, and for many others, it was simple—if you wanted to have that "thing" and be as great as the guitarists you listened to and went to see in concert, then you just had to have that one quintessential piece of equipment: a Marshall. And there were no ifs, ands, buts, or in-betweens about it. So, from that moment on my main goal was to get enough money together to be able to afford one. Needless to say, I went through years and years of trying to get my first Marshall. . . .

I can still remember the first time I ever plugged into one—it was amazing, a truly life-changing experience. The only problem was it wasn't mine; it was someone else's, and that's sort of like driving another guy's Ferrari when your *$#%ing car is a Honda Civic! I eventually got a Marshall of my own and it was, of course, a used one—a 50-watt Super Lead head. It sounded killer, and I'll never forget it because I felt like I'd achieved a lifelong goal.

I find it fascinating that there's this one make of amp that's been the standard of the industry for so long. No matter what people do to try to come up with something that sounds like it, or better than it, or something that's a little more complex or whatever, they always miss the mark. I mean, your typical Marshall is by no means a complicated amplifier, but, at the same time, it has a characteristic to it that seems to be inimitable. There's something so unique about a Marshall that you

High-powered combo: Slash and Jim.

can almost picture the sound, if you know what I mean! It's the only amp that's ever done that.

I'm not totally closed-minded, but I'm also one of those "if it ain't broke, don't fix it" kind of guys, too. I have to admit that I'm a little biased when it comes to Marshall, but I *do* keep my ears and mind open, and I do listen to what people say about this, that, and the other. But, that all said, I still haven't heard anything else that does it for me. There's a relationship between what's going on in your head, what's coming out through your fingers on your instrument, and then what's actually coming out of the speakers. It's all relative and, all things considered, you can play through a whole bunch of different things, but, personally speaking, for me to sound like "me," I have to have a Marshall to do it—that's just the way it is.

In addition to sounding great, Marshall has a visual aura that's *#$%ing larger than life too. To me the all-time best English heavy metal band is Judas Priest, and that wall of Marshalls they had set up on their *Screaming for Vengeance* tour when I saw them at Long Beach Arena in the early '80s, was probably one of the most exciting visuals for a young rock guitar player to ever see. I'll certainly never forget it. And that goes for a lot of other great bands, too, over the years—even on a smaller scale like at the local L.A. clubs like the Troubadour and the Roxy. Even if you didn't know who the band was, they were automatically cool if they had Marshalls. When you're young and impressionable, when you walk into a club and see a Marshall on the stage, you're awed before a single note has been played because you know you're gonna hear some loud guitar! And, back in the day, you also knew that the chances were high that the guy was gonna be great too, because if you could afford to have a Marshall, then you had to be pretty good! That was certainly true on two memorable occasions—Quiet Riot at the Starwood when Randy Rhoads was still in the band, and early Van Halen.

Like I said earlier, it's amazing for a piece of equipment to stand the test of time and become such an iconic thing. I still wonder to this day if Jim realized that he was about to create a musician's staple for the next *$%#ing 40-plus years when he stuck the tubes in his very first amp?!

The equipment aside, over the years I've been fortunate enough to have Jim take me under his wing, so to speak, build an amp for me during a time of crisis, and then put my name on it. That's one of my proudest moments since I got this whole rock thing going and is probably the most flattering gesture ever put towards me. Then, as a bonus, I've gotten to hang out with Jim a bunch of times and discover that he's charming and down-to-earth with a great blue-collar "I work for a living" ethic. He's someone who's never been affected by his success and is still totally focused on the quality of the amps that bear his name. He's also very kind and soft-spoken—not someone you'd expect to make the loudest, rudest guitar amp in the world!

As far as I'm concerned, Jim and Les Paul are kindred spirits. They're definitely cut from the same cloth, and the heart and soul they've both poured into their gear makes me feel very proud to be using it. With all the craziness and bullshit that goes on in this business, it's reassuring to know that the things you keep closest to you are made by genuinely nice people. That's why I'm beyond honored to have been asked to write this foreword.

Thanks for everything, Jim. I'm darn proud to be part of such a great rock 'n' roll story.

Cheers; your friend—

Preface & Acknowledgments

This book is an homage to Jim Marshall even more than to the famous amplifiers that carry his name. Conceived, written, and published in 2003, it's one way of wishing Jim a happy 80th birthday. Eighty years old—and still we were chasing him around the globe to record the story of his life. Happily, there are chapters yet to be written.

A great deal has already been inked about Marshall amplifiers in magazines and in books. However, the details of Jim's life have largely gone untold. Part I constitutes a complete biography as learned firsthand. Part II updates the history of Marshall amplifiers and corrects a substantial amount of erroneous information that has appeared in print or otherwise snuck into Marshall mythology. While not exceedingly technical by design, the section also explains what goes on under the hood of a Marshall. I believe that knowing how an engine works makes one a better driver.

My hope is that *Jim Marshall: The Father of Loud* is enjoyed by amp lovers and gear nuts as well as laymen and fans. If I may suggest, it is recommended for reading the day after a great live show, whether you played it or watched it, when you have a noise hangover and need something quiet to do—or want to know who to blame.

Jim Marshall: The Father of Loud was researched and written inside of two months, which evokes in this writer both pride and deep fear. Two reams of paper and one case of Diet Coke later, I'm finished. It was a welcome assignment I could never have completed on my own.

My thanks foremost to Jim Marshall, who in the summer of '03 graciously endured my endless stream of inquiry. The time spent with him in Bletchley, on a tour of his old West London haunts, and in New York formed the backbone of this book. Thank you, Jim, for your time, for your insight, and for the Scotch (good lord, for the Scotch).

Richard Johnston at Backbeat Books provided the opportunity to write and the freedom to pursue my own vision. An author could not ask for more. For these reasons, among others, he is a prized editor . . . and hereby indemnified. Thanks also to Backbeat's Nancy Tabor and Kate Henderson.

Nick Bowcott has been indispensable from the start and indefatigable to the end. He has opened many doors for me on both sides of the Atlantic, and there would be no book without him. Amid the many long hours he toiled on this project, those he spent on Chapter 5's gear roundups, Chapter 6's amp-anatomy section, Chapter 7's Top 11 list, and Chapter 8's diagrams deserve particular mention. Nick's own adventures, both as a musician and as Product Manager for Marshall, deserve a book of their own.

At Korg USA, Mike Kovins and Mitch Colby championed this project, and Ryan Rhodes, Joe Gilmartin, Jimmy Gumina, Leslie Buttonow, Laura Whitmore, Larry DeMarco, Hugh Gilmartin, and Jennifer Plonski all made crucial contributions.

Thank you to the staff at Marshall headquarters in Bletchley, including Chris Parsons, Emma Lovelock, Paul Hayhoe (whose fine photographs constitute the factory tour in Chapter 6), Steve Greenwood, Gary Lovelock, Phil Wells (product datelines), Bruce Keir, Ian "Binson" Robinson, Joel Richardson, Richard "Dickie" Frost, Paul Tait, and Jon Ellery.

Thanks to Mr. John Kent, who chauffeured Jim, Nick Bowcott, and me around London and tried his damnedest to drive the length of the old Silverdale Road despite the fact that buildings had since been constructed in our path.

My further appreciation to:

Harvey Newquist, who volleyed this opportunity my way; Pete Prown for his research and contributions; Christine Corso for tirelessly transcribing interviews; Pauline Ball; Jean Bowcott; Ann Everitt at Invest In Milton Keynes; Jon Chappell; and the many players who contributed to Chapter 8.

The writers whose magazine interviews have been quoted: Nick Bowcott (Jim Marshall and others), Harvey Newquist (Pete Townshend), Pete Prown (Jim Marshall),

Steve Rosen (Ritchie Blackmore, Jimmy Page), Lisa Sharken (Jeff Beck). Books by Michael Doyle, Ritchie Fliegler, Aspen Pittman, and Gerald Weber have been valuable resources.

The breakfast jerks, for their encouragement; Jeff Higgins for the inspiring Churchill words in the book's final weeks.

Finally, to Kris for the support, the patience, the lost vacations, and for always having understood that music is the other woman.

This book is dedicated to my parents, Mitchell and Teresa Maloof, who long ago instilled in me the same value I admire most in Jim Marshall: Independence.

– Rich Maloof

Introduction

B.B. King's Blues Bar & Grill
New York, New York, September 2003

Anyone who loyally makes a point of catching Jeff Beck live knows that he's always good—but seldom appears to be having a very good time. While reverent guitarists watch him, dumbfounded, those familiar with his passions can't help but think the man would rather be under the hood of a roadster adjusting a carburetor.

But tonight, at the farewell performance following his terrifically successful U.S. tour with B.B. King, Beck is turned on and turned up. To the thrill of the crowd, he grins like a schoolkid and punches the air to celebrate bandmates Terry Bozzio on drums and Tony Hymas on keys. The trio has been locked in the pocket all night, and Beck is urged to the top of his abilities. His leads are liquid and airy, but he'll stop them mid-arc with a chirp, a squawk, a throaty roar. The odd genius of his playing emanates from a single Marshall DSL50, legacy of the 50-watt Marshalls he first played in the '60s. Even at his most aggressive Beck is all about nuance and inflection, and the Marshall faithfully represents the range of his sonic palette, from bruising rock jabs to crystalline funk rhythms to the round, gentle melodies he delivers in quieter moments.

In some ways Beck is the prototypical Marshall player; in other ways, the antithesis. His image deserves to be chiseled alongside the other Mt. Rushmore guitarists: Hendrix, Page, and Clapton. But he is also the perpetual outsider who has spent years looking for a comfortable home for his music. Onstage at B.B. King's club, Beck is right in character. It's as if he is forever looking for a better way: His lines are deliberate, but searching; confident, but phrased more like questions than statements.

The tireless pursuit of his own voice is what the crowd loves him for, and the room is full of disciples who have studied his chops through two, three, even four decades of mastery and risk. All these years later, they respond with the familiar blend of inspiration and resignation—filing out of the club, they'll decide whether to dust off their guitars tomorrow, or sell them, or hand them over to their kids. Such is the fate of the non-Becks. They admire him not for accomplishments recalled from their own glory days, but for his continued dedication to creative independence.

The resilience of Marshall Amplification matches Beck's own, note for note and year for year. While still prized among the heavy set, Marshalls have long been objects of desire across rock's wide spectrum. Forty years after Mr. Jim Marshall sold his first JTM45, three generations of guitarists and fans revere the name. It's the amp of the baby boomer's hero, the baby boomer, and his kid.

It's a simple story, really. A handful of brash British youths needed a new sound for a new kind of music. They marched into a music store in their blue-collar town and asked the gentleman behind the counter to build them an amplifier with leg-shaking power and jaw-dropping tone. So he did.

Marshall Amplification may have had modest beginnings, but they weren't humble. From the start, Marshall was the Father of Loud.

Part I

Chapter 1

A Young Man in London

For most, North Kensington is a place to pass through on the way to somewhere else. That is the legacy of the town, which sits about 20 minutes outside of downtown London, England. It lies along an historically well-trod path between London proper and Oxford. The Grand Junction Canal, dug early in the nineteenth century, before the railways, once provided the only route for transporting coal to and from the Midlands. Today, the low-running canal is little more than a traffic problem, its bridges congested throughout most of the day.

The working-class town is just a few miles from the upscale Kensington area off Hyde Park, but a world apart. It's classic blue-collar: modest, neatly kept row homes neighbored by the carbon-stained walls of industry. A mix of immigrants, predominantly Caribbean, Spanish, and Irish, share the town while keeping to their own, though racial clashes flash every quarter century. Light trucks wend their way through the streets, dodging the freeway's perpetual traffic jam and off-loading at metal shops and construction depots. A corner pub fills up with factory workers after the 5:00 p.m. whistle. Some kids kick a dirty ball around a clearing that's sadly lacking in grass. It's home to some, for others a place to leave at the end of the day. North Kensington is rough around the edges.

The first door on the left is 19 Snarsgate Street, where the Marshalls lived in 1923.

The town today is not much different than it was 80 years ago, when Beatrice and Jim Marshall had their first child, James Charles, on July 29, 1923. They lived in a small house on Snarsgate Street, a dead-end street off a dead-end street. The short block is lined with row houses, about 15 on a side, until the low stone wall at the block's end. Here, at 19 Snarsgate, little James was cared for by his mother, aunt, and grandmother alike. "I remember my Aunt Mary carrying me down the stairs," says Jim, recounting his earliest memory. "I was scared stiff. I was afraid I'd fall." But Jim's toddler years were happy ones, spent in the company of his extended family, and his memories are warm. Around the corner from Snarsgate Street stood the Pavilion Pub, a cavernous mahogany room that served relief from the day's labor in

James Charles Marshall at age 3, with his mother and infant sister.

the form of Scotch and pints of ale. On a recent visit, Jim beamed to find the Pavilion still in business.

"We used to come around here every Sunday after church, when the pub opened. All my relations—my father and uncles—used to come here to drink together. We children used to sit around in the space out front and play, occasionally sneaking a peek inside. We'd have soft drinks and, if we were lucky, they'd bring something out for us to eat as well."

Most every pub in London had live music, and Jim remembers the sounds of jazz mixed with the clinking of empty pint glasses inside. His father and uncles were all boxers, and Jim's father was the sparring partner of a prizefighter. He must have enjoyed his Sundays off.

Jim outside the Pavilion, where he used to play with his cousins.

Trapped in plaster

In 1928, at the age of five, Jim was diagnosed with a rare condition known as "tubercular bones." The terminology is unspecific and now antiquated, but the impact was acute: The bones throughout Jim's body were fragile and hypersensitive to pressure. Though he had survived a tumble through a second-floor railing, the boy was in danger of doing himself long-term harm.

It's not overstating to say the condition robbed Jim of his childhood. From the age of five through the age of twelve and a half, his body was encased in plaster. The cast covered him from his ankles to his armpits. Jim lay in Stanmore Orthopedic Hospital for seven years.

Perhaps because those years were so empty, few memories have stayed with Jim. He remembers his uncle tutoring him in the fundamentals of reading and writing. His parents, and later his younger sister, would ride bicycles up to the hospital for visits on Sundays. The nurses were kind and there was a funny man who cleaned the ward, but it was impossible for Jim to develop lasting friendships with kids his age—few of them occupied nearby beds for more than a month or two. Games were limited to those he could manage flat on his back in bed. Every three months Jim was cut out of the plaster so that a new one could be refitted with room for him to grow. His quarterly freedom lasted a few minutes each time.

It must have been a happy day when Jim was finally cut free for good. But it wasn't exactly boon times beyond the hospital doors. The Marshall household was feeling the crush of recession; nearly ten years after the fall of the US stock market in 1929, the Western world was still suffering through the Great Depression. The family had since moved to Western Road in Southall, where Jim Sr. managed a fish-and-chips shop. Jim had been out of the hospital and in school for just six weeks when his father needed to move the family.

"I'd been put in the top class when I came out of Stanmore, but until then I'd really had no education. When we moved to the new location, where my father was going to open another fish-and-chips, he said, 'Right, son, got to find you another school.' I said, 'Dad, is it worth it? I don't understand what they're talking about.' He said, 'I'd have the authorities after me....'"

Jim managed to talk his dad out of school and into his first job. By age 13, young Jim had left school to help make a living for his family and himself working in the fish-and-chips shop. Though it seems an especially young age, students in 1930s England graduated school by age 14, so Jim really missed little in school. Besides, after seven years in a cast, who wants to sit still for arithmetic?

Jim's entrance into the workforce marks the beginning of a versatile and remarkably industrious career. From this time forward, work would define and dominate his life. Maybe there was a great reserve of energy and potential stored up from years in a hospital bed that had to be actualized. Jim asserts that his primary impetus was

Jim's father managed a fish-and-chips shop in a Southall storefront that's now a tailor's.

Jim with friend at age 13.

to build a life better than the one he had. He had seen his father in and out of jobs, battling the Depression economy.

"In my mind I thought, 'I'm not going to be like my father.' Because my father was always out of work, you see. This was 1937, and it was difficult for him to get a job. I thought, 'I'm not going to be like that.' So I worked as soon as I could. Then in the mornings at four o'clock I was filling milk bottles for Idris Jones, who did all the milk for around that area, and I was working at a jam factory during the day."

Boiling jam and pouring milk was just the start. Throughout his teenage years and into his twenties, Jim would hold down two or three jobs at a time. He was routinely up before the sun and working into the night, always spending thriftily and saving his earnings—for what, he did not yet know. He worked in scrap yards and biscuit factories, he sliced meat in a canning factory. He sold shoes and made deliveries and manned machines that built batteries.

Singing

And he sang. Believe it or not, the man behind the world's loudest bands got his start in music as a silky-voiced crooner. The story of his being discovered is a milestone in Marshall's life, and a hopeful tale to most anyone who's played a talent show.

"I was discovered as a singer when I was 14. I had been attending classes at a tap dancing school, and it was parents' night," says Jim, who'd taken up tap at his father's suggestion, to help strengthen his legs after all that time in plaster. "I already knew the girls in the troupe, of course, because we all went to the lessons. Everyone went for individual lessons, and then the teacher would get you as a group. In rehearsal, the teacher had a presentation of girls on the stage at the same time, all

"Heart of Gold" marks the site of Idris Jones's dairy place, where Jim bottled milk.

doing the same routine. When the parents' night was about to come up, she said to me, 'I don't know what to do with you, you're the only boy in the class this year.' Then she said, 'I know. You're going to be our Fred Astaire. You're going to sing three or four numbers with the girls dancing behind you, and then you go into your own dance routine.'

Young Jim resplendent in his tap-dancer togs.

"I said to her, '*Sing?*' She said, 'Yes! I've heard you sing along when the girls were rehearsing. I think it'll be successful.' And on the night we did it, it was quite successful.

"This chappie in the audience said to me as we came offstage, 'You've got a very nice voice, son.' I said thank you and began to walk away, and he said, 'Come back! I'm playing at the biggest dance hall in Southall on Saturday night. If you care to come along, I'll try you out with my 16-piece dance orchestra.' He said, 'I can't promise you anything; you might fall flat on your face. You're okay with a pianist, but a 16-piece orchestra is another story.'"

The chap from the audience, grandfather to one of the young girls, was bandleader Charlie Holmes (not to be confused with the jazz alto sax player of the same name and era). Holmes had the top orchestra in London and regularly played to packed houses. Knowing only that an opportunity had been laid at his feet, Marshall showed up to sing that Saturday night. For a young teenager, it had to be intimidating.

"He didn't try me out—he put me on, straightaway, and I sang in front of four or five hundred dancers in the hall. In those days, that's what we used to do. There was no afternoon rehearsal or anything like that. Not in those days. Musicians had to be sight readers, and the performers had to be able to show up with their charts, hand them over to the band, and perform. The musicians would sight-read and you'd sing.

"So I did a few numbers. At the end of the evening I was putting on my jacket, ready to walk out, and Charlie Holmes shouts, 'Marshall!' I thought, 'Jeez, what have I done wrong?' He said, 'What are you scared of, son?' And I wasn't going to say *You!*, though I was. I said, 'Mr. Holmes, have I made some mistakes?' And he said, 'No, you were really on out there.' I received six or seven engagements a week after that.

"The funny thing was, during the few weeks I went to school, we used to sing in the class as we were getting ready to go into the halls in the morning—songs about 'God save our gracious King or Queen' and such. And the teacher in my class used to say, 'Marshall, please don't sing. You're putting people around you off.' Because my voice was cracking! I was 13, maybe 13 and a half then. But at 14, it had changed."

Jim Marshall hung up his tapping shoes and began a regular gig fronting Charlie Holmes's group. With all due respect, it's kind of funny to think that the boy in tap shoes doing a Fred Astaire routine is the same guy Zakk Wylde says "kicks major fuckin' ass!" But Jim was good, damn good, and his innate musical talent was plainly evident. His music career was off to a strong start.

Regular evening and Saturday night shows began filling Jim's schedule. With Jim behind the mic—his style has most closely been compared to Bing Crosby's—he covered London's big band circuit, performing in halls where 200 couples would dance the jitterbug and the lindy hop. The crowds were big and the performances were long: four- and five-hour shows were the norm in those days, even in the pubs. On a four-hour gig a musician would be lucky to get a ten-minute break.

But there were still weekday hours to fill, and Jim maintained his busy schedule filling milk bottles in the morning, boiling jam at the factory all day, and gigging as frequently as six evenings per week.

"I was working a total of 85 hours a week. Forty-eight hours was the standard workweek in a factory. In the mornings I was with the milk distributor, then at the jam factory, then performing in the evenings and some Saturday afternoons. I was earning as much money at 14 as any adult. Although I only got one shilling—one-and-sixpence, actually—in the morning, and then at the factory something like 80 shillings per month."

Engineering and the war

On September 7, 1940, Word War II fell on London from out of a clear blue sky. Germany's planned invasion of England had for a month been held at bay by the Royal Air Force, who managed to defend the country even though they were outnumbered and outflanked. When Hitler realized his strategy to take the island nation could be foiled by Churchill and the RAF, he began an aerial bombing campaign to terrorize and demoralize the citizens of London. For the two months of the London Blitz, bombs were dropped on the city day and night.

"None of the places I worked or lived were damaged, but I remember the raids," Jim recalls. "Dashing under tables, finding shelter. I remember bombs dropping right behind a house where I was delivering milk. Just as I put the bottle at the door, all of the windows of the house just went *in*. I was frozen to the spot. It was very close."

Like many young men his age, 17-year-old Jim Marshall marched down to the recruiting office to sign up for service. But his medical history made him ineligible. "I volunteered for the Royal Navy, my father having been in the Royal Navy for 14 years. That was the service that I chose. I went to Acton, where you had to go to determine eligibility. I went through the medical okay, and then I had to go through this interviewer. And he said, 'I had your medical report sent to me, and I'm afraid we cannot accept you.' I said, 'Why? I'm perfectly fit now.' He said, 'Yes, but I see you had these tubercular bones. We don't want a recurrence, which could happen. And you're doing a far better job where you are for the war effort."

Jim had since begun a new day job as an engineer, an occupation he would sustain along with several others throughout the war years. His first position as a dilutee was a simple one, working in line with a team of setters who prepared parts to go through an assembly machine. The work was not especially challenging to Jim, so—right in character—he built in a challenge of his own.

"All we had to do was set the machine up so the parts would go through. But I was interested in it, so I bought books on engineering and taught myself how it all worked. I taught myself engineering, and read enough to become quite capable. By the time I left the company, Cramic Engineering, I was the No. 1 engineer.

"Eventually I was getting so many offers, plus I was performing every night. I thought, 'I'm going to leave this job and find somewhere else.' At the time, you had to get all your jobs through the Labor Exchange. I found a place called Heston Aircraft, where they made the wings of Spitfire airplanes and other wings of aircrafts. Cramic had been sending me out as a rep to a competing company, Fairy Aviation, and didn't want me to leave. The boss there stepped in to the Exchange and told them, 'Don't give that Heston job to Marshall, because we want him back!' I started a personnel war between Cramic Engineering and Heston Aircraft! But I did go to Heston and worked on the Spitfires, which were flying in the war. In time I became the top machine man in the company."

Drumming

In spite of the war, London's music scene at the time was in full swing. Every corner had a pub, and every pub had a band. Squadroneers' clubs were full of patriots and families of servicemen, and dance halls housing orchestras provided respite from the gloomy daily news. For a working musician like Jim Marshall, business was good.

Jim had been singing regularly with a septet of players from Charlie Holmes's 16-piece orchestra. The satellite group would play smaller rooms and socials. One gig proved to be a turning point in Jim's career.

"We were playing a club locally every Sunday night. We'd have one ten-minute break in the evening, and invariably during that break, fights would break out. Everybody fought when the music stopped, I suppose because they had no other distractions. We'd seen this happen night after night, so on this particular night the pianist said to me, 'Instead of just being a singer, why don't you come in on drums during the ten-minute break? I know you've done tap dancing and such, and you've got a good sense of rhythm.' I said okay. So we did that while about five members of the group went and had their break. And true enough, it stopped the fighting, because something else was still going on.

"The actual drummer, who led the band, later got called up into the service. We had a meeting and the pianist said, 'Well, what we could do now is instead of being booked as a seven-piece band, we'll be six. With you singing as well as on drums, we'll be able to split six ways rather than seven.' I thought, 'Well, that suits me!'"

Too young to drive (petrol was scarce during wartime, anyway), Jim had to find alternate means of getting himself and his drum kit to gigs. So he built a small trailer to hook up to his bicycle, loaded the kit into the trailer, and started pedaling.

"I vividly remember the Ealing Broadway station. I would cycle up there with my trailer behind my bike, carrying my drum kit, to get on the train to go to London to gig. I'd chain the bike to the railings outside the station and then carry the drums from there.

"The first big drumming gig I did was at a hotel in Hammersmith. I finally got there with my drums, and the bloke at the door said the bandleader was waiting for me. But when he realized I wasn't playing in the headlining band, he motioned toward the rear entrance. 'Round the back, upstairs,' he said. I had to get an entire drum kit up a spiral staircase! I was afraid of leaving anything down bottom, because it was kind of a rough area. Can you imagine, hauling it all upstairs, the bass drum case.... Years later, I was relating this story to a pupil and he said, 'My dad was working the door at that hotel in those days!' Who'd have thought I'd be teaching that doorman's son. He was a fine player, too—voted No. 1 drummer in a *Melody Maker* poll."

It may have been an inauspicious start, but Jim was soon called for bigger and more prestigious gigs. And once it was recognized that Jim could sing and play drums at the same time, he started getting calls to lead his own bands.

"I was sitting in on a gig with the Lou Preager Orchestra. Lou's brother, Alfred Preager, used to run the offshoot bands from the Orchestra, which were called the Lou Preager Ambassadors. Alfred heard me playing that night and said he'd like to use me as a lead in one of the seven-piece Ambassador groups. So one night I was playing and singing with them, and Alfred came along and said, 'I didn't know you could sing as well! You sound so much like Bing Crosby. I'd like to book you and bill you as "the Young Crosby."' And he did!"

Gigging regularly, Jim occasionally crossed paths with another local talent: vocalist Cleo Laine would go on to considerable success singing on Broadway, at Carnegie Hall, and at elite jazz clubs around the world. "Cleo Laine was born two streets from me in Southall. Well, she was born as Clementina Campbell, and then she married a milkman and became Clementina Langridge. Some time after, a bandleader [Johnny Dankworth, who later married Laine] took her on as a singer and said, 'No way I can sell you to clubs as Clementina Langridge!' So she became Cleo Laine. I first saw Cleo Laine sing at the Dominion Cinema, where she was performing with a very large orchestra. And she was really a stunner in those days."

Though his music career was blossoming, Jim's storied work ethic never wavered. He kept up the 18-hour days, and even bounced back after an incident in a canning factory that threatened to end not only his burgeoning drumming career but his ability to sustain most any livelihood at all.

"I was working in a meatpacking plant, where pieces of frozen meat are cut and pushed into cans. I was pushing this piece of lamb through the cutter with a stick, and in those days there were no guards or safety mechanisms whatsoever. My hand slipped on the ice of the frozen lamb and must've gone right straight across the blade."

Today, Jim laughs as he tells the story and traces the blade's track across his lifeline. "You can still see the scar. The flesh over the entire heel of my hand was gone. My family doctor at the time was also the factory doctor. When he came in, I was already laid out on a stretcher. He had a look and said, 'I'll have to have that hand off.' I thought, 'Oh my God, that's the drumming and everything, gone.'

"I was put in this loony asylum—it wasn't an asylum at the time, but the third ward of a mental hospital that had been opened up for servicemen during the war. So they sent me there. Thankfully, this young doctor said, 'I think I can save that hand.' He tried to save the top of the thumb as well, but after my hand came out of the plaster, it had rotted. My hand was all right but I'd lost the thumb tip. Not surprisingly, that ended my brief career as a meat slicer!"

The damage to Jim's hand is in evidence some 55 years later, albeit incidentally. The shortened thumb tempers the strength of his handshake, and he cradles a steak knife between two fingers; were it his left hand, it could be mistaken for a drummer's traditional grip.

Jim's drumming career would not be thwarted, and in fact thrived. Says Jim, "I was singing in cabaret, leading the band, and getting to play with all of these fantastic orchestras. During the '30s and '40s I became one of the top drummers and singers in the UK."

It was quite a bit of success for a young player, especially one who'd been self-trained. For four years he played drums professionally without a single proper lesson, learning instead by watching other pros behind the kit. But that changed after one humbling night onstage.

"I'd started playing drums at 17, but really didn't know what I was doing other than that I could play rhythms because I'd watched people play rhythms. I couldn't read music or anything like that. It was around early 1942 that I was playing at Stains Town Hall. My small band was about to go on, and funnily enough, the big band on that night was Charlie Holmes, the one I started singing with. Now, Charlie was a drummer as well. The MC got up and said, 'The Charlie Holmes Orchestra will play all quicksteps, foxtrots—all modern music. The small group will play all the Latin American, all the old-time dancing.'

"I thought, 'Oh my God, Latin American.' I could get away with 3/4 time and all that, but not the Latin American. I had never even played the rumba. During the interval, before we had to do the session, I went to Charlie Holmes and I said, 'Charlie, I...' He said, 'I know what you're going to say. You can't bloody well play Latin American, can you, mate?' I said, 'You're right, Charlie. Please, will you sit in with the group I'm playing with for the Latin American set?' And he did.

"That night, I packed up drumming and went to Max Abrams in Knightsbridge for lessons. At the same time, Jack Parnell and Eric Delaney were studying with him; all three of us studied with Max Abrams at the same time. Max was the greatest teacher over here, and when top American drummers were over in England, they'd come by for a brush-up because he was so bloody good. Bloody tough to be with, actually!"

Abrams *was* bloody good, and over the course of a long career added many top-shelf players to his student roster, from Ellington's and Basie's drummers up through the decades to Simon Phillips (a session champ with Judas Priest, Jeff Beck, Pete Townshend, and many others) and founding Police drummer Stewart Copeland. But the mentor could not have imagined that the name of his new pupil would far surpass all his students' fame, and grace countless stages the world over.

Chapter 2

Big Ideas

As England was celebrating the end of World War II in 1945, Jim was in top form as an entertainer. Like Charlie Holmes before him, Jim was an uncommon breed of musician in that he was both drummer and singer. Even more uncommonly, he usually performed both at once, leading orchestras and small groups alike from the drummer's throne.

A typical big band drummer does not require much by way of monitors. Given the director's cues and reasonable proximity to the rest of the rhythm section, he can hear well enough to stay on the beat. But singing drummers, like all vocalists, need to hear harmonies, melodies, and their own amplified voices.

Jim needed more from his monitors. Being a self-made man, he took on the task of building a better PA system himself. "From where I sat as the drummer, I was behind the band and behind the PA. I used to say, 'Damn nuisance! I'm singing and playing, I can't hear myself do either.' So I figured a louder PA would help me hear them. I'd started to build it but hadn't put on the backs yet when we had a performance. I got the shock of my life—I did not know at the time that sound comes off the *back* of the speaker as well. Using a PA system with no backs on the cabinets, I could hear quite well."

Ask Jim where he gained the know-how to build PA speakers and you'll get little more than a shrug. "They're not complicated," he asserts, and his engineering background equipped him with more than enough technical chops to knock together a wood cabinet, follow a signal path, and connect speaker leads. But the task he took on is notable for two reasons: Technically, the PA towers he built himself represent the first Marshall cabs, plus the episode evidences Jim's early appreciation for getting loud! Though the most famous Marshall cabinets would have full backs, these primordial homemades also provided a lesson in the way sound projects from a speaker's cone.

Student becomes teacher

By the late '40s, Jim was at the top of his game and visible every night of the week with London outfits at first-circuit clubs like the Savoy and the Paramount. Jim had become a valuable employee at Heston Aircraft in Middlesex, but by 1949, after the war, he could afford to put his machining career on the back burner. His high-profile gigs had caught the eye of aspiring young musicians, and with little self-promotion Jim found his income handsomely augmented by teaching drums.

Jim ended his own lessons with Max Abrams that same year. He had first approached Abrams to master a variety of styles and to learn how his hero, Gene Krupa, worked his magic behind the kit. Being a singularly quick study, he figured he had learned as much as he could after two years of Sunday night lessons. An increasing number of students were beating a path to his door, so he was confident in flipping his role from pupil to instructor.

The early '50s found Jim married and starting a family. The Marshalls—Jim, Violet, and their young boy, Terry—had a modest row house at 48 Lonsdale Road in Southall, just around the corner from the jam factory where Jim held his first job. Like many neighborhoods in the area, residential streets were tucked in among the industrial structures where the locals made a living. The small lot behind 48 Lonsdale, which was framed by a low cement wall, held a few surprises. Maybe more than a few: Jim and Violet kept 200 rabbits and 18 chickens out back. Chalk it up to Depression mentality, or the newly enforced frugality of a young family. They used the chickens for eggs and the rabbits for meat. Like most everything else Jim did, he took his home farming seriously: He was treasurer of the Southall Rabbit and Poultry Society.

Of course, Jim had loftier aspirations, and by 1953 it was clear that he had put his Midas touch on teaching. Dozens of students had come under his private tutelage. From a corner room in the Lonsdale house, Jim was making more money than he ever had before.

"Many students came to me because I was the first one to teach rock 'n' roll in England. I'd listen to and teach any type of music. Once you're a good reader, you

Jim outside of 48 Lonsdale Road, Southall, where he first taught drums in the room above the front door.

can play anything. And so long as I could play anything, I'd teach anything—left, right, and center. I taught from an 8- by 7-foot room. It was on the second floor, in the front of the house. I made the room sound good, and protected it so the neighbors wouldn't complain. You see, I had a single kit in there plus a 35-watt Vortexion amplifier with two speakers for playing along to recordings. This way, students could play along and maintain an overall balance of volume. Funny thing was, with that amplifier, we were so near Heathrow Airport that every now and again we'd pick up the pilot or copilot talking to the ground as they flew over.

"The room worked well, though some of the sound still got through to the next door. It was terraced housing, and I was at the end; there was a gap before the next

Dapper Jim behind the drum kit in the '50s. Note the similarity of the drumhead script to the later Marshall logo.

row of houses. The people further up the road used to complain, I think more out of jealousy than anything else. But the people next door could hear it, and even said they'd missed the music when they were away on holiday!"

Young drummers were lining up. The entrance to Jim's house became a revolving door of students that would in time peak at 64 pupils per week. That's 64 full one-hour sessions every seven days—with hours of preparation, to boot.

"I'd always worked 16- to 18-hour days as it was. And I didn't believe in class tuition, because the top students would be relegated to the pace of the slowest student. I was getting up every morning at three or four o'clock to work out drum scores. I used to sit and take down the parts I heard on record or make notations when I went to see someone play. That's what got the students started; the sooner you can get them onto *playing* something, the more enthusiastic they were.

"With 64 students, I was making 64 guineas [about £67] per week teaching, plus five shillings [£0.25] for every drum score.[1] It was all by hand—at the time we had no Xerox machines or automatic duplicating. And there were no drum scores in print to be purchased, even for the top orchestrations."

West London must have been fertile ground and Jim an inspiring teacher. A surprising number of talented players under Jim's tutelage would go on to great success. Among them: Mitch Mitchell (known as Johnny Mitchell at the time), who came to greatest fame in the Jimi Hendrix Experience; Mick Burt, who played with Chas & Dave, Albert Lee, and the Searchers; Mickey Waller, who played with Little Richard, Jeff Beck, Ronnie Lane (Small Faces), Rod Stewart, Jimmy Page, and Kenney Jones, and was a member of Steampacket (fronted by Rod Stewart); and Mick Underwood, who worked with Deep Purple's Ian Gillan, Roger Glover, and Ritchie Blackmore in his skiffle days.

With a salary topping £5,000 annually—the current equivalent of almost $8,000 U.S. dollars, which was terrific for a West Londoner in the early '50s—Jim was clearing more money than all his other jobs combined. Though he loved the life of the performing musician, the income could not be denied. Jim gradually reduced his gigging obligations to dedicate his time to teaching. He was banking his earnings for The Next Big Thing.

[1] In the old UK monetary system, 1 guinea = 21 shillings and 20 shillings = £1 (1 pound).

Drumming up business

Originally, the plan was to open a drum shop. At 37 years old, Jim Marshall had learned a lot of lessons in his professional life and one idea was plain to him: He wanted to be in business for himself.

It was 1960, and in ten years of teaching Jim had saved enough to map out his own future with an investment of his own choosing. A drum shop made perfect sense. Quite by accident, Jim had already become a one-man sales force. He'd played Premier drums exclusively onstage, and when students saw their mentor behind Premier week after week, they wanted the same. For the drum company, it was better advertising than money could buy. In fact, Premier knew it was exactly that—so they didn't want to spend money on Jim.

"I was an endorser for Premier Drums. In those days, endorsement deals were very much the reverse of what they are today in that the manufacturer felt they were doing the players a favor. I decided that instead of having just one kit in the studio, it would be good to have two so I could actually play with the pupil. So I went to see Fred Dellaporta, the boss of Premier, at 87 Regent Street. I said, 'When I'm teaching, it would be nice to have another kit so I could play with the pupil.' And he said, 'Yeah, it would be nice, wouldn't it?' And he went quiet just like that, didn't say another word. Then he said, 'Well, we've already got you in the advert, that should be doing well for you.' I was explaining that it would be great advertising for them to have 64 students every week playing on their kits! Finally he said, 'I'll tell you what, you go down and talk to Jimmy at Lou Davis's shop. I'll phone him first and tell him to give you 10 percent off for you and for your students.'

"I suppose it was not entirely unreasonable. It's probably what got in my mind [years later] about not giving Marshall gear away. Anyway, Fred didn't give me the kit. What he did do was, on Christmas of that year I received a package from him, all nicely wrapped up. I opened it and there was a pair of drumsticks in it. That was his idea of a joke. It was a pair of Premier E's, their lightest stick—and he knew bloody well that I used Premier B's! What had happened was that another drummer had died, and Fred had his sticks! He had an odd sense of humor."

With Premier's 10 percent markdown available, Jim would regularly take his students down to talk to manager Jimmy Frost at Lou Davis's music store. They'd order the kits at a lowered profit to Davis's store, and Jim would pass the savings on to his students. With his boss frustrated at the situation, it was Jimmy who first said to Jim, "You keep coming here with your students. You could order the kits yourself. Wouldn't you feel better if you opened your own shop?"

Frost was right. Jim knew at least 64 musicians he could count on to help get business started. It wasn't long before he set about finding an appropriate space for his shop.

"I was living in Southall and still teaching out of my home," says Jim. "I looked for a space that would be well trafficked. A place that would be a reasonable commute for me and something the pupils would be able to find easily."

Southall was connected to the neighboring town of Hanwell by the Uxbridge Road. It was a straight shot from Jim's home to the commercial heart of Hanwell, which saw plenty of foot traffic by the locals. He found a vacancy in a narrow, two-floor space along a row of shops and struck a deal for the lease. The Marshall store was to be opened at 76 Uxbridge Road.

A small newspaper ad trumpeted the opening of Jim Marshall & Son on July 7, 1960. Terry, Jim's 16-year-old son, would get his start in business behind the store counter. Jim's old teacher, Max Abrams, lent some celebrity to the ribbon-cutting ceremony and added credibility to the store as a drummer's destination.

Credibility was never much of an issue. From the outset Jim had enough students coming in for sticks, heads, cymbals, and kits to keep the store busy. Supported by his private drum school, he was quickly selling as many as 23 drum kits a month—far more than stores in business for decades and three times his size. Though Jim had imagined a simple drum shop, his students brought greater opportunity right to the doorstep.

Since Jim opened the store, he had been building speaker cabinets at home on Sundays and trailering them up to the store behind his bike. His earliest creations held 18" speakers ("because no one else was making them"), and he made a variety of enclosures for PA, bass, and guitar. Now, Jim's students were showing up at the shop with their band mates; guitarists and bassists started sniffing around the homemade cabs.

One devilish student was a boy by the name of Keith Moon, who brought around the bassist and guitarist from his band. (Moon took a few lessons with Jim, but guitarist Pete Townshend would later say the Who drummer was not so keen on learning rudiments and "more interested in looking good and being screamed at.")

"I taught so many top pupils, and they would bring their guitarists into the shop, saying they'd like to have a word with me. Pete Townshend would come in, as well as Ritchie Blackmore, who was playing with a pupil of mine in a school band. They'd say, 'Why don't you sell amplifiers and guitars?' I said, 'Well, I know drums, but very little about amplifiers and guitars.' They said, 'If you'll stock them, we'd prefer to come to you than go to the West End, where we're treated as absolute idiots.' The West End shops were still only interested in servicing jazz musicians. They weren't going to take rock 'n' roll musicians seriously at all."

Marshall may not have presaged the success of the Who and Deep Purple, but he did know that the scrappy kids walking in his door were an untapped resource. These guys were young, but they were serious. His relationships with students helped him keep a finger on the pulse of their scene, and he had a sense of the Beat Boom movement on the rise. For a retailer, it meant access to a new network of players. Knowing there's no better promotion than word of mouth, Jim began stocking gear for other musicians in his pupils' groups. There wasn't much square footage to the store, but a sizeable buzz had started around Jim Marshall & Son.

"The shop was tiny, just a small store on that little stretch of road. If you whistled, you'd miss it. The bottom, at street level, was all drum kits with a gangway up the middle. Once I began to stock guitars, I had them on the second floor and on the walls on the way up. You'd get seven or nine people in there, and the place was packed solid!

"But the musicians, they loved it. I suppose that was in part because there was a café across the road owned by two Italian brothers, where they'd spend time together. It was like a musician's labor exchange. My shop and the café were drawing a lot of musicians."

It's difficult to believe by today's standards, but banking on drums and guitars was risky business. Music stores were loaded with *band* instruments befitting the musical order of the day, and made their rent on saxes and reeds and trumpets and valve oil. In London circa 1960, the musicians who had paying gigs were dance orchestras still toeing the line with light swing and a catchy melody. The heyday of the big band was over by more than two decades, its last vestiges barely audible in the mainstream's scrubbed-clean "jazz." It was the age of the pop crooner, with heroes like Dinah Shore, Jerry Vale, and Dean Martin. There was a groundswell of rock 'n' roll across the pond, but England had yet to bring its troops to the front lines. The Beatles weren't even the Beatles yet.

So it was with good foresight and good fortune that Jim Marshall had a sense of his store's potential. Homemade cabs were well and fine, but customers also wanted name guitars and amplifiers. They were hot for American brands in particular, like Fender, Gibson, and Gretsch.

"I knew it'd be best to have other lines as well, so I had a couple of Vox amplifiers, a couple of Selmer amplifiers. I never sold one Vox amplifier. But everybody that came into my shop either wanted the Fender amps like the American groups were playing, especially Fender Bassmans and Tremoluxes, or the Selmer because it was a cheaper line."

Young rock 'n' roll kids were becoming the store's bread and butter. The café across the street continued to hum, with musicians swapping info about gigs and gear.

"It was like Archer Street all over again. Archer Street was the main place in London where all the older musicians met. Fixers[2] would go there to pick up violinists for their orchestras, and players would be down there to take a lesson or have repairs done on their instruments. Between my store and the café, it was very much like that."

It was all Jim and son Terry could do to keep up with business. Their crosstown compatriots, content serving the mainstream band and orchestra crowd, were shocked at how much business Marshall & Son was conducting.

"In the West End they thought the real money was with the orchestras and the people playing jazz and all that sort of thing. But these guitarists had told me what they wanted and I'd said, 'Okay, I'll have them for you.' I placed one particularly large

[2]"Fixers" were engaged by orchestra and band leaders to hire musicians on a per diem basis. In the mornings, they would select among the available players and go about "fixing"—or filling the empty seats—in a group that was to perform that evening.

order with Phil Cowan, who was the manager at Selmer [store and distributor]. I went to Phil with an order of guitars and amplifiers worth £12,000—which was a lot of money in those days. He took a look at it and said, '£12,000?! I'll have to check with Ben.' Ben Davis was the boss at Selmer's.

"Phil came back out and said, 'Ben wants to see you.' I went up to Ben Davis's office and the first thing he said was, 'I don't believe you. You don't even have room to show it all in your shop.' But I'd already taken orders for most of it, you see, and the rest of it I knew would sell. 'Here's what I've decided to do,' he said. 'I'm going to put this over 12 months. You'll pay me back £1,000 per month. But if you sell more of it than that in a month, please pay me.'

"Two months later I went up there with a check for £11,000. You should have seen his face—I thought he'd just about fall out of his seat. I'd already been up there with the first thousand, so in 60 days I'd paid off the entire amount. From then on we were great friends. He said, 'I don't know how you're doing it.' I said, 'I'm dealing with a new type of music, you know—rock 'n' roll.'"

Jim grew accustomed to the drive up and back to the Selmer shop. Besides the American gear he purchased, he was selling Selmer amplifiers—and, every Monday, taking a batch back for repairs.

"I used to drive to Selmer's factory, which was right near their shop, on Monday mornings with a van full of Selmer amplifiers that needed repair. I had so much trouble with Selmers. That's why I took on Ken Bran as my repair engineer.

"Ken used to be a roadie with a group called Peppy and the New York Twisters. He used to drive for them as well, and he'd come into my shop buying stuff for the group. Some time before, he'd approached me saying he was looking for an exit from the band, but I didn't need anyone at the time. He said, 'Okay, I'm going to go work at Heathrow in baggage handling, and I'll keep popping in the shop. Should you need someone in repair, will you think of me?' And in the end, what with all these broken-down Selmers on my hands, I took him on."

There was no clue yet that Bran would have momentous influence on Marshall history. Jim was just happy not to be driving around town with a vanload of busted Selmers.

In 1961, the little drum shop was turning into a not-so-little guitar shop. Hanwell's nascent rock 'n' rollers were going crazy for guitars and basses, and Jim got his hands on whatever they wanted: Stratocasters and Telecasters, Rickenbackers, Les Pauls and ES-335s. The amp of choice for most was the Fender Bassman, but for players who wanted a little more sand in the Vaseline, the Fenders were not *quite* right. Big Jim Sullivan (who has played with everyone from the Kinks to Engelbert Humperdinck and is still a first-call session player in the UK) was tone-seeking, and 16-year-olds Townshend and Blackmore were in the shop regularly talking to Jim about what they wanted from their amps. As Townshend recalled:

> I said, "I've got these two American amplifiers, a Fender Pro amp and a Fender Bassman amp. They're great . . . [but] if I'm playing and somebody's in the front row and they say, 'This is junk,' I can hear what they're saying. I don't want to hear them, OK? I need something bigger and louder." [Marshall's] eyes lit up. . . . I was demanding a more powerful machine gun, and Jim Marshall was going to build it for me, and then we were going to go out and blow people away, all around the world.
>
> —*Fresh Air* radio interview, 1993

"These players got onto me about building them an amplifier," Marshall confirms. "They'd say, 'The Fender Bassman is somewhere near rock 'n' roll, but a bit too far away. Will you make a go at making an amplifier for us? Will you do it?' I said, 'Well, all I've got is a man in the shop on repairs. He and I will have a word.' So I went to Ken Bran and said, 'Let's have a go at making this amplifier.'

"Ken said, 'I'm okay at doing basic repairs'—which is what he'd done for the Twisters—'but I'm sorry, I couldn't do a circuit or anything like that.' He thought for a time and then he said, 'There's a kid at EMI who's getting a fantastic reputation. He's only 18, but he's got such a reputation. His name's Dudley Craven. Would you like to have a word with him?'

"I said yes, and Ken arranged to bring this lad along. I asked him, 'How would you like to join the team of five that's going to make the world's first rock 'n' roll amp?'

He was thankful for Ken's recommendation but said he was quite happy at EMI, where they were paying him five pounds a week. So I said, 'Well, supposing I paid you the same as I pay Ken: £15 a week?' And he said, 'Done!' He gave two weeks' notice at EMI and then he got down to work."

#1 is born

It's easy to say in hindsight, but the circumstances surrounding the creation of Marshall's first amp beg a tempting thought: *Jim knew.* There'd been a collision of his talents: engineer, musician, salesman, marketer. Sight unseen, he'd offered Craven a salary that stopped the guy's watch. The musicians had placed their orders, then their trust, then their hopes with Jim.

When Jim took Dudley on, he invited him to join a team of five: Jim Marshall, Ken Bran, Dudley Craven, and the two brothers who regularly worked the counter, Ken and Fred Gallagher. Jim, the ex-machinist, would shape the chassis; Ken would select and install components, most of which were dug from cutout bins in army surplus and electronics stores; Dudley would be the chief designing engineer; and the Gallagher brothers, as well as the team as a whole, would provide extra ears.

Everyone on the team loved the sound of the Bassman, and Bran and Craven studied it down to the last capacitor. They knew the Bassman was close enough that they didn't have to reinvent the wheel—just make it go faster. To some degree, though, Fender had been heading in the opposite direction Marshall intended—while they were cleaning up the amp for their country players, Marshall wanted to add more grit. Plus, Jim had the benefit of knowing his customers intended to play loud, loud, loud.

"I knew the sound was going to come from the valves," says

Like most newborns, #1 was beautiful but not so pretty.

Jim. "The players had told me what they wanted quite specifically, such that I could hear in my mind what it should sound like. I heard it in my head. It was down to the harmonics that are created when the tubes are driven and used in a certain way. It's not just distortion—it's complex, and it's musical."

Whether it was by design, luck, or availability, Bran and Craven chose a 12AX7 tube for the all-important first stage of the amp's preamp section. A 12AX7 delivers more gain than the 12AY7 valves used in the first stage of the Bassman, and a further difference in output transformers, which manage current to the speakers, contributed even more to the warm growl. From July through September of 1962, Bran and Craven tweaked and remodeled the amp five times. Jim listened, hoping the latest version would match the sound he'd heard in his head, but it wasn't there yet. As each new model was ready, Jim would have a customer take it for a spin while he listened.

"Any main guitarist that was in the shop at the time, I'd say, 'Go play this one for me.' I knew it had to be a good rock 'n' roll amplifier, so I made sure it was a good rock 'n' roll guitarist that was demonstrating it. I turned down the first five. Dudley was on number six, and one of the guitarists—I think it was Pete Townshend—played it and I said, 'That's it! That's going to be the Marshall sound from now on.' And it has been ever since."

Jim may have been running the show, but he has always held Bran and Craven up as the R&D team that originated the Marshall sound. "I *never* had *anything* to do with the engineering," he says. "Ken brought Dudley in as his assistant, and Dudley was the chap who managed to put what I was hearing in my head into an amplifier."

In September 1962, a handful of talented men sat grinning at one another, with their ears ringing, in the back room of a small music shop in West London. Today, the famed "#1," their sixth prototype, sits in the Marshall museum at company headquarters, about 20 paces from Jim's office. It belongs nearby. It was the sound he had dreamed.

Chapter 3

Loud and Proud

Jim Marshall's intuition was dead on. Listening to what musicians wanted was the catalyst. In time it would prove to be the thread that strung together Marshall's success.

Taking consultation from the left-of-center teenagers who walked into his store required some foresight, to be sure. Chuck Berry had kick-started rock 'n' roll a good 15 years prior, but most London music stores and instrument manufacturers still sniffed at the noise born across the pond. Certain it was a fad, albeit a stubborn one, they disregarded the coming generation of British R&B players. Even to the degree rock 'n' roll was established, *rock*—its rough-and-tumble younger brother—hadn't yet emerged. Jim was catering to a crowd whose music was unheard and unproven. And the customers were dreamy kids, barely tipping into their 20s.

In September 1962, the first Marshall amplifier was in the window at Jim Marshall & Son. Bran and Craven's sixth prototype had been christened the JTM45 for Jim and Terry Marshall and its 45 watts of potential power (though in truth it topped out at around 35 watts). On the first day, Jim took orders for 23 of them. Marshall recalls that Townshend, Blackmore, and Sullivan were among those first buyers, having heard the amp they'd asked Jim to build.

Up jumped production

Given the team's limited resources, initial production of the JTM45 was slow. When he wasn't minding the shop or keeping up with his drum students, Jim would shape chassis out of aluminum. Bran and Craven would scrounge for components at the army surplus and electronics shops around town and go to work in the small room at the back of the shop. They built one, sometimes two per week.

Shop No. 2, 93 Uxbridge Road, Hanwell Broadway, opened in March 1963.

Word was out about the powerhouse amp, and the musicians who gathered locally were sampling the JTM45 at one another's shows at night. On the following day, with that dully ringing noise hangover that only musicians can appreciate, they'd make their way to Jim's shop to place their orders.

The JTM had helped drive enough business within its first few months that Jim was confident to expand from The Little Shop That Could. In March 1963, retail space became available immediately across the street at 93 Uxbridge Road. Jim scooped it up and opened the store as J&T Marshall. By comparison the space was luxurious, and its benefits were many. The big showroom allowed him to stock and display a broader range of instruments. Drum instruction could finally be run out of the store rather than Jim's home, which also allowed him to bring on other teachers. Drummers shared the shop's back-room space with cabinet building, the majority of which had still been taking place at Jim's home (the neighbors must've loved him). And a retail window to the street three times the size of that at 76 Uxbridge turned the heads of passersby. The smaller space was closed down as a storefront to become a dedicated workspace for Dudley.

The first JTM45s were being sold as heads only; as is the case today, Marshall heads and cabs were available separately. Since 1960, when the store at 76 Uxbridge opened, Jim had been building his own cabinets in a variety of sizes and configurations. Early PA towers and bass cabs were reliable sellers, and interest among guitarists had grown considerably. Some were driven by Marshall amps while others were extension cabs for Fenders, Voxes, and others.

Due in large part to increased cabinet demand, the store at 93 Uxbridge was soon bursting at the seams—with wood sheets being cut and hammers swinging, cab production takes a lot of space. With no lease yet signed on a proper factory, production was temporarily moved to a 20- by 30-foot space off-site (over an engineering company) to meet orders and, presumably, to preserve the sanity of drum students. Six months later, in June 1964, the first Marshall factory cranked into operation on Silverdale Road in nearby Hayes, Middlesex. In the 5,000-square-foot space, Jim employed 15 people to build amplifiers and cabinets.[3] The off-line production rate for amplifiers stepped up to 20 per week (a big splash compared to the two per week maximum they'd managed; a spit compared to the 1,700 products that come off the line in Marshall's main plant currently).

A new slant

The JTM45 amplifier was indisputably a sonic monster, but it did not roar in all its glory until it was married to the 4x12 cabinet.

Having modified PA monitors in his gigging days and tinkered with the Vortexion in his teaching room, Jim knew what he liked in a speaker cabinet. He tried a number of configurations before working on two 2x12 pairs to match the new JTM45 head. But the JTM was too powerful.

[3]It's hard to believe now, but at the time Marshall was far and away the underdog. By comparison: In '64, Fender amplifiers and guitars were being produced in 20-plus buildings, employing 600 people and occupying over 100,000 square feet of manufacturing space.

"Initially I was trying out 2x12 cabinets with the prototype JTM45, but it just wasn't giving us quite the sound or projection we were really looking for—plus the thing kept blowing speakers like there was no tomorrow! At the time, the available [15-watt] speakers could not manage the current coming off the output transformer because the amp was putting out nearly 50 watts of power when it was turned all the way up. So, eventually it became obvious that the only solution would be to build a cabinet containing four 12" speakers because they'd be able to handle the amp's power and also give me the projection I was looking for. That was obviously going to make for a rather large cabinet, so I made it as small as it could sensibly be—my concern, you see, was that they would be difficult to transport.

"I built the first 4x12 cabinet in my garage workshop, and there was nothing particularly brilliant about its design, really. I just made it the smallest, most convenient size I possibly could so that it would be easy for the groups to move around in the sort of transport they had in those days—that's why it's so compact."

By his own account, Who bassist John Entwistle owned some of the earliest Marshall 4x12s—even before Pete Townshend did. Entwistle recalls that the very first 4x12 was purchased by the bassist from a band called the Flintstones, but that he bought the second, fourth, seventh, and eighth Marshall 4x12s. "Pete Townshend bought all the ones in between," he recalled in a 1999 interview. "I'd buy one, then Pete would buy one. I'd say, 'Is it loud enough yet? Fuck, I'll buy two more!'"

The 4x12 cab housed Celestion G12s (which were, for all intents and purposes, identical to the famous "Blue" Alnico speakers[4]) and catered to Jim's particular clientele by further differentiating from the Fender Bassman. One of the most popular Bassmans contained four 10-inch speakers—a little bit country—while the four bottom-heavy 12s in Jim's cabinets were more than a little bit rock 'n' roll. Along the same lines, Marshall's closed-back cabinets made for a more aggressive output, with the speaker's full frequency range pushing right through the grille; the Bassman's open back dispersed some sound.

[4]Celestion had developed the "Blue" speakers for Vox, and didn't want an upstart amp maker to have the exact same speaker as their biggest client. Consequently, Celestion insisted that Marshall's speakers were painted silver and had no rounded cover over the magnet.

"The first 4x12 cabinet I built in my garage had a straight front," says Jim. "But when we put the amplifier head on top of it, I looked at it and thought, 'Oh Christ, that looks terrible. It does not look *designed*—it just looks like a small box sitting on top of a bigger box'—which was essentially all it was. It was too square, and looked as if it might topple over even though it was heavy and quite stable. I thought, 'Well, if I put an angle on the upper half of the front of the 4x12, then the top of the cabinet will appear to "meet" the bottom of the head.' That, to my eye, was a neater package, and it looked *designed*."

The JTM head sat atop the slant cab like a king on his throne. The slant is a credit to Jim's aesthetic sensibilities, and perhaps even more so to his marketing sense—the cab's mid-height taper makes the speaker enclosure as distinctive visually as the JTM45 head is aurally. Its design further branded Marshall for amp/cab separation, at once making combos appear outdated and giving a distinct look to rock 'n' roll's back line. (The angled cab remains popular and has since been imitated by many manufacturers; unfortunately, Jim never acquired exclusive rights to the much-copied design.)

To achieve the slant, he had tilted the baffle of the two top speakers. The decision to angle the front was a matter of appearance, so Jim was pleasantly surprised to discover an acoustic payoff to angling the speakers slightly upwards. The model 1960 angled-front 4x12 had been in production for a time when he was invited to a show by Brian & the Tremoloes. Not only was the band one of the most popular groups in England at the time, Brian Poole also happened to have been one of Jim's first customers.

"I got to the gig while they were setting up, and Brian's lead guitarist, Ricky, said to me, 'What's the idea of the angle on top of the cabinet's front, Jim?' I obviously didn't want to tell him that it was just there because I liked the way it looked, because that would sound rather silly, so I decided that I'd better come up with something that sounded a little cleverer rather quickly. So I said, 'Well, Rick, you must understand that a straight-fronted cabinet just blows the sound straight into the people at the front of the crowd, but the slant on top throws some of the sound up and over their heads, which means the people at the back of the hall can hear it too.' I thought I was talking a right load of old rubbish, but blow me down if I wasn't telling the truth! I went to the back of the hall when the band was playing and sure enough, even though the place was packed with people, you could hear Ricky's guitar as clear

The first Marshall catalogs featured Brian Poole & the Tremoloes touting Jim's PA cabinets.

as a bell. [In those days PA systems were used solely for vocals—miking amps and drums was unheard of.] The angle was working, you see. I just shook my head and thought, 'What a fool I am—it's a pretty clever design in terms of what it does to the sound, and I never even realized it.'"

Breaking the blues

Eric Clapton's influence on Marshall history is almost as legendary as Townshend's, though it came later and was, by comparison, momentary.

The shop at 93 Uxbridge Road and the since-expanded café a few doors down had turned that stretch of road into a musicians' collective. Clapton was 19 in 1964, and though there was a lo-fi buzz about a young guitarist playing blues-inspired rock, he had not yet staked his territory amidst the West London rock 'n' roll crowd.

Often, Clapton would stroll into the Marshall music store and work his chops on the new guitars and amps. He too fell for the warm overdrive of the JTM45, but the split head/cab configuration was not for him. Clapton was gigging regularly and wanted a combo he could easily stick in the trunk of his car.

Jim remembers, "Clapton used to come around quite a bit. He used to practice there in the shop. He asked me to build a combo so that he could put the whole thing right into the boot of his car. That's how the Bluesbreaker, the first Marshall combo, came about."

It wasn't called the Bluesbreaker just yet. The first combos Marshall built were produced between late 1964 and early 1965, and were available in 4x10 (model 1961) and 2x12 (model 1962) configurations. The chassis was pure JTM45—by this time, speaker ratings had improved, and a pair of 2x12s was able to bear up under the amp's output. The combo went through a few minor changes, mostly cosmetic, before Clapton bought his second-series 1962 late in 1965.

The combo's place in history was cemented once the world heard Clapton's tone on the 1966 album *John Mayall Blues Breakers with Eric Clapton*, widely known as the "Beano" album (because Clapton is pictured on the cover reading a comic called *The Beano*). Recorded at full volume, Clapton coupled the amp with a Les Paul and produced a deep, harmonics-rich tone that had not been known before in blues or in rock 'n' roll. The Les Paul/Marshall combination would become as visible and significant a pairing as Lennon/McCartney or Jagger/Richards.

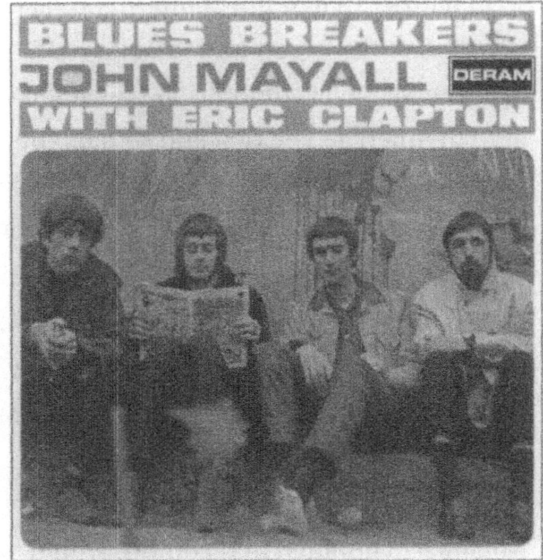

Marshall did not officially name the combo "Bluesbreaker"—that was as much a nickname as was "Beano." Clapton's influence on the Marshall itself has been overstated, but his influence on the company's renown cannot be. In one fell swoop, Marshall and Clapton had gained credibility among a new generation of bluesmen and established the Les Paul/Marshall precedent that still stands.

Eric Clapton (with Firebird I) deployed a phalanx of full stacks with Cream, but he wrung his classic "Bluesbreaker" tones from a 2x12 combo.

Thanks to a handful of international touring acts, word of Marshall was blowing across the ocean and taking seed in the United States. While Clapton's use of the Marshall combo is the most famous, it was Roy Orbison who first took the amp to America. The rich and throaty tone he achieved with his Gibson ES-335 was as integral to his sound as his tremolo-laced voice.

"I met Roy once," Jim remembers, "when he was over here performing. Because of union rules, he had to use British musicians rather than his American band when he was here. Someone in the band backing him was using a Bluesbreaker, and he decided it was the amp he had to have. It wasn't long at all after we'd made it for Eric Clapton. Roy was the first artist to take a Marshall amp back to the States."

Squaring off with Vox

No one had doubted that combos would be popular—the easily portable configuration was a proven winner for a number of makers. In addition to the Bassman, Vox amps were widely popular at the time. Vox had been championed by the Shadows; following their lead, the Beatles acquired a pair of AC30s in 1962 before recording their *Please Please Me* debut. Vox president Tom Jennings was proud to have been in with rock 'n' roll bands at ground zero, and didn't appreciate the encroachment by his West London neighbor.

Says Jim, "I had taken a page ad, a long-page ad, out in *Melody Maker*, which was the No. 1 paper, thanking the musicians that were using our product. That's all it was done for, really. After the page came out, Tom Jennings phoned me and said, 'Get off my shirttails, lad.' And he swore. I never swear, so I listened to him for some time, and he said, 'Listen here, I've got all those groups under contract.' I said, 'I don't feel bad, you've had the Beatles for a very long time.' He began swearing again, and I put the phone down." (Beatles manager Brian Epstein had had a similarly "pleasant" start with Jennings. He went to Jennings Musical Industries on Charing Cross Road and, confident the promotion would pay off handsomely for Vox, asked the manager to give the amps to the band. Jennings' response: "What does he think we are, a fucking philanthropic society?")[5]

"Next I received a call from his solicitor [attorney], who said, 'May I suggest that in the future, should you plan to use the names of any artists in your adverts, you first submit to Mr. Jennings for approval.'"

Long pause.

"I said, 'May I suggest that you, as his solicitor, prepare a document listing the names of all of the artists he has under contract—with your signature as verification.' I knew that as Jennings's solicitor, he wasn't going to sign anything he knew to be inauthentic.

"The following day, Tom Jennings phoned me again, and once again used language. I put the phone down and I went out to my crew and said, 'I'm going into battle with Jennings at Vox, and I'm going to put him out of business.' And it took us six months."

Marshall gave Vox a pounding. No doubt the Bluesbreaker, priced almost 35 percent below the AC30, blew a hole in the side of Vox's business, with another shot following in the form of Marshall's 1958 18-watt combo. Though Vox would survive in

[5]Andy Babiuk, *Beatles Gear* (San Francisco: Backbeat Books, 2001), 27.

name, Jennings fumbled portentously in late 1965. He failed to meet customer demands, the amps became notoriously difficult for owners to maintain, and the quality of manufacturing waned. On the heels of losing control of US distribution, the company was bought out.

The epilogue on the Marshall/Vox rivalry is an amusing one. Vox was bought and sold several times following Jim's initial skirmish with Mr. Jennings, and, with each new owner, the tone of the once majestic AC30 was diminished as a new team of "experts" tried to "fix" something that, although quirky, was never broken in the first place. The quality also took a turn for the worse and at one point one of Jim's dealers sent him a photo of an AC30 with a fire extinguisher mounted on its side. Then, in 1993, a new owner was announced: Korg Inc., Japan—the parent company of Korg USA, the exclusive distributor of Marshall products in North America. Then came the twist:

Because of the relationship that already existed, the first thing Korg did was ask Jim Marshall if he would be willing to return the AC30 to its original glory, and also manufacture the amp in the Marshall factory. "When they first asked me, I thought, 'No way—I don't really want to mess around with Vox,'" Jim recalls. "But then, after thinking about it for a little while, I decided, Why not? It'll be quite a nice challenge to bring back the original sound of the AC30 as it's been missing for many, many years. I was quite appreciative of the tone of the original amp, you see. So, I asked my engineers to give it a go, and I'm quite proud to say that we did restore that original Vox sound. . . . and we did it very quickly, in fact." As a result, to this day the Vox AC30 is manufactured at Jim's facility in Milton Keynes. (To add further irony to the tale, Korg Inc. acquired the Vox name, along with several others, when it bought out another of Jim's nemeses, the ailing Rose-Morris.)

The stack

How do you improve on a JTM45 with a 4x12 cab? For Pete Townshend, the answer was plain: Double the power and double the speaker count.

By 1965, the members of the Who were in an all-out volume war. Entwistle was setting a pair of Marshall 4x12 cabinets side by side in order to be heard above Keith Moon's drumming. Jim had already bumped up the JTM45 to 50 watts (in the form

A 1965 ad from *Melody Maker*. The Marshall pillars—head, combo, slant cab—are already in place.

of model 1987) and sold the head to Townshend, but the guitarist claimed he still couldn't be heard over his own rhythm section. He loved the tone—Townshend heard what Jim had in the overdriven tubes—but he wanted more of it.

"We'd not even thought about making a 100-watt amp until Pete came into my shop and said he wanted us to make him some," Jim states. "So I told him we'd have a go at making one. We made a prototype first and then we made three heads just for him. We were so proud of them when they were finished. There they were sitting on a bench in the workshop with us thinking they looked wonderful, and then Pete's roadie came along and just threw them into the bloody truck! I remember thinking, 'Oh, my God! I can't believe he just did that.'"

For the guitarist, who was slowly growing deaf, there was still the matter of speaker count to consider.

"Then Pete came in again and said he wanted me to build a cabinet with eight 12s to go with his new 100-watt heads—a single cabinet, with eight speakers! I said, 'No problem; what shape do you want them, Pete?' And he went, 'And square, Jim!' When he told me that, I said, 'Look, Pete, if you put a little amplifier on top of a big square cabinet it's going to look ridiculous.' He agreed but was convinced he needed 8x12s, so I said, 'Look, Pete, I'll make a 4x12 with a straight front and then put the angled one on top.' He shook his head and replied, 'No, I don't want that. I want it all in one cabinet.' I told him that it would be ridiculously heavy and difficult to transport, but he didn't care. He said, 'Well, that's what I have roadies for.'

"So, at Pete's request, I built him some 8x12 cabinets, and sure enough they were damned heavy. As I was carrying them out to him with one of my chaps, I said, 'I told you it was going to be heavy, Pete. Your roadies are going to complain like mad.' His reply was, 'Sod 'em, they get paid'—and off he went! But sure enough, he came back a bit sheepishly a few weeks later and said, 'You were absolutely right, Jim, they are flaming heavy, and my roadies are furious. Would you cut them in half for me?' Well, that just wasn't possible because of the way they were made—we weren't using fingerlocked joints in those early days, you see. The cabs were glued together using butt joints. So I told him, 'Look, Pete, I can't do that, because the bloody things will fall apart! Just leave it with me and I'll get it sorted out.' So I ended up doing what I wanted to do in the first place, which was the straight-fronted cab with the angled one sitting on top—it had to be on top both for appearance and for stability. And that was how the stack was born, for Pete Townshend."

> In the old days I used to storm into Jim Marshall's shop and swear at him. They'd run to build something new, and I'd come back the next day to say that it wasn't loud enough, or it wasn't good enough. In the end I got what I wanted. And in so doing, what Jim Marshall did—and consequently the guy who built Hiwatt—was provide English heavy metal and blues players of the mid '60s and early '70s with these *weapons*.
>
> —Pete Townshend, *Guitar Player,* September 2000

The bigger, badder stack was an intimidating sight—and more so an intimidating sound—on the stages of London clubs. But for the rock crowd, enough is seldom enough. Hendrix would later pay his stacks a dubious compliment: "It

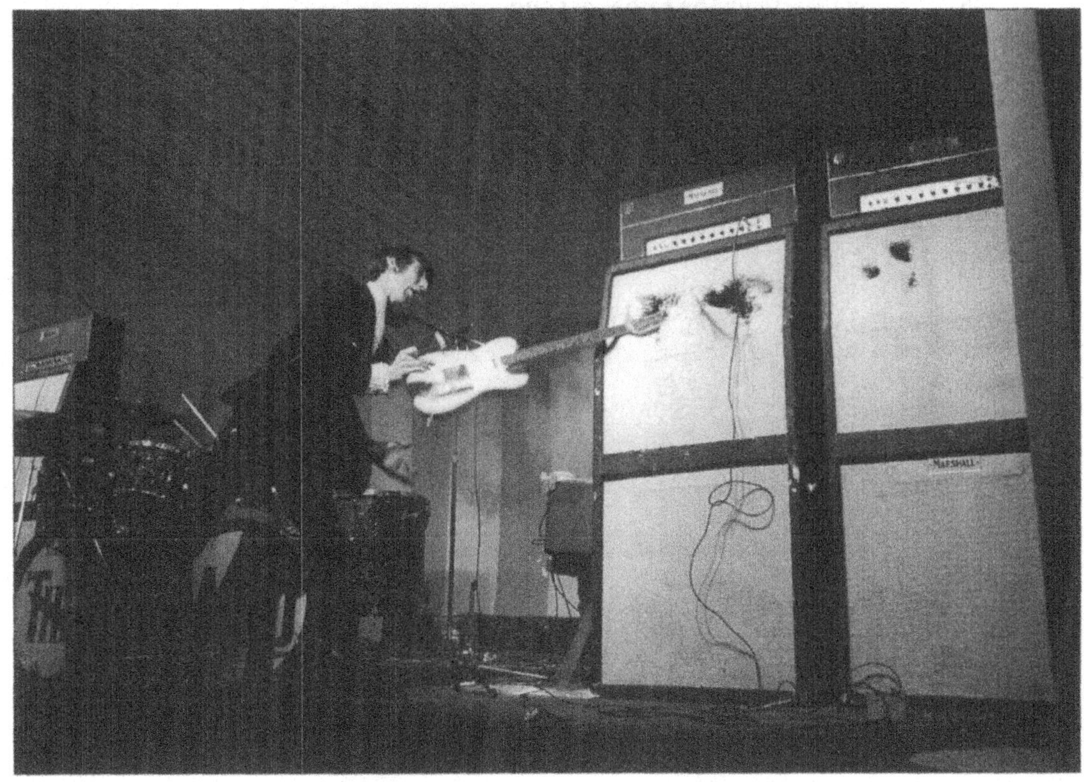

Townshend tearing into a cabinet . . . but carefully.

looks like two refrigerators hooked together." Since then, stack mentality has been multiplied umpteen times, reaching comic levels as walls of Marshall cabs—nine times out of ten they're empty dummies—are used as backdrops for concert stages, photos shoots, and video sets. Kiss, for one, has had up to 44 of them onstage at one time, Zakk Wylde 20; Slayer has been dragging 24 around the world for the best part of two decades; and ex–Van Halen frontman David Lee Roth once did a photo shoot in front of 80-plus Marshall 4x12s. (Not to be outdone, to celebrate Marshall's 30th anniversary in 1992, Jim built a wall of 175 cabinets on the stage of the legendary Hammersmith Odeon in London.)

In a curious display of love for his Marshall stacks, Townshend started shoving his guitar through the grille cloth. (It's worth noting that the first thing Townshend ever smashed was an amp, not a guitar.) Soft-spoken Jim Marshall was all for rock 'n' roll, but as a gentleman who'd made his name in classy jazz joints, it was alarming to see the young mod do a hurricane act on his gear.

Curtain call: For Marshall's 30th anniversary, 175 cabs took center stage (as well as stage left and stage right) at the Hammersmith Odeon.

"I used to play with Pete's father, Cliff, in the big bands. He was a very good saxophonist. When Pete started breaking the guitar, his dad and I thought, 'The kid has gone stark raving mad.' But Pete brought the first two Rickenbackers in to me and he said, 'Can you do anything with these? The idea is, I want them to appear to be the ones I'm using.' What he used to do was, he'd be playing and then at the right time he'd quickly switch to one of the guitars I'd repaired; I had glued it together so it looked to be perfectly normal. And he'd break it again. He was not as stupid as everyone said! When he used to push the guitar through the speaker cabinet, he only used to tear the front baffling cloth. He never used to go through a speaker—we only had to repair the cloth."

No question, Townshend is an MVP in Marshall history, having inspired, played, critiqued, and promoted seminal Marshall products. So astute readers (or Who fans, at least) might be wondering: If Townshend is so central to the Marshall story, why was he using Hiwatt for so many years?

Jim doesn't hesitate. "It was unfortunate, but simply a misunderstanding. The group used to come in my shop, and at one time we were waiting for a check. The check was put in, but my son sent them another bill, thinking they still had a balance due. Pete said they had paid, but Terry swore, 'No, you haven't paid, you haven't paid.' So Pete was upset and went to Hiwatt. And Hiwatt was one of the first copies of us! It was a complete misunderstanding. But knowing Pete, you see, he's an independent individual—same as I suppose I am as well."

The heat has long since blown over. Townshend routinely mentions in interviews that he is proud of his contributions to amp technology and honored to be a friend of Jim's.

> I have the honor of still knowing Jim Marshall and his son Terry very well, and we still get together and go over what really happened with the design of the first really big amplifier. They credit me almost entirely—along with a couple of other people, a couple of bass players—with being the guy that drove them to produce the first four-valve power amp.
>
> —Pete Townshend, *Guitar,* August 1996

Experiencing Hendrix

Seems like the long way around, but Marshall Amplification would never have existed were it not for those young drummers bringing their band mates around. One of Jim's top students had been Mitch Mitchell, who was proving to be a promising musician. Mitchell and Marshall were tight: Mitch had been a longtime student and worked in Jim's shop.[6] He'd even played in a band with Terry Marshall, who was turning out to be a solid sax player.

[6]Jim tells the story of first meeting Mitch Mitchell when the drummer—then Johnny Mitchell—was about 15 years old: "I had just set up a brand new Premier kit in the window of the first shop, at 76 Uxbridge. The window was so small you could barely get the kit in there, with maybe a guitar on either side. I was walking back from teaching at home when I heard this enormous racket going on; I figured whoever it was didn't know what he or she was doing on the drums. I saw this kid sitting behind the kit, in the window, and said, 'What's this?!' He whipped off the drum kit and ran out. About two days later he came in quite sheepishly and said, 'My mum says I have to come in and apologize to you. And she said to please let her pay for any damage I may have caused.' In those days, the skins were easily marked, and if you tightened up the bass drum pedal, it bit into the wooden bass drum hoop. So I had to replace that and all of the skins. But I said to him, 'Tell your mum not to worry. It's in the past, I've forgotten it.' And he said, 'Well, um...would you consider taking me on as a shop boy on Saturdays?' So, Johnny Mitchell became my shop boy when he was around 15. And later on he asked me to teach him to play the drums."

Jimi Hendrix keeps cool in front of the rig he likened to "two refrigerators hooked together."

Having appeared in film and on a children's television series for the BBC as a kid, Mitchell had always seemed destined for something big. As a teenager he played in three bands (according to one account, Mitchell auditioned for the Who after they had posted a notice in Marshall's shop), all of which had small-time hits as British R&B started to take hold. But in 1966, at age 19, he hit on some bad luck: Georgie Fame and the Blue Flames, his latest group, disbanded and left him out of work. The very next day, Mitchell auditioned for an American guitarist whose manager was trying to pull a band together in the UK. In the end, it was down to two drummers. There was a coin toss, and Aynsley Dunbar lost it. Dunbar went on to play with the likes of Jeff Beck, Journey, David Bowie, and Frank Zappa, and Mitch Mitchell became the drummer for one James Marshall Hendrix.

Near the end of 1966, the newly named Jimi Hendrix Experience played one of their first gigs at the famous club Ronnie Scott's.

"Mitch came 'round to the shop one day after having played at Ronnie Scott's with Hendrix," recalls Jim. "He said that there'd been a number of bands on the same night, and the stage was crowded. Jimi said to him, 'I should be playing my Fender [amp], but they told me that I cannot take the Fender up onstage because it means moving all the Marshalls—and there are four stacks of Marshalls onstage. I'd like to play through them.' So he played through them and afterward said to Mitch, 'You know, I wouldn't mind meeting this character who's got my name: James Marshall.'

"So, Mitch brought him along to my shop. And this tall, lanky American said to me, 'I'm going to be the greatest, man.' I thought, 'Christ, another American wanting something for nothing!' And yet a few breaths later he said, 'Now, I don't want to be given anything—I want to pay the full retail price. But what I want is service wherever I am in the world.' I thought, 'Oh no, a service engineer traveling with him, I can't afford that.' But what we arranged to do was to have his roadie come and spend time with Ken and Dudley to learn the amps. And he did, he came for a few weeks and learned really just the basic things, like changing valves, doing solder joints, changing a resistor, and so on. Apparently he did very well—we were never called with any problems on the amplifiers. Like Townshend, Jimi would only tear the grille cloth on the cabinets when it looked as if he were breaking the thing to pieces.

"Jimi bought three stacks. Eventually as I understand it he bought complete rigs to leave on different continents so he would not have to have them carted when he was touring. We became great friends. He had a fantastic sense of humor."

Jim has long credited Hendrix as "Marshall's greatest ambassador." It's no wonder, when the most indelible images of Hendrix onstage—coaxing flames from his guitar at Monterey, or in the morning light at Woodstock—would almost seem incomplete without his stacks as the backdrop.

Marshall rule: Endorsements

Over the course of the late '60s, Jim would see Hendrix at a handful of shows. Like Townshend, Hendrix occasionally appeared to be trashing his gear onstage when he only tore the grille. His contemporaries weren't all so clever.

"There was an enormous concert in London, the first really big rock 'n' roll show in London. There were two stages, with nonstop music all evening. Among the bands were Jimi Hendrix, Procol Harum, and the Move, who were from Birmingham. The guitarist onstage [Trevor Burton] was trying to do a Pete Townshend but he was knocking the stack over." (The Move were known for their adulation of the Who, including the raucous stage antics. When they weren't smashing their gear, the Move were busting up televisions, lamps, and anything else within reach.)

"I'd been at the side of the stage, and ran up behind the stack to hold it up! Hendrix was about to go on, on the opposite stage, but they were still playing. I walked up and said to the guitarist, 'Please, you wouldn't be able to continue playing if the amp were to break down.' He was nice enough about it, and I don't think he'd intended any real harm. But the singer [Carl Wayne] had begun swinging a mic stand around wildly and *just* missed my head. I felt it go through my hair.

"The funny thing was, a couple of weeks later they showed up at the factory at Bletchley. They came in and said, 'We'd like to see Mr. Marshall.' When I showed up—you should've seen the singer's face when he recognized me," Jim laughs. "They'd come to the factory to see if we would sponsor them, give them equipment. And I said, 'No way.'"

Burton, Wayne, and Co. were sure they were being turned down for nearly giving Mr. Marshall blunt head trauma (not unreasonable). But Jim's refusal was not out of bitterness. He had—and has to this day—a strict policy about giving away gear: He never does it. Unless they stole it, everyone you've ever seen playing a Marshall has anted up.

"I've always maintained that policy of no endorsements. The truth is that I don't need [the promotion], and never have. It wouldn't be fair to everyone. I would say to artists, 'If I give you this amp, the next poor schoolboy will have to pay more for his.' They all understand when I explain it to them.

"And it wouldn't be fair to the dealers; it's like giving away their money. What we will do for artists is to sell them the gear at trade rate plus V.A.T. [value-added tax]. But being as we do charge them for the amplifiers, we're quite happy to have them come to the factory when on tour and bring all their equipment to get checked over. We might charge them if there are parts being replaced and so on, but we don't charge them for the hours of labor. Those are our terms, with anyone."

Apparently, players feel Marshalls are worth the cash. The ever-modest Yngwie Malmsteen once put it this way: "Over the years virtually every amp manufacturer in the world has asked me to try their amps.... I'd rather pay for a Marshall than get the other ones for free."

Year of change

The year 1966 was also a big year in that it marked Terry's departure—except for a brief stint in the mid '90s—from J&T Marshall. Looking back now, it's apparent that if Terry was going to follow in his father's footsteps in any manner, it was as a musician: He's currently a successful jazz musician and teacher. Jim and Terry still see one another regularly—both live a stone's throw from the factory.

Terry Marshall performing at Jim's 80th birthday party, July 2003.

"Terry is a good saxophonist—he plays tenor, alto, and clarinet," Jim notes. "He was on the piano at first but he became fed up with it. He earns a lot of money playing and teaching."

Terry's departure came as Marshall was expanding. In 1966, orders for amps and cabinets reached a pitch high enough to justify the opening of an entirely new factory. The company pulled up stakes on Silverdale Road in Hayes and headed out of town, where commercial space was better priced. In June, Marshall Amplification opened a new facility of the same size on Lyon Road in Bletchley. Two years later they would open another location on nearby First Avenue, and in 1984 move again, this time to the huge factory along Denbigh Road where Marshall headquarters currently stands. Jim's home is a comfortable and bucolic five-minute ride from the factory. But in 1966, at 43 years old, he was moving out of West London for the first time in his life.

Misstep: The Rose-Morris deal

Demand was on the rise. Dozens of name acts—Del Shannon, the Animals, the Kinks, the Yardbirds, the Rolling Stones—wanted to be heard through Marshall, increasing the company's prestige and exposure. To date Jim had been taking orders exclusively through his Hanwell shop, but the opportunity for growth led him logically enough to offer product through a number of music retailers. He made a handshake deal with his friend John Jones, who owned Jones & Crossland in Birmingham: John would distribute to the North of England, Jim to the South. But the gears of commerce were in motion, and bigger business came calling.

Marshall's regional success had caught the eye of the Rose-Morris Agency, international distributor of musical instruments, as early as 1964. For two years Rose-Morris would be peripherally involved, promoting and distributing non-exclusively on the domestic market. In 1966, Jim signed a 15-year contract with Rose-Morris to take Marshall Amplification to the next level and distribute worldwide.

In all his years of business, the Rose-Morris deal remains Jim's biggest regret. "The whole thing is, I'd signed this 15-year contract with Rose-Morris, and their markup was outrageous. They were making a very good profit on product sold in the UK, and they took 55 percent on what they sold in the US. Just for what they sent abroad, 55 percent! It breaks my heart. Everybody else was doing that sort of thing for 10, 12.5 percent. But Rose-Morris was making a huge profit, and making an advance on my profit. So the only people that were playing Marshall abroad, particularly in the US, were the people that could really afford it—top-of-the-line stars and that sort of thing."

Marshall's success had been due in large part to affordability. The business had been built on the backs of young players, musicians barely out of their teens who played gigs and worked odd jobs to pull together enough scratch for decent gear. Now, Rose-Morris had set Marshall up as if they were exclusive and high-end, like some boutique manufacturer.

"Obviously, it really restricted the turnover. We never did a really nice turnover. That was stupid, really. We never in a year turned over a million pounds—I think it was usually more like three-quarters of a million. So my costing had to be such that we did not make much profit. I was looking to make it up elsewhere, in resale and in wholesale as well. I started a wholesale business, Cleartone Musical

Jim shows off Marshall Amplification's early-'70s range.

Instruments. I was stocking Slingerland drums, Latin Percussion, all those sort of lines."

In the years to come, Jim would set up a number of businesses to backfill profits lost to Rose-Morris. These included not just music distribution but the opening of two large department stores. Imagine, you're making amplifiers for the biggest bands at the dawn of rock, and to turn a decent profit you start selling socks. Jim leased a number of retail spaces around London, including an enormous 16,000-square-foot showroom for his MBC department stores (named for Marshall, Bran, and Craven). It wasn't until 1979 that Jim would get out of retail. Happily, the business that began in desperation would at its end pay off in spades. Twenty-odd years later, Jim can laugh about it. "When I knew I was near the finish with Rose-Morris, I sold off all the shops. I made so much selling off those leases, as I'd had them since the '60s. When I sold them in 1979, I made far more money selling leases than I ever did from amplifiers."

Park

Rose-Morris had also spelled trouble for John Jones, who lost the right to distribute Marshall to the North. Though Jim could not (or did not want to) allow Jones to control the territory any longer, he sought a means to maintain the friendship and partnership.

"John Jones, who owned shops as well as his wholesale company, was a great friend. When we were preparing the contracts with Rose-Morris in 1965, I said to [president] Roy Morris, 'If I take this contract out, there's one proviso: I do a line of amplification with John Jones.' And reluctantly he had to say yes, because I said I wasn't signing the contract without it. Of course, in retrospect I wished they *had* turned the contract down, because I realized about four months into it what a bad deal it was.

"I built the amps for John Jones to sell wholesale, and we distributed them under Cleartone Musical Instruments, or CMI. I could not use the Marshall name on the amplifiers due to the [Rose-Morris] contract, so we needed another name. They were called 'Park' because I was having dinner one night with him and his wife, and I said, 'I can't call it "Jones Amplifiers," it's too common a name.' And then I turned to his wife, Margaret, and asked, 'What was your maiden name?' She said, 'Park,' and I knew that was it. Because all over the world they know the name Park: a park you walk through, a car park, Park Avenue.... It was familiar and classy at once."

Original Park amps are to this day a great catch for collectors. Produced from 1965 to 1982, Park lines closely mirrored Marshall's own—small surprise, as they were essentially the same amps with a different faceplate—but sales suffered without the benefit of Marshall's celebrated name. Marshall would dissolve Park and CMI, which had come under his control, when the Rose-Morris deal came to an end in 1981. In 1992, Jim resurrected the Park name for a line of low-budget, solid-state amps. The new Parks were a hit, and presaged what was to come at the millennium's turn: the MG line, Marshall's enormously successful line of affordable, all-transistor amps.

CMI, for its part, had opened another income avenue outside the restrictions of the Rose-Morris deal. John Jones held on as director of the small distributor until 1971, when he returned to his Jones & Crossland shops. For the brief period of 1976–1977, PA equipment and a handful of guitar amps were built under the CMI name, to limited success.

What's cooking?: The Kitchen-Marshalls

"Kitchen-Marshall came about through another friend of mine, who owned Kitchen's of Leeds, a big retailer," Jim explains of this curious and brief little venture,

A singer-drummer who gave up playing instruments . . . to sell them

The sound of music means money for Jim Marshall

by MICHAEL NEWBERRY

PALTRY PAY

'LIKE A BOMB'

'NO DEAL'

BIGGER STAFF

The *Sunday Express* of September 27, 1970, recounts Jim's story as a businessman.

which began in 1966. "He was purely a retailer, but he had a commercial section where he outfitted all these clubs with lights and soundboards and PAs. And he didn't like the PAs he was using. I was in his store one day and he asked if I would make a PA for him. I told him, 'Sure, I've got a Marshall PA, we've been doing it for ages.' He said, 'No, can't have that. I want Kitchen's name on it because we do all the clubs locally, and I'd like to have our name up there.' I said the only way I could see doing it was to have the word Kitchen somewhere *in* it, but not as the sole name; I hated the idea of something going through my works with the name 'Kitchen'! I suggested we combine the name, so we made it Kitchen-Marshall.

"We only did two or three years of PAs, and a few guitar cabinets, because he died, you see. His son took over. His son, who was stone deaf, went about closing down the Kitchen business and opening a massive keyboard showroom. It was full of grand pianos and upright pianos. Didn't sell a thing. That's a tough business, and a very expensive operation. His father would never have done it. It's a shame, the company had been over 100 years old."

The bands from Marshall's home turf of West London were enjoying unprecedented success both at home and, increasingly, in the US. Britain's Beat Boom sound had spread like mad, broadening not only at its center, where the Beatles, Zombies, and Hermits thrived, but at the surrounding edges where the rock was getting harder and louder. In some cases, *much* louder.

A leap in the quality and power of Marshall's amp lines also made 1966 a milestone year. With a design re-think on tubes and transformers, the new 50- and 100-watt heads peeled back another layer of overdrive punch. These amps would be the stuff of legend. Nicknamed "Plexi" amps for the gold-colored "Plexiglas" (actually Perspex—causing some folk to refer to it as "Perplexi") on the control panel (used from 1966 through 1969), they remain the most coveted Marshalls of all. A series of lower-wattage head/cabs and combos were offered beginning in 1966 as well, though they weren't to be widely appreciated for a good 30 years. The capability of 18- and 20-watt amps to heat up output tubes and deliver Marshall's distinct crunch at lower volumes would make them highly collectible among studios and musicians playing smaller rooms. For decades, though, "louder = better" was the winning formula. Few players made this clearer than Ritchie Blackmore.

Blackmore

Jim had always kept an ear to the ground, and so long as enough interested customers were there to make a production run profitable, the Marshall team would knock out most any configuration with most any specs. There weren't many asking for 200-watt heads, but Ritchie Blackmore was one of them. He'd known Jim for years; he'd been in the shop back in 1961 with his contemporary, Townshend, asking Jim to build a better amp.

Early in his career, Blackmore had used Vox AC30s in sessions (including sit-ins with Tom Jones) with bands like the Outlaws and Screaming Lord Sutch, and even through his first two years in Deep Purple. But in 1970, he switched to Marshall. Making a 200-watt amp that didn't overheat in about five minutes was a challenge to the team at Marshall, but it was the *look* of the amp and slanted cab that first drew Blackmore. He liked the design so much, in fact, that for years his favorite old Vox was hidden onstage, housed in a Marshall cabinet.

In the '70s, Ritchie Blackmore pushed his Marshalls to the fringes of high performance.

The 200-watt Marshall Majors pushed his buttons, but not hearing the precise tone he wanted, Blackmore approached Jim again.

> So I went back to the factory because I knew Jim and I said, "Look, I want this changed and I want that changed." And I used to play in front of all the people that were there working; there would be women there assembling things, and I had the amp boosted to 400 watts. So I would be playing away right in front of all these people and they'd be trying to work. I'd go, "That's not right, more treble," and they'd take out a resistor. I had to play full blast or otherwise I couldn't know what it was going to sound like. The people hated me.
>
> —*Guitar Player,* 1978

Quite insanely, Blackmore would modify the 200-watters on his own, adding an extra two valves to the output stage to get even more juice from the heads—by his account, the amps he used regularly ran 300 watts. "I'm not saying I play the loudest," he remarked in 1978. "It depends on how many you use. But one on its own is the loudest amplifier in the world."

Page

> "I introduced Marshalls to my backline in 1970. I've used them ever since and probably always will."
>
> —Jimmy Page, from Marshall's 30th anniversary catalog, 1992

Jimmy Page, a friend of Blackmore's from their concurrent session work, had caught the Marshall bug a few years prior. He had admired the tone Eric Clapton introduced with the Paul/Marshall combination, and wanted a piece of it. On the heels of releasing Led Zeppelin's debut in 1969, he equipped himself with a 100-watt Marshall. That June he told *Guitar Player,* "You get a Marshall with a Gibson and it's fantastic, a perfect match."

Like Blackmore, Page would later soup up the head. This was done by the use of KT-88 output tubes, which boosted the SLP's power and also provided a crisper, cleaner sound. And as with Townshend before him, the impetus to go Marshall in the first place had come from within his own band:

> I was going to build up a big bank of four [AC30's], but Bonzo's kit is so loud that they just don't come over the top of it properly.
>
> *What is the amplifier setup you're using now?*
>
> Onstage? Marshall 100s that are customized in New York so they've got 200 watts. I've got four unstacked cabinets, and I've got a wah-wah pedal and an MXR unit. Everything else is total flash [*laughs*]. I've got a harmonizer, a theremin, a violin bow, and an Echoplex echo unit.
>
> *Are there certain settings you use on the amp?*
>
> Depending on the acoustics of the place, the volume is up to about three, and the rest is pretty standard.
>
> —*Guitar Player,* July 1977

Jimmy Page doing voodoo on a Theremin in the early '70s, while his Marshalls look on.

Later in 1969, Page debuted his Marshall on the famous "Heartbreaker" solo and on "Bring It On Home" on *Led Zeppelin II.* For recordings to come, Page would often rely on his favorite older setup, a Telecaster through a Supro amp. But if you caught Led Zeppelin onstage, you caught him with Marshall. And for the brilliant solo in "Stairway to Heaven," Page plugged a Telecaster into a Marshall.

Beck

Jeff Beck had beaten both Blackmore and Page to the punch. He too had played Vox in the past, most famously during his tenure in the Yardbirds, before switching to a 50-watt Marshall (for those keeping count, that's a Yardbirds trifecta: Beck, Page, and Clapton all played Marshall). Beck reinvented his tone and style to launch his solo career, committing his reborn sound to tape in 1968 on *Truth.* The album is largely uncredited as a prototype for heavy metal.

In a 1999 interview, Beck differentiated between the Fender Bassman, which he had also used, and his Marshall:

Jeff Beck, with a Les Paul acquired from Rick Nielsen, fronts a pair of full stacks at a 1968 California gig.

> Let's put it like this: Buddy Holly would not have sounded the way he did with a Marshall. He has the crisp and sparkly thing, which is what the Fender does best. Hendrix couldn't have sounded as good with a Fender—it has diamond sparkles all over it. That crystal clarity is fine for country bands and Fleetwood Mac, but if you want to get a little bit rude and loud, you've got to have a Marshall. The Marshall sound is the balls. It's the big daddy, and it has that growl that no other amp has.
>
> —*Guitar Player,* May 1999

Beck has many amps at his disposal, but he's long stood by Marshall 50-watters. In recent years he's played a JCM2000 (DSL50). "It sounds like you're playing at a million watts," he says, "with a nice, agreeable amount of distortion that can be continuously varied. I love it."

Going stateside

Rose-Morris may have been a rotten deal, but the Marshall name was along for the roller-coaster ride that was the British Invasion. As the Kinks, the Who, the Hollies, Manfred Mann (Marshall players all), and others continued their reign over America, Marshall Amplification multiplied sales by a factor of six between 1964 and 1967.

To support US sales, Jim planned a British Invasion of his own in 1966. From his drumming days, he had a relationship with Al Wolf, the owner of a drum store on New York's famous 48th Street, long known as an instrument retail strip. Jim had sold his amps through Wolf for a few months, and figured him as a shoe-in for moving his amps across the country—but the retailer's own vices unwittingly cost him the deal.

"I had phoned Al Wolf in advance, with every confidence the business would be his. But when I arrived in town for our scheduled meeting I was told he was in Vegas. Al was a big gambler, so Vegas used to take him, pay for him, give him a room at Caesar's Palace. I reluctantly agreed to wait until the next day, but still he did not show

MARSHALL AMPLIFICATION EQUIPMENT

Price Schedule - July, 1968.

		Suggested Retail Price. £.	s.	d.
BASS, LEAD & ORGAN AMPLIFIERS				
1967 Lead 200 Watt Output		158.	11.	6.
1978 Bass 200 Watt Output		158.	11.	6.
*1959 Lead 100 Watt Output		112.	2.	6.
*1992 Bass 100 Watt Output		112.	2.	6.
*1987 Lead 50 Watt Output		77.	7.	6.
*1986 Bass 50 Watt Output		77.	7.	6.
*1989 Organ 50 Watt Output		77.	7.	6.
*Available with tremolo and remote control footswitch at an extra cost of:- To order - prefix model number with 'T' e.g. - T1959		6.	19.	6.
BASS, LEAD & ORGAN [illegible]				
1982 Bass, Lead & Organ	100 Watt Output	122.	4.	6.
1982B Bass, Lead & Organ	100 Watt Output	122.	4.	6.
1990 Lead	80 Watt Output	99.	16.	0.
1960 Bass, Lead & Organ	75 Watt Output	99.	16.	0.
1960B Bass, Lead & Organ	75 Watt Output	99.	16.	0.
1935 Bass	75 Watt Output	99.	16.	0.
1935B Bass	75 Watt Output	99.	16.	0.
1972 Lead & Organ	40 Watt Output	74.	0.	0.
1988 Bass	40 Watt Output	76.	4.	6.
BASS, LEAD & ORGAN COMBINATION AMPLIFIERS				
1961 Lead	50 Watt Output	130.	1.	0.
1962 Bass & Lead	50 Watt Output	135.	13.	6.
*1958 Lead	18 Watt Output	65.	1.	0.
*1973 Bass, Lead & Organ	18 Watt Output	81.	16.	6.
*With reverberation unit extra:-		13.	9.	0.

/Contd..................

			Suggested Retail Price. £.	s.	d.
P.A. (PUBLIC ADDRESS) AMPLIFIERS					
1966	200 Watt Output		177.	3.	6.
1968	100 Watt Output		112.	2.	6.
2003	100 Watt Output		123.	6.	6.
1963	50 Watt Output		95.	6.	0.
1985	50 Watt Output		77.	7.	6.
2002	50 Watt Output		103.	3.	0.
1917	20 Watt Output P.A. System complete with one pair 2 x 10" Columns.		93.	6.	0.
P.A. (PUBLIC ADDRESS) SPEAKER CABINETS					
1976	200 Watt Output	Per Pair	233.	4.	6.
1969	160 Watt Output	Per Pair	188.	7.	6.
1983	80 Watt Output	Per Pair	104.	5.	6.
1991	80 Watt Output	Per Pair	89.	14.	0.
1975	Supafuzz		13.	12.	6.

ROSE, MORRIS & CO. LTD.,
32/34 GORDON HOUSE ROAD,
KENTISH TOWN, LONDON, N.W.5.

....

The July 1968 Rose-Morris price list—a 100-watt 1959 head for £112!

up. So I went to see another wholesaler I knew, and the two old boys there were over the moon when I gave them the offer. But they had a nephew who worked with them, and he walks in and says, 'Forget it. We'll buy stock and it will probably sit on the shelf.'

"My third call was to Sidney Hack, who was the boss of Unicord. Sidney knew I was in New York specifically to set up this operation and had an order for amplifiers all ready for me. Sidney was smart, and it was a shrewd move on his part."

Jazz sounds
JAZZ NEWS
By John Jack
Lady has her day
Systems come systems go
Marshall goes on forever

The full stack reigns in a 1973 *Sounds* ad.

Hack got the deal, contributing greatly to the success of Unicord. At the time, Unicord was a Gulf & Western company. In 1985, twenty-four years after its inception, Unicord was bought by the Japanese-owned Korg Inc. Today, Marshall is distributed in the States exclusively by Korg USA.

To a degree, the Rose-Morris deal overshadowed the Golden Age of Rock for Jim, but it was still a well-gilded Golden Age. For Marshall Amps to have succeeded on such a grand scale, some enormous pieces had to fall into place. An amp was made for some underdog musicians in West London; a riptide of talented and decidedly loud bands rose all around London and were swept to unforeseen suc-

A decidedly groovy ad in *Sounds*, circa 1975, for the 100-watt 2098 (lead) and 2099 (bass) solid-state heads. Both had been discontinued by 1977.

cess; and a generation of liberation-seeking youth on both sides of the Atlantic welcomed the thunderous new music with open ears and flailing arms. Without taking anything away from Jim's business acumen or the capabilities of his R&D teams, a great deal of Marshall's success was "right place, right time." Through the Golden Age and well past, Marshalls were ubiquitous.

Mick Jones, Paul Kossoff, Billy Gibbons, Steve Marriott, Mick Ralphs, Marc Bolan, Tony Iommi, Robin Trower, Gary Moore, Peter Frampton, Al Di Meola, Angus Young, Alvin Lee, Ace Frehley, Paul Weller, Eddie Van Halen—the names of Marshall players from the late '60s through the '70s would fill the next two pages. The gear they were seen playing had perennial influence on rock instrumentation.

All along, Jim and his crack R&D teams kept pace by continually modernizing and bettering available lines. Most notably, the development of the 2203 master-volume head in 1975 by design engineer Steve Grindrod allowed for maximum overdrive without maximum volume; the master-volume design would become an industry standard. For well over a decade, the stages of rock's elite were ringed with Marshalls.

In 1981, the Rose-Morris contract expired at last. Without the distributor's usurious markup on export, Jim was free to price and distribute equilaterally. He immediately produced a stack that represented Marshall's best at a reasonable price. At the dawn of the '80s, an avalanche of JCM800s tumbled into garages and rehearsal studios across the United States. With his hands untied, Jim could offer the Marshall sound at a price most any serious player could manage. The affordable amp hit the amateur and semipro market square in the face. Marshalls ruled supreme in the metal-dominated rock scene of the '80s, as evidenced by a "who's who" of groups with stacks in their back lines: Iron Maiden, Judas Priest, Guns N' Roses, Anthrax, Def Leppard, UFO, Metallica, Megadeth, Yngwie Malmsteen, Ted Nugent, Ozzy Osbourne, Quiet Riot, Bon Jovi, Saxon, Slayer, Rush...the list goes on and on.

The success of the JCM800 drove Marshall Amplification to win the Queen's Award for Export, of which Jim was supremely proud.

"As soon as we finished with Rose-Morris, I reduced the export price by 25 percent straightaway. To win the Queen's Award, a company has to increase their export substantially for three consecutive years. With Rose-Morris, it just was not possible to achieve, but as of 1981 it was. Although I'd reduced the price, the turnover went up 360% over three years. So I walked away with the Queen's Award in 1984. It meant very much to me personally, and to the employees it was a source of pride as well."

Chapter 4

Looking Back

Rock 'n' roll gear, like the music itself, is continually revisiting its own past. The phenomenon may be inescapable under rock's reign. Seems every time a new amplifier, guitar, or effects unit is introduced, it is measured by its capacity to reproduce the characteristics of a small set of tried-and-true products, most of which have been around for decades. Even software-driven instruments and hard disk recorders—the very nature of which begs us to invent, morph, and interface anew—are typically evaluated by their ability to recreate vintage gear.

That is to say, in many ways the dust has long ago settled on rock 'n' roll instrumentation. As anyone in or out of the musical instrument industry can attest, the names of three men—above all others—have had enduring and universal influence: Leo Fender, Les Paul, and Jim Marshall.

It's an exclusive and revered club. To this day, Fender's name is on thousands of guitars and amps that come off production lines around the world. Were it not for the basic model and scheme of Fender's Bassman amp, the JTM45 would never have been made. Les Paul is owed a debt by anyone who has built, played, or daydreamed about a solidbody electric guitar. Plus, his contributions to recording revolutionized the way records are made. Marshall, the company, has been known for 41 years for "the sound." Marshall, the man, is renowned for leaving it the hell *alone.*

The Marshall sound

"I've never wanted to say there was something magical about building an amplifier—amplification dates back so long ago," Jim says. "Since 1962, we've basically made the same amplifier. There's hardly any difference. What we do is about getting the Marshall sound."

And what is *the* Marshall sound? "It really depends on who you ask," Jim answers. "In the early days they were built purely for rock 'n' roll, but nowadays they're capable of doing any kind of music—from very heavy rock to blues and even jazz and country. If I had to pick one amp that defined the Marshall sound, I'd have to say it was the first amp that we ever built back in 1962, the JTM45. To my ears the complex harmonics and musical overtones of that amp when it is driven hard are the very essence of 'the Marshall sound' because that's where it all started."

The evolution of tone has found that sound manifested in a broad selection of players and amps over the years. Some would point to Eric Clapton's "woman tone" or Eddie Van Halen's legendary "brown sound." Slash would describe the raunch of his 2555s, Zakk Wylde would cite the woody roar of his 2203s, and the current crop of players would probably list the hellish tone that Daron Malakian of System of a Down derives from his Mode Fours, or the tight, low punch of Wayne Static's MG100HDFX.

The musical instrument playing field is wide today, and second- and third-generation manufacturers of rock equipment have attached their names to excellent and popular instruments, from Mike Soldano to Paul Reed Smith to Hartley Peavey. They tip their hats to the past while keeping a keen eye on the future, making instruments that are ever smarter, faster, easier, and cheaper. Their names may survive and thrive just as the Three Kings' did—you'll have to wait another 40 years or so to find out.

Fender and Paul were inventors nonpareil and terrifically successful, but both eventually lost control of their prize creations. Leo sold to CBS in 1964, reportedly due to health concerns. A non-compete agreement would prohibit the master craftsman from building amps and guitars for years (he later resumed at Music Man and then G&L). Les spent years convincing Gibson to build the solidbody electric, then spent decades in push-and-pull relationships with Gibson presidents who opposed him on everything from design to manufacture and promotion.

In 1989, Jim was approached by Harmon Instruments, best known for their brass and woodwinds, to sell his company. "The president of Harmon came to see me and offered £100 million, cash, for the business. In addition he also offered to sign me up for 15 years to stay on at £1 million a year."

Imagine it. Jim was 66 years old—comfortably into the retirement years by anyone's standard. If he ever had anything to prove, it had been proven. He'd banked enough to keep the next five generations of Marshalls in luxury. His reputation in business was impeccable and his legacy was safe. No matter what was to follow, Jim could ride into the sunset with his head held high. His reaction to the offer?

"I said, 'Sorry, it's not for sale.'"

Why?

"It's *my* name. And I wouldn't want to be told what to do by somebody else."

Ladies and gentlemen, *that* is rock 'n' roll.

"For me, it was never about turning a profit," Jim says plainly. "Everything I've done, all the money I've made since I was 14, I've saved for all my life. I've never been interested in money, really. Take the shoes I'm wearing: they're Bally shoes from Italy. I bought them in 1970. The clothes I wear all the time I bought back in the 1970s. I don't spend money on myself.

"The only money I spend on myself is for cigars, really—and I don't spend much money on them, either! My girls in Spain, who handle distribution there, buy a handful for me every month and send them over. They only cost me about £2 10P [about $3.50] each. In the whole of England you couldn't find them for that price! I wouldn't pay the £8 15P [about $13.50] they cost in England. I would sooner give up. I enjoy them, and I can afford it, but I just can't see paying that money just for a cigar."

Jim's discreet financial sense has guided his leadership of Marshall. Whenever purchases are required—from new equipment to expanded factory space—he waits until the company can afford them outright and completely. Never does he borrow money from banks or seek investors. "I always save money until I've got enough to make the next money," he notes. "I don't want to be beholden to anybody. I'm very independent, and I don't believe in borrowing money."

Jim also stands in philosophical contrast with those for whom "business planning" becomes a goal in itself. "I've known far too many companies that spend all their time in meetings worrying about the future and coming up with five-year plans and such. How do I plan for the future? By making sure I do everything right today. *Nobody* knows what's going to happen in five years."

Value and production

It's safe to say the man can indeed afford his own cigars. His personal net worth is a private affair, though one can surmise a ballpark considering company output, evaluation, and longevity.

Marshall Amplification is privately held, in its entirety, by Jim himself. Years ago, Jim made three employees (including Ken Bran) directors under him and held out an offer of stock for their loyalty. He offered 2.5 percent of the company to each director, with the condition that they work with him until the age of 51. At that point, each would be offered a quarter of a million pounds in shares. By September of 2003, the only shares left were the quarter million owned by director Kelvin Hack. As this book went to press, Hack cashed in his chips and retired.

As of this writing, the *Financial Times* of London put Marshall Amplification's worth at £30 million (at the exchange rate of 1.6046 pounds sterling to the dollar, that's $48,138,000 USD). Marshall's baseline performance has been steady, and dependably on the rise in the US. The main factory on Denbigh Road in Bletchley, Milton Keynes, produces 1,700 units weekly across Marshall's middle and top-end product lines. A whopping 4,800 additional units are produced weekly overseas, bringing Marshall's total worldwide output to 6,500 units every week.[7] The MG line is produced in two foreign factories: Those made in Korea are shipped to North America (Canada, the US, Mexico, and Central American countries), and a factory in India ships MGs to all of Europe. Marshall pedals and acoustic amps are manufactured in China and shipped worldwide. The US is the chief importer of Marshall equipment, absorbing an impressive chunk of both UK and OEM (original equipment manufacturer) output. Korg USA, Inc., is Marshall's exclusive US distributor.

[7]For perspective, and for insight into Rose-Morris's negative impact, consider that in 1970 the company was valued at £600,000, with over £2 million in overseas sales (per *Sunday Express*). At the time, they were producing 200 amps and 500 speaker cabinets per week.

Even the OEM products made overseas are built under Jim's watchful eye. His staff closely monitors OEM production, and all such units and their accompanying literature state, "Designed, Engineered and Quality Controlled by Marshall Amplification, plc., Bletchley, Milton Keynes, England."

Jim confirms, "I'll only allow my name to go on something if I'm 100 percent sure it's a quality product in all areas—sound, looks, reliability, and roadworthiness."

All told, Marshall products are sold in 87 countries (can you even *name* 87 countries?), with the company currently exploring deeper inroads on the continent of Africa.

As a man of 80, Jim has of course given thought to the long-term future of his company. Marshall Amplification will go into family trust. He is currently engaged to Ms. Pauline Ball, though he already refers to her as his wife. And Pauline keeps him young—at last sighting she was headed to an Eminem show. (Pauline will be Jim's fifth wife. "I was good with business," Jim says, "but never very good with picking women.") Victoria Rose Marshall, Jim's daughter from his second marriage, works at the Bletchley headquarters as sales director. Terry Marshall, who was invited into the business at age 16, lives nearby; he is in touch with his father but not the business. Jim regularly sees his siblings—all six of them—for birthdays and holidays, as well as the aunt and uncle who helped raise him back on Snarsgate Street.

Jim's health is good. A recent tumble down the stairs has crimped his walk a bit, and his doctor occasionally asks him to ease back on the Scotch, but his pace of work, travel, and productivity is yet to be curbed. (There's a bit of black comedy to this, but the day after he declined Harmon's £100 million offer in 1989, he had an aneurysm. It was a frightening episode, but Jim recovered fully.) Asked if he worries that the name or direction of his company might be spoiled when he's gone—that someone might make the kinds of mistakes that ruined Kitchen's of Leeds—Jim's reply is succinct: "It would be idiotic to do anything else."

Charity

Through performances, donations of gear and instruments, and monetary gifts, Jim finds ways to support a number of charities. "I give away about a half million pounds a year to charities," he states. Most are local charities, with a majority going to the Buckinghamshire Association of Youth Clubs ("They used to call it 'Boys Clubs,'" Jim laughs, "but you're not allowed to now because there are girls in there"), London Federation of Youth Clubs, and the Variety Club. In 2003, Jim's contributions actually topped 1.5 million pounds, with another eight hundred thousand to Macmillan Nurses and another two hundred thousand to hospice care. For over ten years he's been a proud member of the Grand Order of Water Rats, a charitable group of 200 world-class entertainers from Britain and Hollywood. The group allows a maximum of 200 members; most recently they were down by one when Bob Hope passed away. Next time you see Jim at a trade show with a golden rat pendant around his neck, you'll know why.

JIM DIVES IN TO HELP CHAMPION PAUL

at ex-hospital

Cops hunt racists

The Citizen extols Jim's philanthropy.

In September 1993, Jim was celebrated in *The Citizen* newspaper for having helped a sufferer of cerebral palsy. Paul Hancock had been crowned Disabled Swimming's World Champion, but almost didn't make his meet because his car had been breaking down. The paper read:

> And in stepped philanthropist Jim Marshall, head of Bletchley's world-famous Marshall Amplification, and no stranger to success himself. After being contacted by us, he agreed to buy a sparkling white Metro car with special adaptations for Paul.
>
> —*The Citizen*, September 9, 1993

Paul and Jim were photographed alongside the Metro—in front of four full Marshall stacks.

Of the ways in which Jim likes to give of himself, none beats a song. Jim had given up performing back in 1953 to teach drums full time. He hadn't sung a lick for 20 years when, at a charity for boys clubs, he was asked to support a friend who was headed to the stage. Frankie Vaughan hadn't sung in some time either, and his wife, Stella, urged Jim to get up there with him. "Walking from the edge of the dance floor to the stage, I thought, 'I'm getting a little nervous. Am I going to be able to remember the words? Can I hit the notes?' But funnily enough, as soon as I got onstage I was *back*. Just like that, I remembered every word and hit every note. From then on I sang quite a lot for charities."

Performing runs thick in Jim's veins, and the fact that he relates to musicians at eyeball level is an invaluable asset to his business. In addition to the now regular singing at charity events, Jim likes to keep his drum chops at the ready as well—every so often he knocks the dust off the Slingerland kit in his office. He's particularly proud of the cymbals given to him by friend Bob Zildjian.

On few occasions has Jim's love of the stage been more evident than on a stop in New York City in the summer of 2003. Fresh from the Expromusic trade show in Mexico, where he'd been honored with a commemorative trophy and by getting his handprints in a "Walk of Fame," Jim had an extended layover. He found himself in town over a Monday night and seized the opportunity to do what he'd wanted to for years: see Les Paul perform.

Since 1995, Les Paul has been playing back-to-back sets on Monday nights at Iridium in midtown Manhattan (and for a decade before at the defunct Fat Tuesday's downtown). Tourists, players, guitar junkies, and fans from the old Les Paul/Mary Ford days fill the dinner club to see 88-year-old Les at work, and he always slays the house. He brings up a steady stream of young talent, alternately encouraging and barking his blue humor across the stage. The crowd loves him for the laughs, and leans back in a nostalgic glow when the inevitable "How High the Moon" comes around.

Though Les's guitars and Jim's amps have been a pair since Eric Clapton wed them in 1966, the gentlemen themselves weren't friends until they both put their handprints in Hollywood's Rock Walk of Fame in 1985 (along with Leo Fender, Eddie Van Halen, Stevie Wonder, Robert Moog, and Bill Ludwig). "That was the first time Les and myself met," Jim recalls. "We hit it off straightaway; he has a great sense of humor. It was wonderful; he's somebody I've looked up to for many years because I

Three for the road: (l–r) Les Paul, Bill Ludwig Jr., and Jim Marshall put their mitts in wet Rock Walk concrete, 1985.

used to play his recordings. Les is a true innovator, and I admire anybody like that—especially when he's such a nice chap." Some 18 years later, Jim was looking forward to seeing his friend—and busting to join him onstage. Late into the second set, Les called him up.

"Ladies and gentleman, Jim Marshall!" Though there were some identifiable gear-heads in the crowd, applause was at first scattered. Then Les clarified, "The man behind the Marshall amp!" The crowd roared. They knew they were witnessing a once-in-a-lifetime sight as the two greeted one another with wide smiles and a hug. Nervous for her fiancée, Pauline blushed and buried her face in her hands. But Les counted off a Gershwin tune, and Jim was in the moment. Casually cradling the mic like a too-cool Dean Martin, his milky voice rode over the top. Les, ever in character, peppered the tune with good-natured razzing to the crowd, but Jim was lost in the music. He swayed and gestured with a fluidity that belied his octogenarian bones.

Among the admirers at Iridium was Marilyn Manson guitarist John 5, who also had an opportunity to sit in with Les: "That was definitely one of the best nights of my life. I met Jim and Les, and that in itself made the night perfect. But what sent it into orbit was getting up there and playing with Les and then, just when I thought it couldn't get any better, seeing Jim and Les onstage together—I swear to you, I had tears in my eyes."

"People that hear me sing now tell me I'm better than I was years ago," Jim would say later. "I think when you are doing it for money, there's a little tension there all the time. Today when I go on, I'm so relaxed up there. It's like I'm sunning myself onstage."

The ultimate pairing: Marshall and Les Paul at New York City's Iridium, 2003.

His follow-up comments were even more telling. "If you can really do your job as an entertainer, it's very difficult to break away from it. It doesn't matter if you're my age or even older. I've always looked upon it as if, if everything else folded, I'd be quite happy to go back to performing. In one way, I would sooner do that."

Jim reflects on the ways in which he and Les are alike: independent, tenacious, driven to see their visions through. While together in New York there was talk of a Les Paul model Marshall amplifier, and whether it was a lark or a serious plan, the prospect jazzed both of them. More than all that, though, Les Paul and Jim Marshall share a timeless love of the stage.

Looking back

The stretch of Uxbridge Road that runs through central Hanwell hasn't changed all that much since Jim owned his first two shops there. It's more crowded, for sure, and a steady stream of slow-moving cars chokes the town's narrow main drag. Local factories and small stores employ the locals in what remains a working-class town.

Jim's limousine raised eyebrows as he cruised through on a recent visit. With the shop names all changed it's tough to get one's bearings at first, and the limo almost passes by 93 Uxbridge. It's been more than ten years since his last visit, but the shop's oversized windows catch Jim's eye. The limo pulls up on the curb and Jim emerges, wearing a grin, to survey the old block.

The site of the first Marshall & Son, 76 Uxbridge Road, later became Dudley Craven's workshop.

The former site of J&T Marshall is now London Drivetime. You used to be able to learn the drums there for one guinea per hour; now

Driven to success: Jim in 2003 at the site of his second shop on Uxbridge Road.

you can learn to drive for £17.50. A deli selling bottled Starbucks stands where the musicians' café used to be, two doors down. Straight across the street, a big sign runs over the window of Flying Pig Instrument Supply Company at 72–74 Uxbridge. Jim has a laugh that all these years later, a music store still sits on the block. Here at his old stomping grounds he may as well be the Mayor of Hanwell (it's fitting that John Kent, his big-hearted driver, should call him "Guv'nor"), and he marches into the music store to introduce himself. Of course, Marshall amps are on the showroom floor, surrounded by a half-dozen other makes. The kid behind the counter, nonplussed at first, trips over himself when Jim identifies himself, then clamors to find something to have autographed.

Immediately adjacent to Flying Pig is 76 Uxbridge, site of the first Marshall store and Dudley's workshop. It really is tiny. At maybe ten feet across, the space is just wide enough to fit the barber's chair and the barber now working there.

"I believe some people used to like coming into my small shop because they were then talking to the boss of it, straightaway," Jim remembers. "It was more like a family affair. In the bigger shops now, that's gone. It was the same way in America, when I first went over. They were very small stores, and it was the same feeling there."

The Official Jim Marshall Nostalgia Tour led to remembrances of the old shops and the people who worked in them. To his disappointment, Jim has lost track of Dudley Craven. "He'd gone to work at Heathrow. I'd formed another company selling housewares and fancy goods and everything else you can think of—that was

Driver John Kent and Jim take a photo break during their 2003 London tour.

MBC, for Marshall, Bran, and Craven. I named it to try and give him something to stay in touch for. I wanted to keep him. He became 21 and was just itching to get back to London. He went to Heathrow and worked in radar.

"The last I'd heard of him, he'd moved to Canada. Whenever I've done interviews there, on television and on radio, I've always said, 'Dudley, where are you? Come and see me.' He was a mad car driver—he'd had two accidents in the time I'd known him—and all I can imagine is that he had a bad motor accident. With all the advertising I've done for him to come back, to see him, I've had no success whatsoever."

Bran stayed on at Bletchley for years as Jim's head of R&D, though he retired in the '70s before collecting on that quarter of a million in stock. In 1974, he was central to a well-designed but ill-fated line of amps known as Narb.

"The Narb line came about because Ken Bran, when we moved into Bletchley, said Marshall was becoming an old name. 'We have to change the name,' he'd said. I told him I didn't see it that way and he went away a bit downcast. And then I thought, 'I'll

In 1974 Ken Bran devised his Narb line of amps to stand apart from Marshall's.

have him back.' So I said, 'We can't call the name "Bran," because people will think of Kellogg's All-Bran or something like that. But reversing your name, as Narb, that'd be okay.' So we did. We built a few in production, but they didn't sell. And yet it was all the same parts—they were the same amplifiers as Marshall. The only thing different was that instead of building 50-watt heads, we did a 75-watt head."[8]

Many of Jim's employees stayed with him for years. Back at the factory, the longest tenured employee is wood machinist Andy Lambourne, who still works for Jim after 31 years. Nearly all of the folks who had worked at the first factory on Silverdale Road made the move to Bletchley when Jim took the company out of West London.

[8]Bran's account of Narb's origins, as told to Michael Doyle in *The History of Marshall* [Hal Leonard], deserves mention. Bran told Doyle a dealer on Charing Cross Road had requested a Marshall amp with a different name.

Pop went for sound of success

profile

JESTER MINUTE!
Have you been to see us yet. We have got a lot to offer
Ladies' & Gent's Fashions
Shoes, Linen and Blankets

In May 1974 Jim told the *Gazette*, "I live for music"...

Perennial success

Were there a list of Jim Marshall's rules for success, numbers one, two, and three would be the axiom he repeats clearly: "I will not have a dissatisfied customer."

From the start, customer satisfaction has been fundamental to the success of Marshall Amplification. Townshend and his decibel obsession, Clapton and his trunk, Blackmore blowing out the walls of the factory—Jim has built his business around the wishes of his clientele. When there was no amp, he built it for them. When it wasn't right, he made it better.

"The very first Marshall amp came about because I listened to what the lads who came into my shop wanted, and I still do the exact same thing to this very day because I believe that doing so is very important," Jim asserts. "As a company we keep in daily touch with musicians from all over the globe via our distributors, who are the best in the world in my opinion. We also keep in regular contact with the general public through road shows, trade shows, dealer presentations, and our website, which is incredibly active [www.marshallamps.com boasts 3,000-plus hits a day]. Plus our artist liaison department supports major acts worldwide and gives us regular communication with players from the past and present.

"Basically we just listen to everybody—from the rank beginner to the top professional, and all points in between. If they make a viable suggestion, we will always follow it up. I always encourage my people to keep their eyes, ears, and minds open to

. . . and in 2000 his dedication to musical instruments made him the industry's Man of the Century.

everybody and everything. Don't think for one minute that you're the best—and always remember that you don't know everything!"

Jim's first order of business when he gets in every day at 6:30 a.m. is to open the mail. As you might imagine, letters pour in to Marshall headquarters by the hundreds every week, even more as new lines are unveiled. While he could very well bring in a team of high schoolers to open envelopes, he insists on doing it himself. He wants no interruption in the customer feedback line.

"I do it because if there is a complaint and the letter were to go directly to that department in the factory, the complaint might never be heard—if it were detrimental to a friend in the department, they would slip it under the carpet. I will not have dissatisfied customers. Anybody that complains is invited to the factory, given a tour, and invited to have lunch with me. They bring their amplifier in that they're complaining about—usually, it's their own fault or the fault of the leads from the guitar—and Phil Wells, my top repairman, will go right through it. Then, once Phil is done, we'll take the customer into our theater and let them play through it. I always make sure the customer is 100 percent happy before he leaves the factory that day. It may seem like a lot of work, but as I always tell my people, it's well worth it."

Few things seem more enjoyable to Jim than meeting Marshall players. At trade shows around the world, people queue up by the dozens to shake his hand, take a photo, and get an autograph. In advance of traveling to shows, he spends hours and hours signing thousands of publicity photos. (Will someone please buy that man a photocopier?) "Why do I do it? Because I just love work; plainly speaking, I am a workaholic," Jim explains with a chuckle. "I love meeting my fans and friends all over the world, because if it wasn't for them I wouldn't be there in the first place. I also like to hear what they have to say about their amplifiers because they are all part of what I call the 'world Marshall family.'"

Generations

Anyone running a company that's been in business more than ten years knows that success relies not just in pleasing customers but in rediscovering customers. Jim is not ignorant of consumers' ongoing fascination with the vintage gear that put him on the map, but he's managed to reinvent Marshall Amplification for successive generations.

Revisiting those Bletchley production numbers, one has to wonder: Are there 6,500 guitarists *being born* every week? Who's buying all those amps?

"Don't forget we're all over the world," says Jim, who notes that he's never really had time to learn to play guitar. "And then consider how many 12-, 13-, 14-, 15-year-old kids want to start up a new instrument and decide to have a go at guitar. The parents are looking for something affordable, of good quality, and maybe they've heard the name or recognize it from album covers, concerts, maybe even from their own youth. The parents have seen *their* heroes play Marshalls. But they don't want to spend an enormous amount of money for a first amplifier; they don't know yet whether the kid will carry on with it."

Jim estimates that more than 70% of his current business comes from the low end of the market. While it's always been his goal to produce affordable amps—the first JTM45 was dubbed by some "an affordable Bassman clone"—he really had his finger on the pulse when he launched the Valvestate line in 1991. Valvestates debuted a hybrid design featuring a single 12AX7 tube in the preamp section and a solid-state power section. Having reduced expensive tube circuitry while maintaining much of the classic Marshall sound, Valvestates and the AVT lines that followed opened the path to a new customer base and led the company to unprecedented success. In 1992, Marshall Amplification won its second Queen's Export Award (the first having come in 1984 on the heels of the JCM800) for increasing export three years in a row.

To date, Marshall amps costing more than $1,200 represent a far smaller piece of the company pie. "The older players who can afford $2,000 for a high-end amplifier, they want the old stuff. They don't buy as many new models, they're hunting through vintage shops and trading and so on—although we've had tremendous success with our Vintage Series reissues, so we have captured some of that market. And now, many of those people who bought their first Marshalls 20 or 30 years ago are buying the newer lines—either for themselves or for their children, because they know to trust the name."

Marshall cast an even wider net in 1999 by introducing the MG amp line. With the most affordable Marshalls ever on the marketplace, Jim has made a significant step toward securing the next generation of customers. His awareness of a broader market and his ability to reach out to it nearly guarantee that the principle of selling

Crowning achievement: Jim receives his second Queen's Award for Export in 1992.

generationally will perpetuate itself. If those MG buyers continue playing, chances are good that they will explore higher-grade Marshalls when they're ready for their next amp. They won't grow out of Marshall—on the contrary, they'll grow into it.

As in several other industries, the perpetual growth—or imminent demise—of a musical instrument company is dependent on existing trends in pop culture. Musicians may be a relatively independent lot, but few will deny the influence of their heroes. Jim got his first lesson in this when his pupils sought the same Premier drums he was playing.

Considering how many incarnations hard rock has assumed over the last 41 years, it's notable that so many key players in each successive movement have chosen Marshall amps. Clearly the guitarists of the British Invasion were customers. As their sound gradually capitulated to the earthy, crunchy rock of the '70s, milestone bands from Thin Lizzy and Bad Company to Kiss and Van Halen churned away on Marshalls. The dark lords of metal and thrash, from Black Sabbath and Metallica to

Anthrax and Slayer, stacked their Marshalls high. Shredders like Yngwie Malmsteen, Joe Satriani, and Eric Johnson (a complete nut for tone) as well as the hair bands (Ratt, Dokken, etc.) that chased their virtuosity, sought the same power. Even when guitar technique went out of fashion and Seattle slew the hair bands, the Marshall script logo lurked in the background for players like Kurt Cobain, Tom Morello, Dave Navarro, Mike McCready, and Jerry Cantrell, and Billy Joe of Green Day. In 2003, the appearance of Marshall lines onstage with a new breed of players represented by the likes of System of a Down, Static-X, the Deftones, Staind, Gomez, Papa Roach, Hatebreed, and the Used—as well as more established crowd pleasers such as Iron Maiden, Jeff Beck, Billy Gibbons, Zakk Wylde, Slash, and Slayer—attests that there's really no end to Marshall in sight.

"You can always learn something new," Jim says with his ready smile. "We've worked with so many great talents through the years. I'm constantly hearing new bands, and that's why I've been doing this for so many years, because I love the music. I believe you should always keep your eyes, ears, and mind open to everybody and everything."

With full faith and trust in his work force—from the teams in his factories to distributors and retailers worldwide—Jim truly sees nothing difficult about running his business.

"There's no difficulty to it at all, as long as you take pleasure in what you are doing. I should do as much as I can all of the time. I've only had four holidays total, including the last one I took which was in 1948. I thoroughly enjoy myself as long as I'm working. To me, every working day is a holiday.

"I would have to say that as of this time, my goals in business have been met, yes. But I don't believe in standing still. I'm always looking forward to something else."

Back at Iridium, Jim and Les are winding down the Gershwin brothers' "'S Wonderful." Flushed with adrenaline, and maybe a little Scotch, Jim suns himself onstage. It's past midnight, and for the first time all evening the crowd is up on its feet. As he exits stage right, he's swarmed. Clubgoers extend their hands for a shake, offering words of praise and asking Jim to sign their tickets, a photograph, even a few Les Paul guitars.

Singing, shaking hands, greeting gracious fans—these are the moments Jim loves most. Ultimately he is a performer through and through, even more so than a man of business. He's been successful in both, but nothing means more to him than the music. You can see it on his face.

Part II

Chapter 5

Marshall at the Millennium

As Marshall Amplification entered the new millennium it was enjoying an era of unprecedented success. On the high end, its critically acclaimed JCM2000 took the all-tube Marshall sound to jaw-dropping new levels of toneful, high-gain crunch and, believe it or not, crystalline clean tones, while the limited-edition, handwired JTM45 offset head and matching "offset" 4x12 successfully revisited the holy grail of warm Marshall overdrive that started it all. More affordably, the Valvestate, AVT, and MG lines had successfully departed from prior all-tube designs while still maintaining that all-important "Marshall sound" and look, making the company's amps available at every price point. The company had also successfully expanded its product line with two signature models, more sophisticated rack gear, and painstakingly accurate reissues of several highly-sought-after classics from yesteryear.

Since Marshall gear from its inception in 1962 through the 1980s has been covered in great detail elsewhere (nowhere more thoroughly than Michael Doyle's *The History of Marshall* [Hal Leonard]), this chapter will focus on equipment from the early '90s forward, detailing many of the Marshall heads, combos, rack gear, and effects of the latest era.

Crunch Time

The JCM900 Series

As they had in the '80s with the JCM800s, Marshall brought out a new tube-driven line for the 1990s. The JCM900 line attempted—and largely succeeded—at creating officially hotrodded Marshalls. During the '80s, many owners sent their precious vintage and new Marshall heads to exclusive amp boutiques to have them modded to supposed perfection. More often than not, though, the amps were either mangled or manipulated to such an extreme degree that their original tone was not only lost, it was irretrievable. To halt the trend, Marshall decided with the JCM900 series to have these amps "pre-modded" out of the box by adding the most common mods—namely more gain and an effects loop.

> "Shredders of the world, please note: The JCM900 saves you the trouble and expense of having your amp hotrodded."
>
> —Art Thompson, *Guitar Player*, 1991

The JCM900s came in two flavors: the single-channel Hi Gain Master Volume MKIII models (evolved from the popular 100-watt 2203 and 50-watt 2204 heads, both of which first came out in 1975) and the two-channel Hi Gain Dual Reverb models (based on the JCM800 100-watt 2210 and 50-watt 2205 split-channel heads). As the "Dual Reverb" in the name suggests, the latter amps boasted two Reverb controls, one for each channel. To capitalize on the metal phenomenon of the 1980s, Marshall borrowed a joke from Spinal Tap lead guitarist Nigel Tufnel (a.k.a. actor Sir Christopher Guest), whose legendary Marshall, as depicted in the heavy-metal send-up *This Is Spinal Tap*, had a gain knob that went up to 11. Not to be outdone, Marshall gave the JCM900 a gain dial that spun all the way up to *20*. To hammer home the point, Marshall's American distributor, Korg USA, had Mr. Tufnel unveil the JCM900 series at a star-studded event at Guitar Center's renowned Hollywood location, and ran an ad that featured Tufnel saying, "Now it goes to '20'—that's 9 louder, innit!" To top off the over-the-top launch, Korg sponsored a Spinal Tap performance at the January 1990 NAMM trade show. (Tickets for the Tap show were the hottest items at that year's NAMM.)

JCM900 100-watt head.

"The JCM900 launch in LA was great fun, and Christopher Guest was just fantastic," Jim recalls. "As soon as he stepped out of the limo that took us to the event, he instantly became Nigel Tufnel and stayed in character, without even the slightest slip, for the entire time!"

The JCM900 line came in a wide variety of 100- and 50-watt heads and combos with accompanying extension cabinets of different configurations. Although the 100-watt, dual-channel (with shared EQ) Hi Gain Dual Reverb head, the 4100, proved to be the most popular amp in the JCM900 range, of special interest are the turbo-charged versions of the Master Volume MKIII heads introduced in 1993: the 100-watt 2100 SL-X head and the 50-watt 2500 SL-X. This evolutionary pair were sometimes referred to as the MKIV Master Volume amps—even though "MKIV" didn't appear on either front panel—and SL-X stood for "Super Lead eXtended." The key difference between the MKIII and the MKIV? The addition of a fourth 12AX7 (ECC83) preamp tube to further increase gain and warmth.

All JCM900 models shared several features (in addition to Gain knobs that went to 20). Lurking on their rear panel you'll find:

- A series effects loop with fully buffered send and return and variable level that can be set anywhere between -10dB (for stompbox effects) and +4dB (for rack-mount effects) via a Loop Level control.
- A High/Low switch. The Low position halves the amp's output power by switch-

ing the output tubes from pentode to triode operation. How does this work? Some tubes, such as the EL34 or EL84, have five active elements, while others only have three. Based on the Greek words *pent* (five) and *tri* (three), "pentode" means—you guessed it—five active elements and "triode" means three. So when the JCM900 High/Low switch is set to Low, it shuts off two elements in each of the output tubes, causing them to run as triodes. In addition to the lower power output, the amp's tone and feel changes. The pentode mode sound is brighter and more aggressive, while the triode is smoother, with a silkier high end.

- Two line outputs. One is Direct (i.e., "as is") for slaving other power amps, the other Recording Compensated (i.e., "EQ'd") so it can be run straight to a mixing board or recording console.

The JCM900s also feature failsafe output protection circuitry that's based on the fact that, as in most all-tube Marshalls, the power tubes work in pairs in what is known as "push/pull" operation: If an output tube fails, a fuse immediately blows, taking the tube's partner out of the circuit and thus protecting the amp. In addition, a Fail LED lights on the rear panel, letting you know that a tube failure has occurred. Here's where it gets clever: On any 100-watt JCM900 (i.e., an amp with four output tubes) there are two fuses and two Fail LEDS. So, since the tubes work in pairs, if one tube fails only one of the fuses blows, leaving one pair of tubes on and allowing the amp to continue operating at half-power. This means you're still in the game during a performance—unless one tube in each pair fails simultaneously. The Fail LEDs also let you know which pair of tubes—the outer (1 and 4) or inner (2 and 3)—contains the guilty party.

Even though the reverb-less Hi Gain Master Volume amps only had one channel, they all featured an extra Master Volume control that was footswitchable. This allowed the player to switch between two predetermined volumes, or, as was often said, "Go from loud to very loud."

An instant success, the JCM900s were, in the minds of many, the "industry standard" professional tube amps—until they were usurped by their replacement, the JCM2000. In addition to enjoying great reviews and excellent sales, the 900s amassed a pretty impressive users list, including Dave Murray of Iron Maiden, Brad Whitford of Aerosmith, Motor City motormouth Ted Nugent, Bruce Kulick of Kiss, Dave Navarro of Jane's Addiction, Tom Keeley of screamo mavens Thursday, Trey

Guest star: Spinal Tap's Nigel Tufnel points out his favorite feature.

Azagthoth of Morbid Angel, super-shredder Jason Becker, and that bearded Texan tone maven, Billy Gibbons of ZZ Top. According to one reviewer, the amps were "the best new Marshall I've heard in years. . . . Marshall has successfully reinvented itself."

"The channel switching on the 900 offers the option of switching from 'Crunch' to 'Torch' with no more difficulty than driving a high-performance elevator."

—Billy Gibbons, *Marshall Law,* 1991

"Amps for the road—0 to 20 in under 2 seconds!"

—Dave Murray, Marshall 30th anniversary catalog, 1992

"My Marshall 900s are the foundation from which I build, because I can always rely on them to spit out that classic thickness. When I stand in front of the thing, I can feel it rearranging my chromosomes."

—Ted Nugent, *Marshall Law,* 1991*

"The greatest thing since I don't know what. All the volume you need and maybe more."

—Nigel Tufnel

JCM900 Models

Hi Gain Master Volume MKIII Heads

2100 100-watt, single-channel tube head with series effects loop (1990–1992)

2500 50-watt, single-channel tube head with series effects loop (1990–1992)

Hi Gain Master Volume MKIII Combos

2101 100-watt, 1x12 single-channel tube combo with series effects loop (1990–1992)

*Note: Though the bow-hunting guitarist has since moved on to endorse another manufacturer's amps, we thought his quote was too good to hit the cutting floor.

2501 50-watt, 1x12 single-channel tube combo with series effects loop (1990–1992)

2502 50-watt, 2x12 single-channel tube combo with series effects loop (1990–1992)

Hi Gain Master Volume (MKIV) Heads

2100 SL-X 100-watt, single-channel tube head with series effects loop (1993–1999)

2500 SL-X 50-watt, single-channel tube head with series effects loop (1993-1999)

Hi Gain Dual Reverb Heads

4100 100-watt, dual-channel head with reverb and series effects loop (1990–1999, 2003–present)

4500 50-watt, dual-channel head with reverb and series effects loop (1990–1999)

Hi Gain Dual Reverb Combos

4101 100-watt, 1x12 dual-channel combo with reverb and series effects loop (1990–1999)

4102 100-watt, 2x12 dual-channel combo with reverb and series effects loop (1990–1999)

4501 50-watt, 1x12 dual-channel combo with reverb and series effects loop (1990–1999)

4502 50-watt, 2x12 dual-channel combo with reverb and series effects loop (1990–1999)

Marshalls for the Masses

Valvestate

With the all-tube Marshall JCM900s handling the top of the marketplace, the company created the Valvestate line in 1991 to cater to the all-important middle- and lower-priced sectors. Aside from a few smaller 10- and 20-watt models and a pair of rackmount power amps, the Valvestate hook was to put a single 12AX7 (ECC83) tube into the preamp of an otherwise solid-state amp, making them hybrids. A rather clever electronic design incorporating something Marshall called "the Valvestate bipolar, high impedance circuit" was employed in Valvestate amps' power stage to

>>> Tubular Alarm Bells <<<

The EL34 crisis: 1994–1996/97

In keeping with what had become a celebrated Marshall tradition, all JCM900 amps boasted power-amp sections driven by EL34 tubes—a pair in 50-watters and a quartet in the 100s. However, this all changed for a worrisome period in the mid '90s because of a worldwide EL34 shortage.

In the not-so-distant past there was a time when tubes (or valves, as they're known in the UK) were everywhere—TVs (the nickname "the tube" did not come from just the picture tube), radios, hi-fi systems, telephone exchanges, and even the first computers. In fact, you used to be able to buy—and test—tubes at your local drugstore. Then, in 1948, the smaller, cheaper, cool-running, and service-free transistor was born, and tubes quickly fell from favor. By the mid '70s tubes had been purged from virtually all modern-day electronic devices, except for certain extremely high-end hi-fi components—and rock 'n' roll amps like Marshalls.

As the transistor took over, companies stopped manufacturing tubes, and before long a once-plentiful supply of good-quality tubes had dwindled to almost nothing, and prices had skyrocketed. The majority of Western tube manufacturers vanished, with the only factories still making the tonally desirable "glass bottles" located in Eastern Europe, China, and Russia. When the Berlin Wall fell, so did one of the few remaining manufacturers of quality EL34s, and by the early '90s the only place Marshall could get a plentiful supply of good-sounding, reliable EL34s was from the Tesla factory in the country known as Czechoslovakia. Then communism fell, and the Tesla factory—and Czechoslovakia—ceased to exist. By the autumn of 1994, with their once-huge stockpile of EL34s virtually nonexistent, Marshall had no choice but to start using Russian-made 5881s. (A Chinese factory was making EL34s, but their product was substandard.) As a result, the Sovtek 5881 (a tube similar to the 6L6) was the only game in town.

As a result, from late 1994, the majority of all-tube Marshalls that once boasted EL34 power tubes were loaded with 5881s, and their front panels carried a sticker that read "Marshall 5881 Power Valve Equipped." Ironically, when Jim and company made the first Marshalls, the JTM45, back in 1962, the power tubes they used were American 5881s. But because this tube was imported, expensive, and hard to get in quantity, Marshall had to find another power tube to use, and after trying a few different ones—most notably the KT66—settled on EL34s in the mid '60s. So 30 years later, history repeated itself, but in reverse.

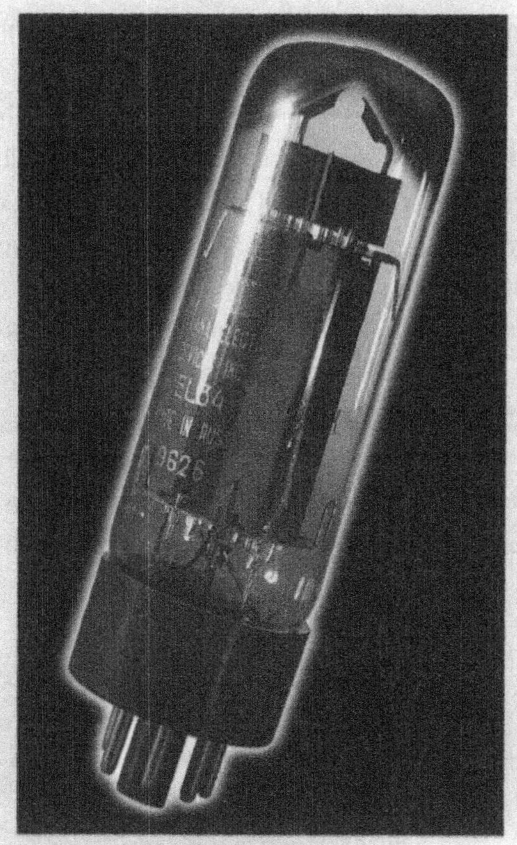

When the change from EL34s to 5881s was announced, many Marshall fanatics panicked because they felt the EL34 was responsible for a good portion of the "Marshall magic." However, though the EL34 was important, it was only one of many ingredients that made the "magic" happen. As a result, although a tonal difference could be detected (the 5881s have more lows and more highs, the EL34s have more of a midrange "bark"), the 5881-loaded Marshalls still sounded like Marshalls—which should come as no surprise, given the power-tube listing of the JTM45.

Thankfully, by the time the JCM900s' successors, the JCM2000s, were being designed, Marshall's engineers had already spent two years working closely with Russian tube manufacturer Svetlana, and an extremely consistent and reliable EL34—a close copy of the original and much-respected Mullard—was available in large quantities.

Marshall's chief designer at the time, Steve Grindrod, was so impressed with the reliability of the Svetlana EL34s that in 1997 he told the UK magazine *Guitar*, "You'll notice that the JCM2000 amps don't have valve-failure LEDs—that's how confident I am in these new EL34s."

Crisis over. . . touch wood.

—Nick Bowcott

help conjure up the sound and the feel of a tube-driven power-amp circuit. Whether this was successful or not is, of course, a subjective matter, but the reviews were extremely positive and, if sales are any yardstick, Valvestate's tube emulation was definitely "close enough for rock 'n' roll." The series sold extremely well, quickly becoming an important part of the Marshall amp family. (The fact that one Billy Gibbons harbors a host of 8008 power amps in his current live rig indicates that Valvestate was definitely onto something.) The world's guitar press has since praised the Valvestate, with one scribe noting, "The company revolutionized the industry with its affordable Valvestate amps. . . . If the amps didn't quite match their tube brothers tone for tone, they came close: more important, their sound was shaped by the same ears that made Marshalls special."

The Valvestate Series included a variety of configurations: small combos, large combos, stereo chorus combos, a compact 4x12 cab, two heads, and a couple of power amps—plus the short-lived, half-pint 8001, a 10-watt micro-stack.

Valvestate 8080 80-watt combo.

> "A lot of heavy-duty all-tube heads just don't seem to be able to deal with real low notes. To my ears, tube-driven power amps tend to 'flutter' when you hit 'em with a low *E* string tuned down to *C*, or even lower. I don't like my signal to alternate in that way, and because of this I use Marshall 8100 Valvestate heads, which have solid-state power amps. They give me a tight, modern guitar sound—to me that amp is perfectly designed for this type of music. The 8100 does have one tube in it, though, a 12AX7 in the preamp, which helps give some of that classical Marshall tone to my sound."
>
> —Tommy Victor, Prong (1994)
>
> "A beast destined to become a 'must have' for many merchants of metal mayhem."
>
> —*Guitar School,* September 1991

One of the most popular Valvestate features was the Contour control, found on all models except the two 10-watters and the rack power amps. The Contour control reshaped the mids, giving a bluesy bump at one end and a vicious, modern scoop at the other. As a result, Contour was often referred to as the "old guy, young guy" control. And while the appeal of Valvestate was wide, its ability to create an extremely aggressive, in-your-face tone made the 8100 100-watt head the amp of choice for many early '90s metal mavens, including Tommy Victor of Prong, whose fans include Wayne Static of Static-X and Dimebag Darrell of Pantera.

Another 8100 evangelist was the late Chuck Schuldiner, the twisted mind behind the band Death and a forefather in the dark domain of death metal. Chuck bought his 8100 on the recommendation of producer Scott Burns, who told him, "As far as I'm concerned, the best head for dialing in the perfect death-metal tone is the Marshall 8100 head." Regarded as the George Martin of death metal, Burns's production credits include Sepultura, Obituary, Deicide, and, of course, Death.

On a lighter note, members of the electro-pop band Depeche Mode were spotted with a Valvestate combo.

"First Generation" Valvestate models

(1991–1996, unless otherwise stated)

Combos

8010 10-watt, 1x8 single-channel combo

8020 20-watt, 1x10 channel-switching combo-with reverb

8040 40-watt, 1x12 channel-switching combo-with reverb*

8080 80-watt, 1x12 channel-switching combo with reverb and parallel/series effects loop*

Stereo Chorus Combos

(1993–1996)

8240 40+40–watt stereo 2x12 channel-switching combo with chorus, reverb, and parallel/series effects loop*

8280 80+80–watt stereo 2x12 channel-switching combo with chorus, reverb, and parallel/series effects loop*

Heads

8100 100-watt channel-switching head with reverb and parallel/series effects loop*

Stereo Chorus Head

(1993–1996)

8200 100+100–watt stereo, channel-switching head with chorus, reverb, and parallel/series effects loop*

Cabinets

8222 2x12 stereo extension cab for the 8280 combo (or 8200 head) (1993–1996)

8412 140-watt, mono 4x12 straight-fronted, compact cabinet for the 8100 head

Power Amps

8004 40+40–watt stereo, 1U (unit, or rackspace) rack power amp (1991–1997)

8008 80+80–watt stereo, 1U rack power amp (1991–2000)

Misc.

8001 10-watt micro-stack with two 1x8 cabs (1991–1992)

*Preamp contains 12AX7 tube.

Completely Racked

The JMP-1 Preamp

As a great number of '80s players deconstructed the traditional guitar amplifier into separate preamp and power-amp components to fit into their ever-growing racks (the rest of which were often filled with tone-sucking digital effects units), Marshall joined the fray with their 9000 series rackmountable amps. In 1992 they upped the ante with the JMP-1 Valve MIDI Preamp. Combining MIDI programming, four channels (two dirty, two clean), and that classic Marshall crunch, the preamp quickly became a bestseller and remains in production over a decade later. Indeed, at the time of this writing, the membership of The JMP-1 Users Club included Steph Carpenter of the Deftones, both guitarists in Def Leppard, all three axemen in Iron Maiden, Jerry Horton of Papa Roach, Dave Mustaine, John 5 of Marilyn Manson, Mike Mushok of Staind, and the ubiquitous Billy Gibbons.

For rack users, the JMP-1 is ideal. With two 12AX7 tubes warming up its tone and authenticating its overdrive capabilities, the single-rack-space unit offers 100

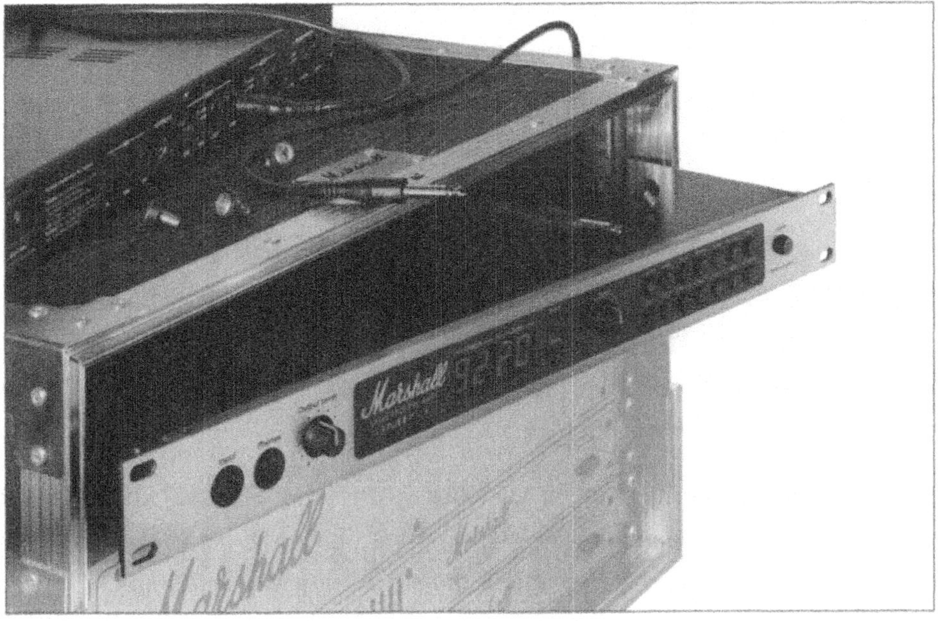

JMP-1 Valve MIDI Preamp, in its natural habitat.

Chip off the old block: a JMP-1 ad that imagines micro-heads.

locations for saving settings, and it switches swiftly and silently. Other features include a stereo effects loop with its own programmable Mix control, a Bass Shift button, MIDI mapping, and stereo line outputs featuring Marshall's much-praised speaker-emulation circuitry.

To further cater to the rack crowd, over the past decade Marshall has created several all-tube stereo power amps to complement the JMP-1: the EL84 20/20, a compact, single-rack-space unit offering 20+20 watts of EL84-driven stereo power; the 9100, a 50+50–watt 5881-driven, three-rack-space unit boasting a Dual Monobloc design; and the 9200, a 100+100–watt 5881-driven, three-rack-space Dual Monobloc behemoth. And, once the EL34 crisis was resolved (see Tubular Alarm Bells sidebar, page 104), the 9100 and 9200 were redesigned with EL34s and renamed the EL34 50/50 and EL34 100/100.

By the way, the hi-fi term Dual Monobloc simply means that each side (channel) of the stereo power amp operates as a completely independent unit, with nothing shared.

To round out their rack attack, in 1995 Marshall came out with the JFX-1 Signal Processor. Designed by the same guy responsible for the JMP-1, the JFX-1 was a single-rack-space digital effects processor that only offered four effects—Reverb, Delay, Chorus, and Flange (or a mixture of them)—but did them all incredibly well. Despite getting rave reviews (*Guitar Player* dubbed it "the best in its class"), the JFX-1's limited effects menu didn't appeal to the public at large, and it was discontinued in 1997.

Rack products

Preamp

JMP-1 Valve MIDI preamp with four channels, stereo parallel/series effects loop, and 100 memory locations, 1U rack (1992–present day)

Effects Processor

JFX-1 Digital Effects Processor 1U rack (1995–1997)

All-tube Stereo Power Amps

EL84 20/20	20+20–watt 1U rack w/EL84s (1997–present)
9100	50+50–watt Dual Monobloc 3U rack w/5881s (1993–1996)
9200	100+100–watt Dual Monobloc 3U rack w/5881s (1993–1996)
EL34 50/50	50+50–watt Dual Monobloc 3U rack w/EL34s (1997–present)
EL34 100/100	100+100–watt Dual Monobloc 3U rack w/EL34s (1997–present)

The Party Line

Marshall's 30th Anniversary series

In 1992, 500 hundred years after Columbus sailed the ocean blue, Marshall made its own global conquest with its 30th Anniversary series of amps. Billed as "The Pinnacle of Valve Technology" as well as "The Ultimate Marshall," these amps were designed to provide *all* of the previously available Marshall tones, combining vintage sounds with modern features such as MIDI channel switching and advanced tone-shaping options. All the series' amps (essentially two: a 100-watt head and a 100-watt 1x12 combo, both of which appeared in various cosmetic guises) sported—for the first time in Marshall history—three totally independent channels for switching among clean, crunchy rhythm, and searing lead tones. In classic Marshall tradition, each channel was directly routed to the power amp in order to minimize signal degradation and create the warmest tone possible.

During the first year of production, all the amps came covered in snazzy blue vinyl. For an even more stylish note, the hand-built Limited Edition (LE) line of 100-watt heads and 1x12 combos featured brass plating on everything metal on the chassis—including the tube retainers. The script Marshall logo was solid brass. Marshall produced a total of 800 LE heads and 500 LE combos; all 1300 were snapped up immediately, making LE a much-sought-after collectible. After the first year of production (1992) subsequent amps in the 30th Anniversary line were covered with standard black vinyl.

Both the head and combo units came laden with *seven* (yes, seven!) 12AX7 preamp tubes and four EL34 power tubes. Due to the mid-'90s EL34 shortage, however, Marshall for a time used Sovtek 5881s in the power stages of the 30th Anniversary amps.

Beyond the traditional Treble, Bass, Middle, and Presence knobs, the 30th Anniversary line included a number of additional tone-modifying controls. In Channel 2, for example, a Mode A–B–C selector switch gave guitarists a choice among tones reminiscent of vintage Super Leads, the Master Volume amps that dominated the late '70s and '80s, plus JCM900-style high gain. Channel 3 included Gain Boost and Contour switches, which provided extra midrange control and was perfect for the mid-scooped, dropped-*D* metal riffing that was gaining popularity in the '90s. The Master Output section contained a sensible button called Low Volume

6100LM three-channel 100-watt head.

Anniversary Series 6100/6960 full stack and 6101 combo.

Year of the blue: a dramatic 30th-anniversary ad.

Compensate, which made the amp sound full and fat when it was being used at very low (read: bedroom) volumes. Other features worthy of mention:

- In addition to being able to switch channels with the supplied LED footswitch (MPM3E), you could do so via MIDI.
- A Damping Select switch with three settings: High, Auto, and Low. This switch altered the speaker-damping characteristics of the amp's power section. High was perfect for punchy, bright, Fender-like clean tones, while Low produced that slightly loose yet tight low-end "growl" that Marshall is famous for. Most clever of all was the Auto setting: When chosen it would automatically select High damp-

ing for the Clean channel and Low damping for the Crunch and Lead channels, giving you the best of both worlds.

- A sophisticated effects loop that was switchable between Series and Parallel operation.
- Four Switchable Power Options: 100 watts (all four tubes), 50-watt Pentode (two tubes), 50-watt Triode (all four tubes in Triode mode, giving a smoother tone than Pentode), or 25-watt Triode (two tubes in Triode mode). This was possible via two switches: Pentode/Triode and High/Low Power.

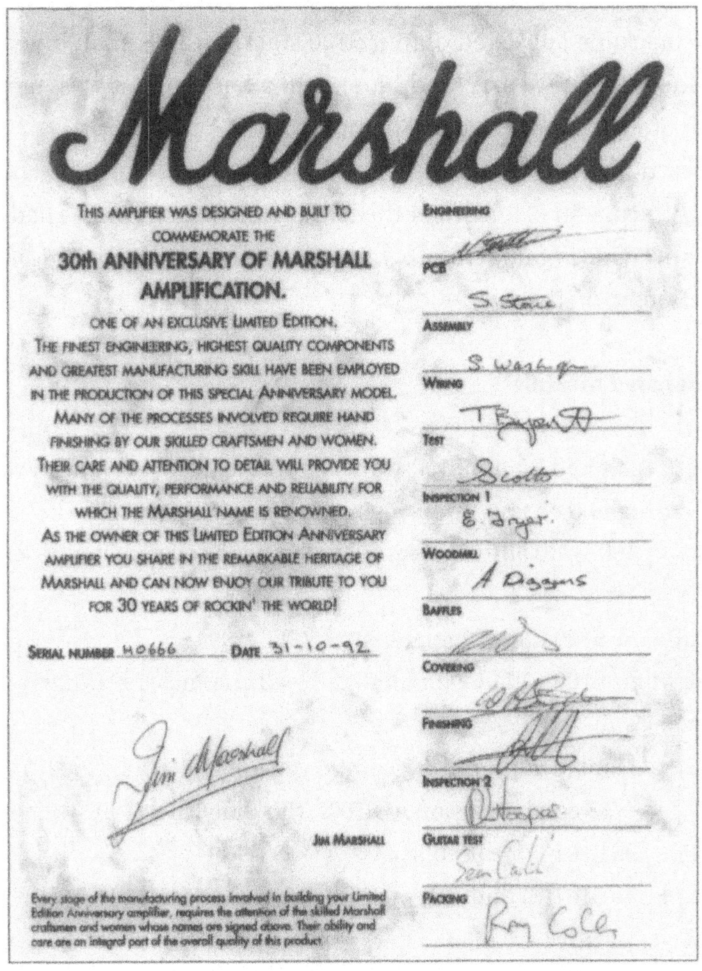

Marshall

THIS AMPLIFIER WAS DESIGNED AND BUILT TO COMMEMORATE THE

30th ANNIVERSARY OF MARSHALL AMPLIFICATION.

ONE OF AN EXCLUSIVE LIMITED EDITION.

THE FINEST ENGINEERING, HIGHEST QUALITY COMPONENTS AND GREATEST MANUFACTURING SKILL HAVE BEEN EMPLOYED IN THE PRODUCTION OF THIS SPECIAL ANNIVERSARY MODEL. MANY OF THE PROCESSES INVOLVED REQUIRE HAND FINISHING BY OUR SKILLED CRAFTSMEN AND WOMEN. THEIR CARE AND ATTENTION TO DETAIL WILL PROVIDE YOU WITH THE QUALITY, PERFORMANCE AND RELIABILITY FOR WHICH THE MARSHALL NAME IS RENOWNED.

AS THE OWNER OF THIS LIMITED EDITION ANNIVERSARY AMPLIFIER YOU SHARE IN THE REMARKABLE HERITAGE OF MARSHALL AND CAN NOW ENJOY OUR TRIBUTE TO YOU FOR 30 YEARS OF ROCKIN' THE WORLD!

SERIAL NUMBER H0666 DATE 31-10-92

JIM MARSHALL

Every stage of the manufacturing process involved in building your Limited Edition Anniversary amplifier, requires the attention of the skilled Marshall craftsmen and women whose names are signed above. Their ability and care are an integral part of the overall quality of this product.

ENGINEERING

PCB

ASSEMBLY

WIRING

TEST

INSPECTION 1

WOODMILL

BAFFLES

COVERING

FINISHING

INSPECTION 2

GUITAR TEST

PACKING

The lads in the shop and Jim Marshall signed the Limited Edition's certificate.

Not surprisingly, Marshall introduced the feature-laden 30th Anniversary series in the US with an ad that bore the bold headline, "What's blue, has 17 knobs, 22 switches, variable damping factor, effects loop, 11 tubes and sounds like God?"

Despite being high-ticket items (in the US the 6100 head had a list price of $1999 and the 6101 combo a staggering $2399), the 30th Anniversary amps sold well and attracted a goodly amount of pro users, including super-shredder (and Kirk Hammett's one-time teacher) Joe Satriani, and Alex Lifeson of Canada's finest-ever rock export, Rush. Satriani used the 6100's Clean channel exclusively, preferring to get his dirty tones by stomping on a Boss DS-1 distortion pedal. At one time, Lifeson's live backline consisted of four 6100 stacks—three main ones, named after the Three Stooges (Curly, Larry, and Moe), and a backup that was named after that "fifth Beatle" Stooge, Moe's brother Shemp.

In a hotrodding move reminiscent of the one made on the Hi Gain Master Volume MKIII heads in '93, in 1994 the 30th Anniversary amps' Lead channel was modified for even more gain. This upgrade was designated by the addition of the LM (Lead Mode) prefix on the two models.

30th Anniversary models

Heads

6100LE Limited Edition, 100-watt, all tube, feature-laden head with brass-plated chassis, brass logo, and blue vinyl (1992)

6100 100-watt, all-tube, feature-laden head covered in blue vinyl (1992–1993)

6100(B) As 6100 but with black vinyl (1993–1994)

6100LM As 6100(B) but with modified lead channel (1994–1999)

Combos*

6101LE Limited edition, 1x12 combo version of 6100LE (1992)

6101 1x12 combo version of 6100, with blue vinyl (1992–1993)

6101(B) As 6101 but with black vinyl (1993–1994)

6101LM As 6101(B) but with modified lead channel (1994–1999)

*Loaded with a specially designed Celestion G12 Gold speaker, except those sold in the USA where an Electro-Voice EVM 12L was used.

Cabinets

6960ALE	Limited Edition 300-watt mono/stereo, angled 4x12 cabinet with blue vinyl and brass logo to match 6100LE head (1992)
6960A	As 6960ALE but with regular logo to match blue 6100 head (1992–1993)
6960AV	As 6960A but with 70-watt Celestion "Vintage 30" speakers (1992–1993)
6960BLE	Limited Edition cabinet, as 6960ALE but with straight front (1992)
6960B	As 6960A but with straight front (1992–1993)
6960BV	As 6960AV but with straight front (1992–1993)
6912LE	Limited Edition blue 1x12" cabinet with brass logo for 6101LE (1992)
6912	Blue 1x12" cabinet with white logo for blue 6101 (1992–1993)
6912(B)	As 6912 but with black vinyl (1993–1999)

Entering the Entry Level

Park: Son of Marshall

Even though Valvestate—the most affordable Marshall line to ever hit the stores—proved incredibly successful, it still wasn't inexpensive enough to be considered a player in the entry-level market, where cheap and cheerful offshore amps ruled. To address this substantial area of the marketplace, in 1993 Marshall resurrected the Park name it had used from the mid '60s to 1980, and placed it on a line of Korean-built solid-state guitar and bass combos. This new line was launched with a Dr. Frankenstein–themed ad that showed a lab-coat-wearing JCM900 stack creating a Park combo in a horror-movie laboratory.

Initially three Park guitar combos were offered: the G10, a 10-watt, 1x8" single-channel combo with dual Gain controls and a headphone output; the G10R, the G10 with spring reverb added; and the so-called "flagship" of the Park Guitar range, the G25R, a 25-watt, 1x10" two-channel combo with reverb.

Park was pushed as "a division of Marshall Amplification," with that phrase appearing in small print on the front panel of the amps, and "Designed, Engineered, and Quality Controlled" by Marshall stated on both the back panel and in literature. Nonetheless, the public didn't make the connection or know, let alone care, about the respected Park heritage. As a result, while Park sales were good, they didn't exactly break any records.

Achtung! The German edition of Nick Bowcott's Park guitar-lesson book, with Frankenstein-themed cover.

The "Park Guitar" range received a facelift in 1997 when the old trio of models were replaced with four new ones. First up was the G10MKII, a no-frills, three-control (Gain, Contour, Volume) 10-watt, 1x6½ combo with a Boost switch an headphone output. Next came the G15RCD, a 15-watt, 1x8 combo that was essentially the old G10R with 5 watts more power and a CD input so you could jam along with your favorite recordings. Then came the G30RCD, a 30-watt, 1x10 combo with two independent channels, reverb, CD input, and a line out. And, last but not least, the G215RCD, a 15+15–watt, 2x8 version of the G15RCD boasting stereo chorus.

Even with the new, lower price of the stripped-down 10-watter, and a white script Park logo on the speaker grille that stated "by Marshall" below it, this new series was considered another cheap, "no-name" amp by the vast majority of consumers and so, once again, sales were respectable but hardly earth-shattering.

Park Guitar combos

G10	10-watt, 1x8 single-channel combo (1993–1996)
G10R	G10 with reverb (1993–96)

G25R 25-watt, 1x10 two channel combo with reverb (1993–96)

G10MKII 10-watt, 1x6½ combo (1997–1998)

G15RCD 15-watt, 1x8 single-channel combo with reverb and CD input (1997–1998)

G30RCD 30-watt, 1x10 two-channel combo with reverb and CD input (1997–1998)

G215RCD 15+15–watt, 2x8 version of the G15RCD with stereo chorus (1997–1998)

(l-r) The adorable Park G10R, G10, and G25R.

Barney

The giant purple Plexi Limited Edition stack

In 1994 Marshall created an eye-catching, supersized Limited Edition 100-watt Plexi stack. Clad in purple vinyl with a "light straw" basket-weave grille cloth and boasting an "extra tall" straight cabinet, this skyscraper was seven feet high. Only 200 were made, 100 of which went to the US with a retail price of $4,000 each. They sold out

Purple craze: Jimi Hendrix's shadow looms in the background of this glamour shot of the 1959LTD/1982 full stack..

instantly. The stacks' size and color garnered them the nickname "Barney," after the popular children's TV dinosaur character. Because of its extra-tall base cabinet, it was also affectionately known as "the Hendrix stack."

1959LTD Limited Edition, 100-watt, purple Plexi head (1994)

1982ALTD Limited Edition, 100-watt, purple, angled 4x12 loaded with 25W Celestion Greenback speakers (1994)

1982BLTD Limited Edition, 100-watt, extra-tall, straight 4x12 loaded with 25W Celestion Greenback speakers (1994)

Portable Power

The JTM Series

The JTM Series was introduced in 1995 to provide guitarists with affordable, all-tube amps. This vintage-look range was divided into two distinct groups, the 30-watt JTM30s and the 60-watt JTM60s. The 30-watters featured two footswitchable channels with shared EQ, spring reverb, Speaker Emulated output, and a series effects loop, plus two 5881 power tubes and three 12AX7 preamp tubes.

In addition to having twice the power, the 60-watt JTMs had a different tube complement—four 12AX7 preamp tubes and a pair of EL34 power tubes—and some extra bells and whistles, including totally independent channels, dual Reverb controls, and two effects loops, one series and one parallel. The JTM610 succeeds, opined one journalist, because it "offers the distinctive Marshall sound in a portable, manageable package at an appropriate price."

JTM Series

(1995–1998)

30-watt combos

JTM312 1x12 two-channel combo with reverb and series effects loop

JTM310 2x10 two-channel combo with reverb and series effects loop

60-watt combos

(1995–1997)

JTM612 1x12 two-channel combo with dual Reverb controls and two effects loops, series and parallel

A JTM610 and JTM615 flank (from top) a JTM622, JTM 2x12 cab, and JTM612.

JTM610 3x10 two-channel combo with dual reverb controls and two effects loops, series and parallel

JTM615 1x15 two-channel combo with dual reverb controls and two effects loops, series and parallel

JTM622 2x12 two-channel combo with dual reverb controls and two effects loops, series and parallel

60-watt Head

(1996–1997)

JTM600 Two-channel head with dual reverb controls and two effects loops, series and parallel

Cabinets

JTMC12 70-watt, 1x12 cab for the JTM312, JTM612, and JTM600 (1995–1998)

JTMC212 140-watt, 2x12 cab for the JTM622 (1995–1997)

JTMC410 120-watt, straight-front 4x10 cab (1996–1997)

More Bang for the Buck

Valvestate II

As we've noted, the sound, features, and, most important, lowball pricing made the first-generation Valvestate (1991–1996) a huge success, quickly coming to represent a decent chunk of Marshall's business. Being a savvy businessman, Jim reinvested some of the Valvestate profits into continued R&D, figuring the line could be made even better in terms of both sonics and features. As a result of this diligent self-improvement scheme, in the mid '90s Marshall seamlessly revamped the entire line

The Valvestate II clan, from baby 1x8 15-watter to big daddy 100-watt full stack.

into what is today known as Valvestate MKII or, simply, Valvestate II. Using "Valvestate" technology, Jim's designers revamped the amps internally and externally, offering more guitarist-friendly features and an even more tube-like experience without the corresponding price tag of full tube amps.

Once again the lower end of the new Valvestate II line comprised small combos, including the 15-watt VS15, the 30-watt VS30R 1x10, and the VS65R, a mid-sized 1x12 with 65 watts, two channels, reverb, a line out, and a footswitch. In the 100-watt range, the VS100R and VS102R were 1x12 and 2x12 combos, respectively. A 100-watt head, the VS100RH, was also available, complemented by a pair of compact 4x12 Valvestate cabinets, one angled, one straight. A big selling point of these 100-watters was their three-channel capability, a luxury feature for many performing guitarists. Another 100-watter bonus was a nifty front-panel button labeled Power Dimension. When activated, it simulated the saturated sound of an all-tube amp being pushed to the limit, without the associated high volume.

As was the case with the first generation of VS amps, the Contour control proved popular for its dramatic array of midrange colors. Thrash-metallers particularly appreciated the sucked-out-mids sound it gave them when copping Metallica and Anthrax riffs. One such VSII fan was J. (Yuenger) of White Zombie fame, who used a VS100RH head as part of his live rig during the band's heyday in the mid '90s.

> "Marshall tubes are the sound of rock. Marshall Valvestates are the sound of the future—it's a completely different thing and it's what I'm looking for."
>
> —J., *Marshall Law*, 1996

A trio of stereo chorus combos rounded off the line, including the two-channel, 2x10, 30+30–watt VS230R, the VS232R (same amp as the VS230R but with two 12" speakers), and the big mama VS265R—a 65+65–watt brute with a pair of 12" custom-voiced Goldback speakers. Players could extend the latter combo with a 2x12 cabinet called the VS212 to enjoy the 4x12 Marshall experience. And, speaking of the 4x12 experience, the old VS412 remained the same except in 1997 it was renamed the VS412B, the "B" standing for "base" (straight front), in order to distinguish it from the new VS412A, its angled-front brother.

"For head-twisting chunk, the Valvestate is the grand mufti of hybrid amps. Its rawness is evenly distributed across the frequency spectrum, making it exciting to play and hear. Simple, logical controls permit a wide range of assertive voices—a veritable choir of ale-drenched soccer louts. The VS100 looks serious and sounds scary."

—*Guitar Player*, November 1997

"Whether you're into Gary Moore, George Harrison, Nirvana, George Benson, Van Halen, Cheap Trick, or half-a-dozen other styles, this 2x12 version [VS232R] of Marshall's versatile and well-conceived VS230 will do the business."

—*The Guitar Magazine* (UK)

"To bastardize a famous lyric from Elton John's 'Honky Cat,' extruding a tube tone from a transistor amp can be like trying to get whiskey from a bottle of wine. But the latest addition to Marshall's Valvestate series, the VS265R, has managed to achieve the impossible. Not only that, but the whiskey is smooth, goes down easy, and doesn't leave an unpleasant aftertaste."

—*Maximum Guitar*

Valvestate II

(1996–2000, unless stated otherwise)

Combos

VS15 15-watt, single-channel 1x8 combo (1995–2000)

VS15R Same as the VS15 but with spring reverb (1995–2000)

VS30R 30-watt, dual-channel 1x10 combo with reverb (1995–2000)

VS65R 65-watt, dual-channel 1x12 combo with reverb

VS100R 100-watt, triple-channel 1x12 combo with reverb

VS102R 100-watt, triple-channel 2x12 combo with reverb (1998–2000)

Stereo Chorus Combos

VS230 30+30–watt, dual-channel 2x10 combo with reverb and stereo chorus

VS232 30+30–watt, dual-channel 2x12 combo with reverb and stereo chorus (1998–2000)

VS265 65+65–watt, triple-channel 2x12 combo with reverb and stereo chorus

Head

VS100RH 100-watt head version of the VS100R

Cabinets

VS112 80-watt, mono, 8-ohm 1x12 cab for the VS100R

VS212 160-watt, stereo/mono 2x12 cab for the VS265

VS412 140-watt, 8-ohm, mono 4x12 cab with straight front (1996)

VS412A 140-watt, 8-ohm, mono 4x12 cab with angled front (1997–2000)

VS412B 140-watt, 8-ohm, mono 4x12 cab with straight front (1997–2000)

Power amp

VS Pro 120/120 120+120–watt stereo power amp, 2U rack (1998–2000)

One for the Roses

JCM Slash Signature Limited Edition

In January 1996, Marshall introduced their first-ever "signature" amp, with Slash of Guns n' Roses fame: the 2555SL Slash Signature head. As Jim himself wrote in the foreword of the accompanying literature, the 2555SL was "the first-ever Marshall to bear a signature other than mine in our 34-year history!" It was billed as "a deadly accurate reissue" of the all-tube, 100-watt Marshall Silver Jubilee 2555 head released in 1987 to celebrate two memorable landmarks in the company's history: Jim's 50th year in the music business and Marshall Amplification's 25th anniversary—hence the term "Jubilee."

Jim has confirmed that the company resurrected this classic model at the guitarist's behest; the road had been rough on Slash's gear. An Axl Rose–induced riot had reduced his stockpile of 2555s considerably, and the top-hatted guitarist was afraid of not being able to reproduce his trademark tone without his beloved Jubilees. Production of the JCM Slash Signature Limited Edition was confined to 3,000 units; all were snapped up immediately, making it highly collectible.

Best seat in the house: Slash aboard his signature halfstack.

Just like the original 2555, the tube payload of the two-channel Slash head was three 12AX7s in the preamp and four EL34s in the output section. Other features included a series effects loop, input gain control (for more dirt), a high-power/low-power, pentode/triode switch that dropped the head's power from 100 to 50 watts, and a DI output jack. Accompanying Slash Signature cabinets (angled and straight) came fitted with 70-watt Celestion Vintage 30 speakers and a special plaque featuring the signatures of both Slash and Jim. To top it off in genuine Slash style, his signature amp and cabs came with sleek faux-snakeskin covers.

2555SL 100-watt head.

"The Slash's ease of operation makes it an obvious choice for those who dig the sound and simplicity of an 800 Series Marshall, but want the ability to switch between sounds. If you've been wishing for a new rock amp that can fill the gap between retro and modern, the Slash may do the trick. Now if Marshall would just keep making them."

—*Guitar Player*, July 1995

"This is the amp that has made six pretty successful albums, done countless sessions, and survived two riots, three world tours, and my inflexible approach to a particular sound. It's been flawless the entire time; I wouldn't even consider trying something else—something that consistent you just don't *%$# with."

—Slash, 1996

Slash Signature Series

2555SL Limited Edition Slash Signature 100-watt, two-channel 2555 head (1996-1997)

1960ASL Limited Edition Slash Signature 280-watt, mono/stereo 4x12 cabinet with angled front (1996–1997)

1960BSL Limited Edition Slash Signature 280-watt, mono/stereo 4x12 cabinet with straight front (1996–1997)

White Noise

The 35th Anniversary Series

In 1997 Marshall produced a Limited Edition run of reissues to commemorate the company's 35th birthday. Clad in regal white vinyl, these handsome amps included the 1959WSP 100-watt Super Lead Plexi head, the 1987XWSP 50-watt Super Lead head, and the 1962WSP "Bluesbreaker" combo.

Behind the velvet rope: The Anniversary Series amps and cabinets all dressed up for their NAMM-show debut. (Note stack of Parks, right background.)

Complementing the two heads was the 1960AXWSP angled cabinet—a 100-watt, 16-ohm, mono 4x12 loaded with four 12" 25-watt Celestion Greenback speakers, covered in white vinyl and sporting an original-style metal handle, salt-and-pepper fret cloth, and a "100" logo in the top lefthand corner of the grille. As a change of pace, Marshall also included in the series a PB100WSP Power Brake power attenuator that was similarly finished in white. (Connected between the head and cabinets, Marshall's PB100 Power Brake unit allows the guitarist to crank the volume on the head for warm, natural, output-tube overdrive, and then reduce the overall volume to lower levels. Eddie Van Halen used a Variac voltage controller to similar effect on his old Plexis, achieving the renowned "brown sound" he favored on Van Halen's early recordings.)

Although the 1962 combos were sold as separate entities, the heads were sold paired with 1960AXWSP cabinets as half-stacks—with the 1959WSP/1960AXWSP combo including the PB100WSP. Only 250 sets were produced (meaning a total of 500 cabs were made), making them instant collectibles.

35th Anniversary Limited Edition Series

Heads

1959WSP Limited Edition 100-watt Plexi head in white vinyl (1997)

1987XWSP Limited Edition 50-watt Plexi head in white vinyl (1997)

Combo

1962WSP Limited Edition 1962 2x12 "Bluesbreaker" combo in white vinyl (1997)

Cabinet

1960AXWSP Limited Edition 100-watt, 16-ohm, mono angled 4x12 in white vinyl (1997)

Power Brake

PB100WSP Limited Edition PB100 power attenuator with white finish (1997)

A Smaller Stack

The JCM600 Series

In 1997 the JTM Series was replaced by the much more streamlined and modern-looking JCM600 range that comprised just three 60-watt amps (the JCM600 head, the JCM601 1x12 combo, and the JCM602 2x12 combo), and four cabinets (the

JCM600 60-watt full stack.

JCMC12 1x12, the JCMC212 2x12, and an interesting 4x10 set, the angled-front JCMC410A and the straight-front JCMC410B). The amps were fueled with a pair of EL34 power tubes with four 12AX7 tubes in the preamp. Other amenities included two independent channels, three-band EQ, separate reverb controls for each channel, a Master Presence on the back panel, both series and parallel effects loops (with Mix on the latter), and XLR outputs with Marshall Speaker Emulation. The 12" and 10" speakers used in the JCM600 range were all custom-voiced Marshall/Celestion Heritage models.

Despite the surfeit of features, the JCM600 series did not have the staying power of its larger Marshall brethren; it was discontinued in 1999 to make way for the far superior TSL60 range. Short lifespan notwithstanding, players did like them.

> "An excellent example of what an amplifier should be. Classic tones, classic styling."
>
> *Guitarist* (UK), 1997

JCM600 Series (1997-1999)

Combos

JCM601 60-watt, dual-channel 1x12 combo with reverb and two effects loops, series and parallel

JCM602 60-watt, dual-channel 2x12 combo with reverb and two effects loops, series and parallel

Head

JCM600 60-watt, dual-channel head with reverb and two effects loops, series and parallel

Cabinets

JCMC12 70-watt, 16-ohm, mono 1x12 cab for the JCM601

JCMC212 140-watt, 16-ohm, mono 2x12 cab for the JCM602

JCMC410A 120-watt, 16-ohm, mono 4x10 cab with angled front, for the JCM600 head

JCMC410B 120-watt, 16-ohm, mono 4x10 cab with straight front, for the JCM600 head

Into the Deep End

The JCM2000 Series

In the summer of 1997 Marshall unleashed the first of the all-tube JCM2000 amps—a comprehensive series that married the high gain and features of the JCM900s and the 30th Anniversary amps with the larger-than-life, organic power-amp punch of the Plexi and the JCM800s. In the space of a mere two years the JCM2000 family grew to be nine strong, consisting of two distinct groups.

Double Trouble. The company's opening JCM2000 salvo was the DSL100 head. DSL (Dual Super Lead) connotes its two footswitchable channels: Classic Gain and Ultra Gain. Like its predecessor, the JCM900 4100 head, each of the DSL100's channels has independent controls for Gain Volume and Reverb while sharing common EQ controls for Bass, Middle, Treble, and Presence. For additional tonal flexibility, each channel has two modes, selectable via the front panel. The Classic Gain channel's modes are Clean and Crunch, for the warm vintage-style overdrive of a souped-up vintage Super Lead Plexi. In the Ultra Gain channel, the Lead 1 mode is reminiscent of a hotrodded JCM800 model 2203, while Lead 2 is pure metal meltdown. The head uses four EL34 power tubes and four 12AX7 preamp tubes, and boasts a series effects loop plus some highly versatile tone-shifting options—all of the features that serious rockers demand for live performance.

The amp's secret sonic weapon is a button labeled Deep: a resonance control that significantly pumps up the bottom end while keeping it tight and focused. The Tone Shift button carves out mids for that thrashy, pre-'90s Metallica-approved tone.

The amp received superior reviews for its tone and versatility, with *Guitar Player* running a provocative subhead on the cover of its September 1997 issue: "The Ultimate Marshall?"

> "The best Marshall ever? [The DSL100] combines the best tonal qualities and features of both modern and vintage Marshall amps in one package."
>
> —*Guitar Shop*, October 1997
>
> "While many consider the 1959 Super Lead Plexi or the JCM800 Master Volume 2203 to be the epitome of tone, James and Co. might have just reinvented their own Holy Grail with the JCM2000 Dual Super Lead head."
>
> —*20th Century Guitar*, July 1997

Typically with Marshall's all-tube heads, the DSL100 has a 50-watt deadringer, the DSL50—the amp of choice of revered 6-string virtuoso Jeff Beck.

> "Are we enjoying the DSL50? You bet we are. Even though it's well into its seventh year of production, the Dual Super Lead sounds fresh and inspiring, proving that when Marshall gets it right, they really deliver the right tools for the job. . . . When you turn up for your next gig armed with this rig, nobody will question that you really mean business."
>
> —*Guitar Buyer* (UK), July 2003

Subsequent members of the Dual Super Lead family were a pair of compact, twin-channeled 1x12 combos with EL84-driven power stages: the 20-watt DSL201 (2xEL84s) and the 40-watt DSL401 (4xEL84s). These two combos shared a number of features, including two independent channels, footswitchable spring reverb, and a parallel effects loop with a front panel FX Mix control. In addition to its two channels—Clean and Overdrive (OD1)—the DSL401 also features a third footswitchable sound, OD2. The difference between OD1 and OD2? The 20dB of boost that kicks in whenever OD2 is selected.

> "Their tight, punchy tones are Marshall through and through—these new combos are the mightiest minis that Marshall has ever made."
>
> —*Guitar Player,* July 1999

JCM2000 Dual Super Leads

Heads

DSL100 100-watt, dual-channel head with reverb (1997–present)

DSL50 50-watt, dual-channel head with reverb (1997–present)

Combos

DSL201 20-watt, dual-channel, 1x12 combo with reverb (1998–2001)

DSL401 40-watt, dual-channel, 1x12 combo with reverb (1998–present)

JCM2000 DSL100 full stack.

Triple Threat. A year after the DSL100 hit, Marshall released the JCM2000 Triple Super Leads, a range of feature-laden all-tube monsters with, as their moniker suggests, three channels: Clean, Crunch, and Lead. First up came the all-tube TSL100 100-watt head and the TSL122 100-watt combo, both housing 4x12AX7 tubes in their preamps and 4xEL34s in their power stages. In addition to their three totally independent, footswitchable channels, these two monsters offered a host of other features:

- Two parallel effects loops—Loop A and Loop B—each with its own front-panel Mix control. The way these two loops operate together is clever: When only Loop A is used, it acts as the master loop for the whole amp; when Loop B is used by itself, it only affects the Crunch and Lead channels—the Clean channel remains "dry" (no effect). When both loops are used, Loop A is dedicated to the Clean channel while Loop B affects Crunch and Lead.
- A universal VPR (Virtual Power Reduction) switch. When engaged it modifies the TSL's power amp so that it emulates the sound and feel of a 25-watt power amp, allowing you to rock out at a much lower volume with the tone and dynamics you'd get if the thing were cranked to a Tufnel-approved 11.
- An Output Mute button, which—guess what!—mutes the output for silent tuning and guitar changes. And, as the next feature will reveal, it's useful for late-night recording.
- An XLR Emulated output featuring Marshall's acclaimed and popular speaker-emulation circuitry. This feature works when the Output Mute is engaged, so you can do that late-night recording session without having to worry about your neighbors calling the cops.
- A Mid Boost button on the Clean channel and two Tone Shift buttons, à la the DSL heads—one for Crunch, the other for Lead.
- Two Deep buttons for tight, resonant, low-end beef. One works on the Clean, the other on both the Crunch and Lead channels.
- Built-in footswitchable Accutronics spring reverb with two level controls, one dedicated to the Clean channel and the other shared by the Crunch and Lead.
- A 5-way LED footswitch that comes with both models, allowing you to change channels as well as switch both the reverb and the effects loops on and off.

The Marshall team tried the TSL122 with a host of different speakers, agreeing that this 2x12 combo sounded best when loaded with Celestion Vintage 30 (rated at 70 watts, despite the "30" designation) or Celestion Heritage speakers, which, as we noted previously, were specially voiced for the JCM600 series. But the team couldn't decide which speaker was "the one," so they loaded a TSL122 with one of each—which turned out to be the best of both worlds. The same mix-and-match approach was taken on the TSL122's 2x12 extension cab, the TSLC212, which adds to the TSL122's already impressive air-moving capabilities. Like the combo it pairs with, the TSLC212 houses one Vintage 30 and one Heritage.

Although their impressive array of 21 knobs and nine switches intimidated some and just plain befuddled others, the two 100-watt TSLs were quickly crowned as Marshall's new "flagship" models. The reviews reflected their lofty status within the line—as did their hefty price tags. (The award for the most amusing TSL100 review goes to the *Guitar World* writer, who, noting that Marshall had "achieved the impossible" and built a versatile amp, ended his write-up with the line, "Hopefully pigs won't start flying out of my butt.")

JCM2000 TSL100 halfstack.

> "The TSL122's pristine clean sounds and cranium-crushing distortions will both surprise and delight hardcore Marshall fans."
>
> —*Guitar Player*, November 1998
>
> "The TSL122 is far more versatile than any other Marshall out there, and offers many ways to tweak your tone. . . . It'll be tough for them to top this one."
>
> —*Guitar Shop*, January 1999

The following year, 1999, the JCM2000 family welcomed its final three members: a trio of 60-watt, all-tube TSLs—two combos (1x12 and 2x12) and a head. In terms of features these amps can be considered identical triplets, and those features can be thought of as a simplification of the knob- and button-heavy TSL100s. Although the TSL60s have three-channels—Clean, Crunch, and Lead—quite a few items are shared. For example, there's only one Deep switch and one parallel effects loop, both working on all channels. Also, the Crunch and Lead channels share tone controls and the Tone Shift button. This yields a simpler, less-cluttered front panel, making the amp a little less intimidating for the less-is-more brigade. Useful TSL features like dual reverb controls (one for Clean, the other for Crunch and Lead), XLR Speaker Emulated Out, and a supplied 5-way LED footswitch remain.

JCM2000 Triple Super Leads

Heads

TSL100 100-watt, all-tube head with three independent channels, reverb, and two parallel effects loops (1998–present)

TSL60 60-watt, all-tube, three-channel head with reverb and parallel effects loop (1999–present)

Combos

TSL122 100-watt, all-tube 2x12 combo with three independent channels, reverb and two parallel effects loops (1998–present)

TSL601 60-watt, all-tube, three-channel, 1x12 combo with reverb and parallel effects loop (1999–present)

TSL602 60-watt, all-tube, three-channel, 1x12 combo with reverb and parallel effects loop (1999–present)

Cabinets

TSLC212 150-watt, 2x12, 16-ohm mono extension cab for the TSL122 combo (1998–present)

Marshall for the Masses

The Marshall MG Series

Ever since the offshore-built Park line was introduced in 1993, Jim Marshall kept a watchful eye on all aspects of it—tone, looks, construction, consistency, and reliability—as did his R&D staff, who not only designed the amps but also played an integral role in setting up and then closely monitoring production lines and quality control procedures. All were more than pleased with what they saw—the Park amps sounded good, looked good, were sturdily built, and had a remarkably low failure rate. In fact, Mr. Marshall was so impressed that in the summer of '98 he deemed the line worthy of bearing his name. And so Park became Marshall and, literally

G30RCD 30-watt 1x10 combo.

overnight, sales went through the proverbial roof—such is the power of that famous white script logo.

The rebadged line, initially known as the Marshall Park Series, consisted of the same four models that wore the Park logo: the G10MKII, G15RCD, G30RCD, and G215RCD. In 1999, however, following the introduction of three new models—the G50RCD and G80RCD combos plus the G100RCD head—the line became known simply as the MG Series. Like its predecessor Park line, the MG's literature had a B-movie horror theme, with an image of an ivy-covered MG combo in a graveyard, next to a zombie hand emerging from the ground holding a Les Paul neck. The slogan was also Vincent Price–approved: "Tone that'll wake the dead, at a price that won't kill you!"

The three new MG models—the G50RCD, G80RCD, and G100RCD—were based on three of the most popular models in the first generation of Valvestate: the 8040, 8080, and 8100, respectively. The only real difference, apart from the name and the fact that the G50RCD had 10 more watts than the 8040, was the fact that the MG versions didn't boast a 12AX7 tube in their preamps; they were 100% solid-state. These new models were extremely well received—especially the G100RCD head, which mimicked the 8100 so well that many would fail a blind-folded A/B test. As a result, just like the 8100, the G100RCD quickly became the head of choice for hard-hitting, down-tuned modern artists like Wayne Static of Static-X and Riggs of Rob Zombie, both of whom appeared in US ad campaigns for the head. The delightfully ghoulish Riggs ad fit perfectly with the tongue-in-cheek horror-movie spin.

> "This amp is a corpse grinder—it gives you bone-crushing terror and spine-tingling chills!"
>
> —Riggs, *Marshall Law*, 1999/2000

In 2001 the popular MG line became complete with the introduction of two compact, Celestion-loaded, 140-watt 4x12 cabs: the angled MG412A and the straight MG412B. Unlike the Korean-made G100RCD head they stacked with, though, these affordable cabs were built in Milton Keynes, England.

Killer tone: Rob Zombie's Riggs haunts a United States MG ad.

Note: To round out the line in style, Marshall added the G15MS Lead 15 Micro Stack in 1999. Essentially a head version of the G15RCD with two 1x8 cabinets—one angled and one straight—just like the Lead 12 3005 Micro Stack before it, this good-sounding little beast quickly found a home in bedrooms, dressing rooms, and tour buses the world over—a purple micro-half-stack with light-straw grille cloth has taken up permanent residence in Zakk Wylde's tour bus.

MG Series

Combos

G10MKII 10-watt, 1x6½ combo (1998–2001)

G15RCD 15-watt, 1x8 single-channel combo with reverb and CD input (1998–2001)

G30RCD 30-watt, 1x10 two-channel combo with reverb and CD input (1998–2001)

G215RCD 15+15–watt, 2x8 version of the G15RCD with stereo chorus (1998–2001)

G50RCD 50-watt, 1x12 two-channel combo with reverb and CD input (1999–2001)

G80RCD 80-watt, 1x12 two-channel combo with reverb and CD input (1999–2001)

Head

G100RCD 100-watt, two-channel head with reverb and CD input (1999–2002)

Cabinets

MG412A 120-watt, 8-ohm, mono 4x12 cab with angled front (1999–present)

MG412B 120-watt, 8-ohm, mono 4x12 cab with straight front (1999–present)

Micro Stack

G15MS 15-watt head version of the G15RCD and two 1x8 cabs, one angled, one straight (1999–2001)

The Holy Grail Revisited

The Limited Edition Offset JTM45 Halfstack

At the January 1999 Winter NAMM show in Los Angeles, Jim and Co. were responsible for inducing mass drooling when they unveiled the hand-wired, Limited Edition Offset JTM45 Halfstack. Why did they do it? Because they could! "Only a few of these heads and cabinets were ever constructed," Jim explained in the accompanying manual. "A few years ago one of these extremely rare offset halfstacks came into my possession, and I immediately placed it in the Marshall Museum at our headquarters in Milton Keynes, England. Since then, all who have seen and heard it have commented most favorably—not only on its unique looks but also on its rich, fierce, majestic tone."

To say this eye-catching reissue was painstakingly accurate would be a gross understatement. "We have sought out and reproduced all of the original components and methods of construction we used back in '62," Jim pointed out in the manual. "From the hand-wired tag board housed in an aluminium [not a typo—that's the UK spelling of "aluminum"] chassis, through to the original silver Celestion

Alnico loudspeakers. We have even resurrected the original 'coffin' logo!" For purposes of absolute authenticity, the reissue had a pair of KT66 power tubes, and both the cabinet for the head and speaker cabinet featured traditional butt joints (so-called because the pieces of wood were literally butted against each other and glued) as opposed to the fingerlocked ("comb") joints Marshall has been using since 1966. To ensure the butt-jointed cabinets were square, a special jig was used while the glue dried.

As you can see from the photo, the "offset" designation came about because the head's chassis is offset to the side as opposed to being in the middle. The reason the accompanying 4x12 is also called "offset" becomes immediately apparent if you sneak a look at the back of its partially open-backed cabinet—the four 12" Celestions (15-watt, silver-painted, alnico-magnet G12 Blues—just like in the originals) are arranged in a staggered fashion, making the cabinet longer and lower than if the speakers had been in the usual "square" speaker arrangement.

Limited Edition Offset JTM45 Halfstack.

Only 300 of these beauties were made, and, because of many countries' regulations concerning electrical equipment (which we'll discuss shortly), they were only available in America (where 250 ended up) and Japan. How much did they cost? $5,000 a pair—but worth every penny to the lucky buyers.

Why was the chassis offset in the first place? Explains Jim in the manual: "The reason the amp's chassis was offset like this was to help ensure that the head balanced properly when carried. Despite the practicality of this design, however, we quickly discovered that most people preferred the symmetrical look of a centrally placed chassis, so that's how we've been building heads ever since."

21st-Century Hybrid

The AVT Series

Building on the popular Valvestate line, in 2000 Marshall created the AVT Series (Advanced Valvestate Technology), as Jim's engineers further refined their expertise in tube/solid-state hybrid amp design. Like the majority of their predecessors, all AVTs have a single 12AX7 preamp tube that plays a vital role in the gain and tone-generating circuitry and, according to Marshall, isn't "merely acting as a pilot light as in some so-called 'hybrid' amps." The real reason for AVT's "advanced" tag, however, is what's going on in the power amp. Using their newly developed "dynamic clip" technology, which Marshall claims "emulates the HT supply of a valve amp," coupled with the frequency-dependent power-amp damping that's been the backbone of Valvestate, the result is a more realistic tube sound—which all players crave—at a very reasonable price. All models over 50 watts include digital effects and other exclusive EQ features, adding further value to the AVT package.

On the bottom end is the diminutive AVT20, a two-channel, 1x10 combo with speaker-emulation output, Master Volume knob, headphone jack, and Accutronics spring reverb. There are three 1x12 combos in the lineup, each different from the next. AVT50 starts the group with 50 watts, two independent channels, spring reverb, and a series effects loop. The AVT100 jumps up to 100 watts and offers more sophisticated features like three channels (Clean, Overdrive 1, Overdrive 2), a parallel effects loop, and Scoop and Bright switches to further tweak the EQ. It also packs

16 digital effects (DFX) controlled by Mix and Adjust controls, has a Speaker Emulated Line Out, and comes with a 4-way LED footswitch for channel switching plus DFX on/off.

The 1x12 AVT150 has 150 watts of power and *four* channels. This unprecedented fourth channel, called Acoustic Simulator, is a sophisticated EQ circuit that allows an electric guitar to sound similar to an acoustic-electric guitar fitted with a piezo pickup. And, for more flexibility, the AVT150 has two DFX sections: one for its Acoustic and Clean channels, the other for OD1 and OD2. The big brother of the combo line is the powerhouse AVT275, which includes all of the AVT150's features, but with the stereo power amp pumping out 75 watts per side. Both the AVT150 and the AVT275 come with a 5-way LED footswitch for channel switching and DFX on/off.

Two heads top off the AVT series: the AVT50H and AVT150H, which are head versions of the AVT50 and AVT150 combos. They are made to be paired with the

AVT100 three-channel 100-watt combo.

compact AVT 4x12 straight (AVT412B) and slanted (AVT412A) cabinets, which are rated at 200 watts and come loaded with four 12" Celestion speakers.

All AVT combos feature a closed-back cabinet design and house specially designed Celestion speakers with "extended bass response." This allows the AVT combos to have the sort of low-end thump and projection normally associated with a 4x12.

How true is Marshall's bold claim that AVT's "emulation of the sound, feel, and projection of an all-tube amp is the best there is"? Judging by artists' reaction and the positive reviews the series garnered, it could well be justified. In fact, the write-ups were so glowing that Marshall ran a double-page ad featuring AVT review excerpts in the US for several months.

"The AVT20 is a great tool for me—it's a really good-sounding practice amp that I use to work on new ideas or warm up before a show. I play Marshall live, and it gives me a great representation of my live sound in a small, sturdy package."

—Mike Mushok, Staind, Marshall 2001 catalog

"The AVT is easily the most impressive hybrid amp I've heard to date. . . . By cloning the best of its breed, Marshall has graced the AVTs with the dynamic and harmonic power to blur the barrier between tube and solid-state. If the AVT150 is any measure of things to come, one's decision to buy a tube amp can now be steered by *choice* rather than necessity."

—*Guitar Player*, March 2001

"The AVT20 is the best small combo I've ever heard. It sounds a lot bigger than it is."

—Jerry Horton, Papa Roach, Marshall 2001 catalog

AVT Series

(2000–present)

Combos

AVT20	20-watt, two-channel 1x10 combo with spring reverb
AVT50	50-watt, two-channel 1x12 combo with spring reverb
AVT100	100-watt, three-channel 1x12 combo with digital effects
AVT150	150-watt, four-channel 1x12 combo with two digital effects sections

Stereo combo

AVT275	75+75–watt, four-channel 2x12 combo with stereo digital effects

Heads

AVT50H	50-watt, two-channel head with spring reverb
AVT150H	150-watt, four-channel head with two digital effects sections

Cabinets

AVT112	100-watt, 8-ohm, mono 1x12 cabinet for the AVT100
AVT412A	200-watt, 8-ohm, mono 4x12 cabinet with angled front for the AVT50H and AVT150H
AVT412B	200-watt, 8-ohm, mono 4x12 cabinet with straight front for the AVT50H and AVT150H

More Bang for Yer Buck

The MG Series gets digital

From little acorns grow mighty oaks. In January 2002 Marshall unveiled the latest and definitely greatest generation of their incredibly popular MG (Marshall Guitar) series of introductory-level amps. Made offshore and priced to encourage brand loyalty in new players from their very first purchase, the line comprises eight solid-state combos, one head, and two 4x12 cabs. Of the nine amps, six of them boast built-in digital effects—designated by "DFX" at the end of their model numbers. Combos in the 10- to 30-watt range are the MG10CD, MG15CD, MG15CDR (with reverb), MG15DFX, and MG30DFX. All come with useful features like a CD input (for jamming along to favorite discs), "Emulated" headphone jack, and, on the two DFX models, four basic but variable digital effects: reverb, chorus, flange, and delay.

MG15DFX 15-watt 1x8 combo

These DFX effects are controlled using what Marshall jokingly refers to as "idiot-proof" editing, which consists of two controls: a Preset/Adjust control with 64 presets for each of the four effects, and an FX Level control.

Larger MG amps are the 50-watt, 1x12 MG50DFX, 50+50–watt, 2x12 stereo MG250DFX, and the 100-watt, 1x12 MG100DFX combos, plus the 100-watt MG100HDFX head. In these bigger models, the digital reverb has its own dedicated Level control so its place on the Preset/Adjust control is taken by 64 preset Chorus/Delay options. All of the MGs, which are made in either Korea (for the US market) or India, feature a technology Marshall uses on AVT called Frequency Dependent Damping (FDD)—circuitry which the company claims "mimics the way an all-valve power amp interacts with the speaker(s) it is driving." However it does what it does, it certainly makes the MGs sound and feel more "tube-like."

If the past three years of MG sales are any indication, the company has been wildly successful roping the next generation of players into the Marshall fold. Special care was taken to ensure the Overdrive channel of the MG100HDFX maintained the unique, aggressive behavior of its two forefathers, the 8100 and G100RCD, and pros like Wayne Static, Tommy Victor, and "Metal Mike" Chlasciak (Halford and Pain Museum) were quick to embrace it.

"In the past there was definitely a stigma attached to transistor amplifiers, but with so many of the high-gain American metal guys going solid-state, things are changing. . . . [the MG100DFX] is loud, punchy, and provides the trademark Marshall sound in an affordable package."

—*The Guitar Magazine* (UK)

"Marshalls are metal—they're the only amps that move air."

—Mike Chlasciak

"I love the old G100RCD head; it has a lot of gain and a really "in-your-face" tone that's perfect for the crunchy, detuned rhythms I do. That said, I think the MG100HDFX is even better, and I really like its 'magic button'—the FDD switch. The HDFX has an even tighter low end and a little more crunch, too. Another thing I've noticed is that in addition to sounding great at stage volumes, the HDFX still sounds great at really low volumes—it maintains its bite and tightness. The built-in effects are nice as well. It's really easy to dial them in, and I've been using some of them for different guitar parts on demos."

—Wayne Static, *Marshall Law*, 2002/3*

*Marshall assured us that no money changed hands in exchange for the above quote but admitted that they did offer Mr. Static a copywriting job after he gave them the quote!

MG250DFX 50+50–watt 2x12 combo.

MG Series: The Second Generation

(2002–present)

Combos

MG10CD 10-watt, 1x6½ combo with FDD and CD input

MG15CD 15-watt, 1x8 combo with FDD and CD input

MG15CDR 15-watt, 1x8 combo with FDD, CD input, and spring reverb

MG15DFX 15-watt, 1x8 combo with FDD, CD input, and digital effects

MG30DFX 30-watt, 1x10, two-channel combo with FDD, CD input, and digital effects

MG50DFX 50-watt, 1x12, two-channel combo with FDD, CD input and digital effects

MG250DFX 50+50–watt, 2x12, two-channel stereo combo with FDD, CD input, and digital effects

MG100DFX 100-watt, 1x12, two-channel combo with FDD, CD input, parallel effects loop, and digital effects

Head

MG100HDFX	100-watt, two-channel head with FDD, CD input, parallel effects loop, and digital effects

Cabinets*

MG412A	120-watt, mono 4x12, Celestion-loaded cabinet with angled front (2002–present)
MG412B	120-watt, mono 4x12, Celestion-loaded cabinet with straight front (2002–present)

Micro Stack

MG15MSII	15-watt head version of MG15CDR with two 1x8 cabs—one angled, one straight.

*As was the case with the first-generation MG cabs, the MG412A and MG412B were made in England. In later 2003, however, to compete with an increasing amount of cheap, offshore-made 4x12 cabinets on the market, production was moved to Korea (US market) and India (Europe).

Bull's-Eye

Zakk Wylde Signature Model

In January 2002, six years after Marshall's first signature amp with Slash, the company released the Zakk Wylde Signature 100-watt JCM2203ZW head, in honor of Ozzy Osbourne's celebrated guitarist. Noted for its distinctive design of gothic lettering, targets, and the "skully" logo from Zakk's "other" band, Black Label Society, the 2203ZW looks and sounds as menacing as the guy it is named after.

2203ZW Limited Edition 100-watt halfstack.

The 2203ZW head is fueled by three 12AX7 preamp tubes and a quartet of 6550s—Mr. Wylde's power tubes of choice. It also boasts a series effects loop with a "true bypass" switch. The 2203ZW came with a bag of collectible Zakk Wylde guitar picks and a certificate of authenticity signed by both Zakk Wylde and Jim Marshall. Only 600 were made, and

Don't back up!: Zakk Wylde guards his signature rig behind the tour bus.

they sold out instantly. Zakk's message to the lucky 600 owners was simple: "I hope the 2203ZW kicks your ass as much as it kicks mine."

Cosmetically matching Limited Edition 4x12 cabinets (but *not* signature models)—the angled-front, 300-watt 1960AF7 and the (extremely limited) straight-front, 300-watt 1960BF7—were also offered by popular demand.

Zakk Wylde Signature head

2203ZW Limited Edition	100-watt JCM800 2203 head with 6550 power tubes (2002)

Past Masters

Reissuing the reissues

The mailroom at Marshall headquarters is routinely deluged with letters from consumers requesting that their favorite old models be reissued. Seizing on a market that would otherwise belong to collectors and vintage shops, the company has exhumed a number of classic amps to satisfy public demand. As Jim puts it, "The continual fascination and love for our vintage amplifiers is a testament to just how relevant and important these models are today. They laid the foundation for much of what followed and represent an important part of our heritage."

The reissues can be thought of as coming in two waves. The first wave was a staggered launch in the late '80s and early '90s, as outlined in Doyle's *The History of Marshall.* It comprised four models: the world-renowned 100-watt 1959SLP Super Lead Plexi head; the 50-watt 1987X Plexi head; the amp that started it all, the JTM45; and the 1962 "Bluesbreaker" 2x12 combo made famous by Eric Clapton in his days with John Mayall, especially on the groundbreaking record *Blues Breakers with Eric Clapton,* a.k.a. the "Beano" album. (Note: The 1987X and JTM45 are both housed in

1959SLPX 100-watt full stack; 1987XL 50-watt halfstack; JTM45/2245 halfstack with 1960TV cab; 1962 2x12 Bluesbreaker combo.

a "small" head box that's about 3" shorter in length than the 1959SLP head box, and 2" shorter in height.)

The second wave, which we're addressing here, hit the streets in the summer of 2002, several years after the first wave failed to pass new, stricter safety regulations in European and many other countries, and were taken off those markets. (This didn't affect America or Japan; both countries continued to sell the first-wave reissues until the second wave was ready to roll). Reissuing the reissues would prove to be a unique challenge to Marshall's design team. While they wanted to reproduce classic Marshalls to spec, they were faced with four major hurdles:

1. The specs varied greatly among the original models. Anyone who has played a handful of Plexis back to back knows the amps' sound can vary widely. Simple factors like parts availability had impact; plus, the design teams of old were constantly refining.

2. Component tolerances also varied in the "good ol' days." In fact, they often varied wildly, so that two seemingly identical circuits could sound and feel very different due to the combined effect of the variances. So, when an old "holy grail" amp was found, the circuit couldn't just be taken at face value—instead, every component had to be stringently tested. "In the early days they were often building the amps with whatever was at hand at the time," reveals R&D's Ian Robinson. "So things like the feedback resistors could change from day to day, week to week, meaning that the amp's all-important damping would change too."

3. Personal opinion: When a so-called "holy grail" original amp was found, Marshall sought the opinions of many players from all over the world to ensure a universal agreement of what is and isn't "classic." "We also had to respect the heritage and avoid the obvious danger of deciding, 'We can improve this,'" Robinson states. "As a department we understand that these amps really can't be improved—they are what they are, and that's how they should always remain. That was our responsibility."

4. Modern approvals: As we've already noted, what was acceptable electrically back then is now deemed illegal in most parts of the world. So duplicating a great old amp is not a simple "copy it exactly as is" exercise, because the resulting replica would not pass the necessary electrical-safety tests. To give you an idea of how strict and ever-changing these tests are, consider that Marshall's reissue amps of the late

>>> 1962JAG Limited Edition <<<

Now *here* is a plush ride. The 1962JAG, built in conjunction with Jaguar Cars Ltd., commemorated Marshall's 40th anniversary in high style. Limited to a very exclusive run of just 40 amplifiers, it is bound to become one of the most collectible amps Marshall has produced.

Manufactured in January 2003, the 1962JAG is a gold-plated, leather-covered beauty based on the 1962 Vintage Reissue "Bluesbreaker" combo. Each chassis was manually punched before being sent for gold plating, and over 150 additional components in all (including the foot pedal) are gilded with a gorgeous mirrored finish. The amps were assembled entirely by hand, right down to the hand-soldered potentiometers and valve bases. Once assembled at the Bletchley factory, the amps were sent to Jaguar's trim shop in Coventry where they were hand-trimmed in white Jaguar leather. A snowy leaping-cat logo is embossed in the upper right corner.

One 1962JAG was given away in a contest in the UK magazine *Guitarist*, as an editor there had first suggested the Marshall/Jaguar collaboration. Only 30 others were made available worldwide. To ensure fairness of availability, Marshall held a promotion inviting anyone who could afford the £5,000 ($7,900 US) amp to register for a random drawing. Sales primarily benefited a charity that provides musical instruments to schools for deprived students.

'80s/early '90s failed new European CE tests introduced later that decade and were taken off the market—except in America and Japan, where they were still deemed "acceptable" by regulators. Likewise, as mentioned earlier, the renowned limited hand-wired Offset JTM45 launched in America in 1999 wasn't available elsewhere in the world, apart from Japan, due to codes.

In the late '90s the first wave of Marshall reissues was unceremoniously swept off most markets by those pesky regulations. Not willing to let modern legislation kill the company's tonal heritage, once again Jim's R&D team went back to the drawing board. They gathered up a handful of universally accepted "holy grail" originals and, after a year's worth of hard graft, emerged with a set of faithful reissues that were once again "legal." This time, though, the lineup featured a newcomer—the much-lauded JCM800 2203. A neat twist was also added to three of the models: the 1959SLP, the 1987X, and the 2203 all featured a series effects loop. And, before you cry foul, note that the effects loop features a "bypass" switch that takes it completely out of the circuit. The reason for the inclusion of this purist-upsetting feature? Public demand—another example of Jim's "listen to what our customers want" credo in action. To designate the presence of the bypassable loop, an "X" was tagged on the end of the model number of the amps in question, except for the 1987X, where an "L" was added instead because it was felt (correctly) that "XX" would look a little silly.

Vintage Reissues

(the second wave, 2002–present)

1959SLPX	100-watt, all-tube Super Lead "Plexi" head (circa 1967-1969)*
1987XL	50-watt "Plexi" head, in small box (circa 1966–1969)*
2203X	JCM800 100-watt, all-tube head (circa 1981–90)*
JTM45/2245	JTM45 head, in small box (circa 1965–1966)
1962	2x12 "Bluesbreaker" combo (circa 1965–1966)

** Features series effects loop with "true bypass" switch.*

Four Amps in One

The Mode Four

In January 2003 Marshall took hybrid amplification to new levels with the Mode Four, representing a leap in design, feature sets, and cosmetic appeal. Providing modern guitarists with maximum versatility, heavy crunch, expansive headroom, and a broad bottom end, the Mode Four MF350 head is driven by a colossal 350-watt solid-state power section. The front and rear sections of this beast are equally unique in design and approach, combining to create what Marshall calls Dual Amplifier Design—one aspect being "classic" (traditional Marshall), the other "modern." The latter's goal is definitely to invade the bottom-heavy tonal territory long owned by Mesa's much-praised Rectifier heads.

MF350 350-watt two-channel/four-mode full stack.

Front end. The Mode Four features two entirely separate preamps, each containing a single 12AX7 tube. Each of the preamps—Amp 1 and Amp 2—has two modes to select between, thus the "four" in Mode Four. For maximum flexibility, all four modes are footswitchable.

Amp 1 features Clean and Crunch modes, closely recreating the tones of a classic Marshall 100-watt SLP and a hotrodded JCM800, respectively. The gain increases vastly when you switch to Amp 2, which features OD1 and OD2 modes. The saturation in OD1 is akin to the modern-metal sound of the JCM2000, while OD2 enables gain so over-the-top it makes the JCM900's "20" knob look like it's missing a decimal point.

Each side features Gain, Volume, Bass, Middle, and Treble controls, individually voiced Scoop switches (to "scoop" the midrange), plus controls for Reverb level and FX Level. To increase Amp 2's tonal range, it includes a 3-way rotary switch labeled Tone Matrix. This switch completely reconfigures the mids, giving three distinctly different distorted tones. Setting 1 produces the "woody knock" associated with high-gain Marshall amps; Setting 2 tightens the low mids, making for a heavier, less "woody" sound; and Setting 3 is the lowest and most extreme of the trio, resulting in an exaggerated low-end "thump."

Rear end. in addition to being capable of delivering a ridiculous 350 watts, the MF350's power amp completely reconfigures itself depending on whether Amp 1 or Amp 2 is selected. According to Marshall's R&D team, whenever Amp 1 (Clean or Crunch) is chosen, the MF's power amplifier reconfigures to create "the unmistakable sound and feel of a 100-watt Super Lead Plexi or 2203." When Amp 2 is selected, it reconfigures itself so it can create "the deep, dark-sounding, loose low end that has proved so popular with modern players who either detune regular 6-strings, or use 7-string or baritone guitars." The MF's rumbling ability can be further enhanced via a Resonance control in the Master section—a four-control area in the middle of the front panel.

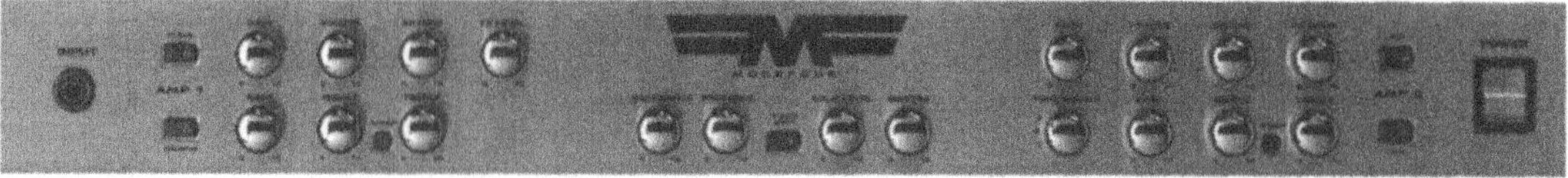

Command central: The Mode Four's sleek control panel.

Whatever the science behind it (and regardless of the "ad speak"), the real test of Marshall's claims for the Mode Four lies in the amp's user list. In less than a year after its introduction (as of the fall 2003 completion of this book), the list included the likes of Daron Malakian of System of a Down, Tripp Eisen of Static-X, Dave "Brownsound" Baksh of Sum 41, John 5 of Marilyn Manson, Dave Navarro of Jane's Addiction, Sean Martin of Hatebreed, and both Mike Mushok (studio) and Aaron Lewis (live) of Staind.

> "The complete rock amp. The clean is really full; the crunch has an attack which is great for fast, heavy-metal type muting; OD1 is just a really cool, all-around rock tone; and the fourth mode (OD2) is the one I'm usually on whenever I'm playing heavy."
>
> —Daron Malakian
>
> "Four sounds, two amps. Everything is huge. After hearing this amp you will cry if you spent your money on [another amp]."
>
> —Dave Baksh
>
> "Nothing beats the crunch sound of a Marshall. I'm really impressed with the tonal versatility of the new Mode Four. The Clean Mode's the best ever—in fact, I like it so much that I used it on the new Staind album, '14 Shades of Grey.'"
>
> —Mike Mushok
>
> "Any head can distort, but not many can produce chunk, and when it's all said and done, that's what it's all about. I just plug straight in and get all the nuts I need."
>
> —Kerry King, Slayer
>
> "My Marshall has enabled me to do away with half of what I used to use on the floor. You'll find that your old distortion and boost pedals will make great gifts."
>
> —Dave Navarro

The Mode Four garnered enthusiastic magazine reviews without exception; one write-up characterized it as "sure to shape the future of amplifier design and modern guitar tone." In addition, *Guitar Player* gave it their prestigious Editors Pick award, and *Guitar One* awarded it their "1" trophy.

> "The Mode Four is exceedingly loud, but a big advantage of all that power is that it allows detuners and 7-stringers to go deep into the chug zone without sounding like their amp is about to implode. In fact, it's funny just how loud and loose you can get without losing definition."
>
> Marshall may be the "sound of rock," but the Mode Four's clean channel offers even more headroom than a Fender Twin Reverb. The sound is rich and dimensional, and maxed-out gain delivers roughly the same level of grind as you'd expect from an early-'70s Marshall. Dial up the mids and add reverb, and you get meaty, clanging Strat tones that are great for hard-driving, SRV-style blues."
>
> —*Guitar Player*, April 2003
>
> [Marshall] focused on very specific musical needs and addressed them by using the best technology available."
>
> —*Guitar One*, May 2003
>
> "The MF350 nails those detuned sounds—and a lot more besides—better than any amp in the world. And it looks almost too cool to be true."
>
> —*The Guitarist* (UK), February 2003

To deal with its enhanced low-end-thumping abilities, the Mode Four head is joined by a quartet of specially designed 4x12 "tall" Celestion-loaded cabinets (two angled, two straight). These super-sized cabs (3" taller than the "industry standard"

Marshall 4x12) help bring out the low-end range of the MF350 head. The 16-ohm, 280-watt-apiece MF280A (angled) and MF280B (straight) cabinets are designed to be used in a full-stack configuration, and are loaded with four 70-watt 12" Celestion/Marshall Vintage 30MF speakers. The 8-ohm, 400-watt MF400A and MF400B cabinets are designed for half-stack operation only, and come loaded with four 100-watt 12" Celestion/Marshall speakers. (The MF350 delivers its full 350 watts of power when presented with an 8-ohm load. It delivers approximately 235 watts when hooked up to a single 16-ohm cabinet.)

Other MF350 features include:

- Built-in "studio quality" digital reverb. This was chosen instead of a more traditional spring system because the designers felt that the amp's propensity to create low-end rumble would play havoc with a mechanical reverb system.
- Two Emulated Line outputs, one XLR and one ¼".
- A rear-panel Tuner Out jack plus a front panel Tuner Mute switch for silent tuning and guitar changes.
- A footswitchable universal Solo Level control that, when activated, can give a boost of up to +6dB (which doesn't sound like a lot, but it actually translates to twice as loud).
- A 6-way LED footswitch that allows you to switch Solo Level and Reverb off/on in addition to bouncing between the four modes.

Mode Four

(2003–present)

Head

MF350 350-watt, two channel/four-mode hybrid head with parallel/series effects loop, footswitchable digital reverb, and Solo Level

4x12 cabinets

MF280A 280-watt, 16-ohm, extra-tall, angled-front Mode Four cabinet

MF280B 280-watt, 16-ohm, extra-tall, straight-front Mode Four cabinet

MF400A 400-watt, 8-ohm, extra-tall, angled-front Mode Four cabinet

MF400B 400-watt, 8-ohm, extra-tall, straight-front Mode Four cabinet

OTHER PRODUCTS

Taming the Beast

The PB100 Power Brake

As we've noted elsewhere, to achieve the full-blown tonal glory of a non-MV, all-tube Marshall like a 1959SLP, 1987, or JTM45, you've got to turn the sucker way up in order to get that inimitable power-tube magic happening. And a cranked Marshall means one thing—volume, deafening volume. This is not a problem for multi-platinum rock stars playing sold-out enormodomes, but for the average Joe in a small club, rehearsal room, or—God forbid—bedroom, it is!

Enter the PB100, a clever little device that sits between the head and cab(s) and allows you to turn the amp to 11 while attenuating (reducing) the volume coming out of the speakers by as much you want—even down to bedroom level. And, thanks to the "reflected inductive load" circuitry, the PB100 does all this without damaging the amp or that all-important tone.

The fact the PB100 is still available 11 years after its 1993 launch speaks volumes (awful pun intended) for how well it does its silencing task.

Strumming Through a Marshall

The Acoustic Soloist series

With the blossoming of acoustic-electric guitars in the 1990s, so too came the so-called "acoustic amplifier." Marshall answered the call with their line of stereo Acoustic Soloist amps. First to the gate, the AS80R stereo (40 watts per side) 2x10 combo came with stereo analog chorus, reverb, an XLR input (for a vocal mic), anti-feedback "notch" filters (which allow cuts to the midrange frequencies—invaluable for amped acoustic players), piezo tweeter, plus stereo effects loops and line-out jack. In 1999 the AS80R went away, and into its place stepped the more affordable OEM 50-watt AS50R combo, which offered similar features with two 8" speakers and a piezo tweeter.

Also currently in production is the high-end AS100D (50 watts per side), which uses two 8" custom-voiced speakers and two polymer-dome tweeters to tailor the tone coming from its four channels. There are also an array of input and output

Acoustic Soloist AS100D 50+50–watt 2x8 combo.

possibilities (¼" cable, XLR, and RCA). But this model particularly stands out for its 16 built-in stereo digital effects. These include good-quality reverbs (halls, rooms, plates, etc.), chorus, flange, delay, modulation, and various mixtures.

Step On It

Marshall stompboxes

Marshall first dabbled with stompboxes in the late '60s, when they offered the self-explanatory SupaFuzz and Supa-Wah pedals. Then, in 1989, the original Marshall Guv'nor pedal was introduced, for the first time offering something akin to Marshall overdrive in a pedal, adopted by no less than Gary Moore. You may recall reading in Chapter 4 that Jim's driver, John Kent, calls him "Guv'nor." But that's not where the pedal's name comes from. Says Jim, "When we first had some players test out the pedals, they tried them and said, 'That pedal's just the guv'nor, innit.' So we said, 'Well, yes, I guess it is!'"

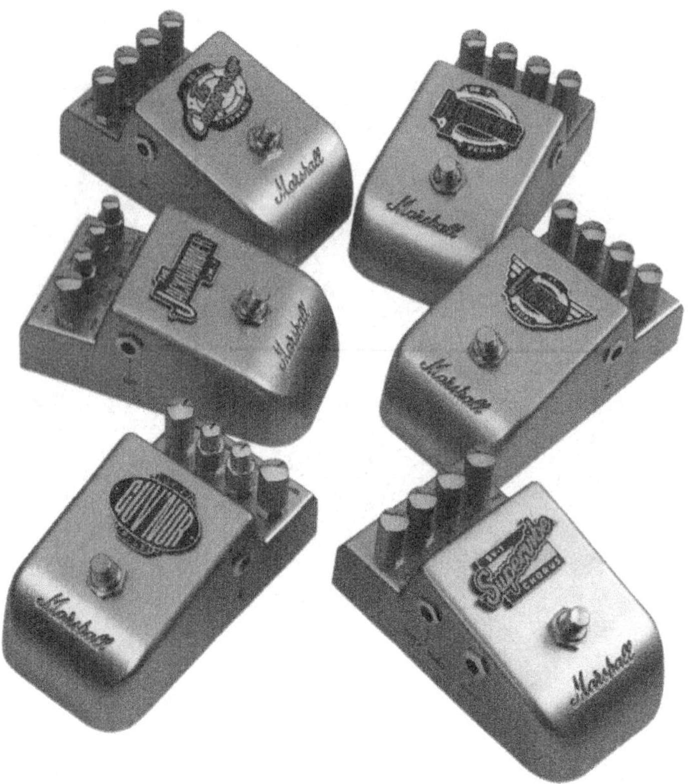

(clockwise from top right) BB-2 Bluesbreaker II; VT-1 Vibratrem; SV-1 Supervibe; GV-2 Guv'nor Plus; JH-1 Jackhammer; ED-1 Edward the Compressor.

In the early '90s the company came out with another three overdrive/distortion stompboxes—the BluesBreaker, the DriveMaster, and the ShredMaster—using a "from the guys who brought you distortion..." advertising line. Five controls on the latter two offered up a host of tonal options. But the housings were neither compact nor sleek and, as a result, this trio hardly set the world on fire.

In 1998 Marshall introduced a range of six new Marshall stompboxes, and this time they looked as good as they sounded—and were compact, too. Not surprisingly, three of the six distorted. Still in production today, the GV-2 Guv'nor revives Mr. Moore's favorite stompbox, adding an inner-dial Deep control on the Bass knob for dialing in more bottom. Another revisited oldie is the BB-2 Bluesbreaker II, an overdrive pedal with two modes: one to produce an actual boost (an output kick to

MS-4 1-watt belt-clip "full stack."

smack the front end of a tube amp and create natural overdrive), as well as a gain setting to create tube-like distortion on a solid-state amp. For metal players, meanwhile, the JH-1 Jackhammer provides all sorts of nu-metal distortion settings for head-banging, skull-crushing, and other cranium-based leisure pursuits.

It's not all about distortion, though: The VT-1 Vibratrem emulates the tremolo-laden, psychedelic guitar sounds of the mid-1960s, while the ED-1 Compressor (with Monty Pythonesque nickname "Edward the Compressor," a play on the early English king Edward the Confessor). Finally, the SV-1 Supervibe offers an array of modulation effects from vibratos to choruses. Marshall's pedals, like the Acoustic Soloist amps, are made in China.

Size Isn't Always Important

MS-4

Marshall's mighty 1-watt battery-operated halfstack-with-a-belt-clip, the MS-2, was an instant hit when it hit the marketplace in 1990, and what's not to like? It looks good and sounds remarkably good too. So, in 1995 came the next logical step—a full-stack version, the MS-4! Just like its little brother, this 25cm no-brainer can be found in bedrooms, in offices, and on guitar techs' workbenches the world over.

Bass-State B150 150-watt 1x15 combo.

Big Bottom

Marshall bass amps

Bassists, too, have enjoyed the benefits of Marshall gear during the past 10 years or so. The now-discontinued Dynamic Bass Series (DBS) featured a number of heads, cabinets, and combos. These included the 7200 head, which used a single 12AX7 tube in its preamp along with a completely solid-state power section that cranked out 200 clean watts (bassists need the headroom). The more powerful 7400 head had similar features, but offered a massive 400-watt output. Features on both included a built-in compressor, Deep and Bright switches, graphic EQ, and preamp Blend to mix the tube signal with the solid-state for just the right amount of warmth.

Cabinet options included the 7152 with a 1x15 and 2x10 configuration in one housing, and the 7041 with 4x10s and a high-frequency horn. The 7015 was more on the compact side, offering a 1x15 setup. Marshall also issues two combos in the Dynamic Bass System, the 72115 (200 watts, 1x15 speaker with a horn) and the 72410 (200 watts, 4x10 speakers with horn).

Naturally, Marshall also makes gear for bassists who lust for all-tube tone. Enter the behemoth VBA400 (VBA stands for "Valve Bass Amp"). This all-tube, 400-watt head uses an amazing *eight* 6550 power tubes with three 12AX7 and one 12AU7 (ECC82) tube in the preamp. Features include active/passive inputs, 3-band EQ, 3-position Mid Contour, Deep and Bright switches, a tuner output, a DI XLR, effects loop—hell, you can even select your preferred fan speed.

Since not every 4- or 5-stringer can afford a high-end bass head with 12 tubes, Marshall also produces the more moderately priced Bass-State series. There are two all-solid-staters in the line: the B30 is a 30-watt 1x10 combo, while the B65 is a 65-watter with a 1x12 setup. Topping the line is the B150, which boasts 150 watts, a 1x15 configuration, and—like the current AVT guitar amps—a single 12AX7 (ECC83) tube in the preamp. Last and also least, in terms of output power, comes the entry-level MB25MKII, a 25-watt 1x10 combo that started out life as a Park and then morphed into a Marshall when the Park guitar amps did the same in '98.

As this book goes to press, Marshall is gearing up to start work on an entirely new line of bass amplifiers and speakers. R&D head Bruce Keir is a bassist himself, ensuring that the forthcoming line will supersede anything Marshall has offered before in this category.

The "Where Are They Now?" File

As Jim has never been afraid to admit, not all of his products are smash hits—the vast majority are, but a few miss the mark. Joining the latter minority are the following three:

DRP-1: Direct Recording Pre-amp

Aimed at the burgeoning home-recording market, this little black-and-gold box entered the fray in 1994. Powerable by a 9V battery or optional AC adapter, it could be used onstage or for headphone practice in addition to being a direct recording device.

DRP-1 preamp.

Time to tune: A CAT-1 awaits its fate amid the knicknacks atop a G100RCD head. The amp is covered in cornstarch from the infamous Riggs ad photo (page 141).

To be frank, its sound was lackluster, and it quickly disappeared. It currently resides in the "clunker" retirement home.

Park 4x12 cabinets

Launched in the mid '90s, this pair of 160-watt 4x12s—the angled G412A and straight G412B—didn't last long. They were too expensive and lacked a vital ingredient, the Marshall logo.

CAT-1 Tuner

A Marshall tuner? It may have looked cute, but this CAT didn't have nine lives—it barely had one. RIP.

Special thanks to Nick Bowcott for his substantial contributions to this chapter.

Chapter 6

Amp Anatomy

"When these young rock 'n' roll guitarists were coming into my shop in the early '60s, they hadn't found the exact sound they wanted from their amplifiers," says Jim, who had been selling amps by Selmer and Fender in addition to the drum kits and guitars that sustained his store. "The closest was the Fender Bassman. I was always partial to the Bassman as well but it wasn't quite the sound they were after."

Though not an amp designer himself—Jim has always given credit to his R&D teams—he knew that the potential to produce the desired sound rested within the tubes. The rich, earthy tone would have to be the result of harmonic overtones generated by overdriven vacuum tubes. To better understand the concepts at work here, first consider what overtones are and how they are produced.

Overtones

Any note—any pitched sound—generates overtones, a series of notes extending upward in pitch from the played, or fundamental, note. Most of those overtones extend well beyond the range of human hearing, but even barely audible overtones contribute to the character of a note. We perceive notes as individual tones, but what we hear is actually a combination of the note played and its overtones.

As a phenomenon of physics, overtones come in reliable intervals that make up the overtone series (sometimes referred to, inaccurately, as the harmonic series). In the overtone series, each consecutive note is the next multiple of the fundamental's frequency: The fundamental is the first note; double its frequency for the second note (which sounds one octave plus a 5th higher than the fundamental); quadruple the frequency for the fourth note (two octaves above the fundamental); and so on.

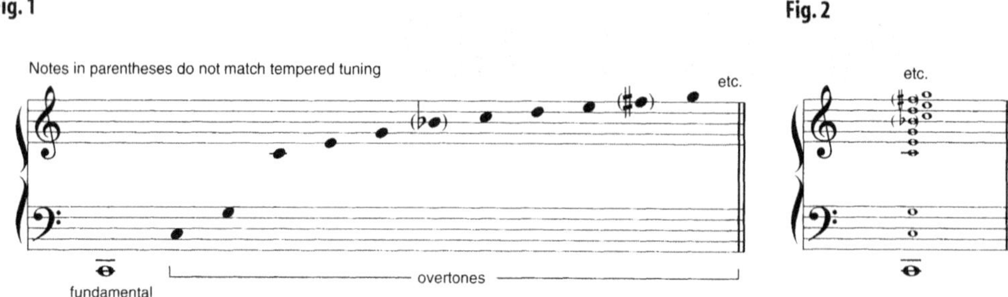

Figure 1. The overtone series, with *C* as the fundamental. Figure 2. Overtones as perceived by the human ear. The energy of each successively higher pitch decreases.

The concept is familiar to guitarists who sound harmonics along a string. The harmonic heard on the low *E* string at the 12th fret sounds one octave higher than the open string. This is because that 12th-fret harmonic is played at exactly the string's halfway point (between nut and bridge): halve the length of the string, and its frequency is doubled. The harmonic at the 7th fret falls at exactly one-third the string's length, tripling the frequency and sounding one octave plus a 5th above the fundamental.

The overtone series comes out of hiding on other instruments as well. Listen to an open *D* being bowed on the wound string of a violin for more than four or five seconds, and you'll hear a high *A* emerge. Hit the middle *C* on a piano and then quickly step on the damper pedal, and the *C* two octaves above is heard; get it just right and you'll begin to hear high, slightly dissonant pitches resonate as well. If you've ever heard a Tibetan monk open his throat and sing remarkably low notes, you know that as many as two or three additional tones are produced. The monk can only sing one note at a time; the overtone series is responsible for the others.

One phenomenon of overtones is that the intervals between consecutive notes get smaller as the series proceeds. Thus, when more overtones are audible, more dissonance is contributed to the note heard. At very high frequencies, the dissonance does not strike the ear as discordant but instead adds richness and depth to the tone.

Driven

We've taken the long way around with the physics lesson, but all in the name of great-sounding amps. Jim Marshall recognized that an overdriven vacuum tube had the potential to greatly enhance the sound coming through an amp by adding—or perhaps more accurately *bringing out*—the electric guitar's harmonic overtones. In almost every other tube-driven application, distortion and coloration of the signal was an imperfection, an undesirable side effect. But for guitar amps, it was perfection.

How to overdrive the tubes? Play that amp louder than life.

Today, guitarists are accustomed to hearing overdrive at even the lowest volumes. The vast majority of modern amps have a control labeled "gain" that can be cranked up to 10, yielding a drenching distortion, while the output volume is set to a whisper (there's also a huge amount of analog overdrive, fuzz and distortion stompboxes, and digital devices that can create a similar effect). What's happening here is that the gain control is determining how hard the preamp tubes are being overdriven, while the power tubes, which regulate power to the speakers, remain undistorted and still have plenty of headroom. But the original and true Marshall sound is the result of overdriving *power amp* tubes as well. With a 100-watt amplifier, that can only be accomplished by playing extraordinarily loud—which for Townshend and company was no problem.

In 1975 Marshall introduced the 2203, which employed a master-volume design in which a pre-amp volume control enabled the user to overdrive the preamp into distortion. That scheme would become almost ubiquitous on amps by Marshall and other amp manufacturers in years to come. But it's still important to recognize and appreciate—and understandable to lust for—the unique and characteristic sound of a Marshall's overdriven Marshall power amp section—a sound so singular and organic it cannot be emulated by a stompbox or preamp alone, regardless of what a manufacturer may claim.

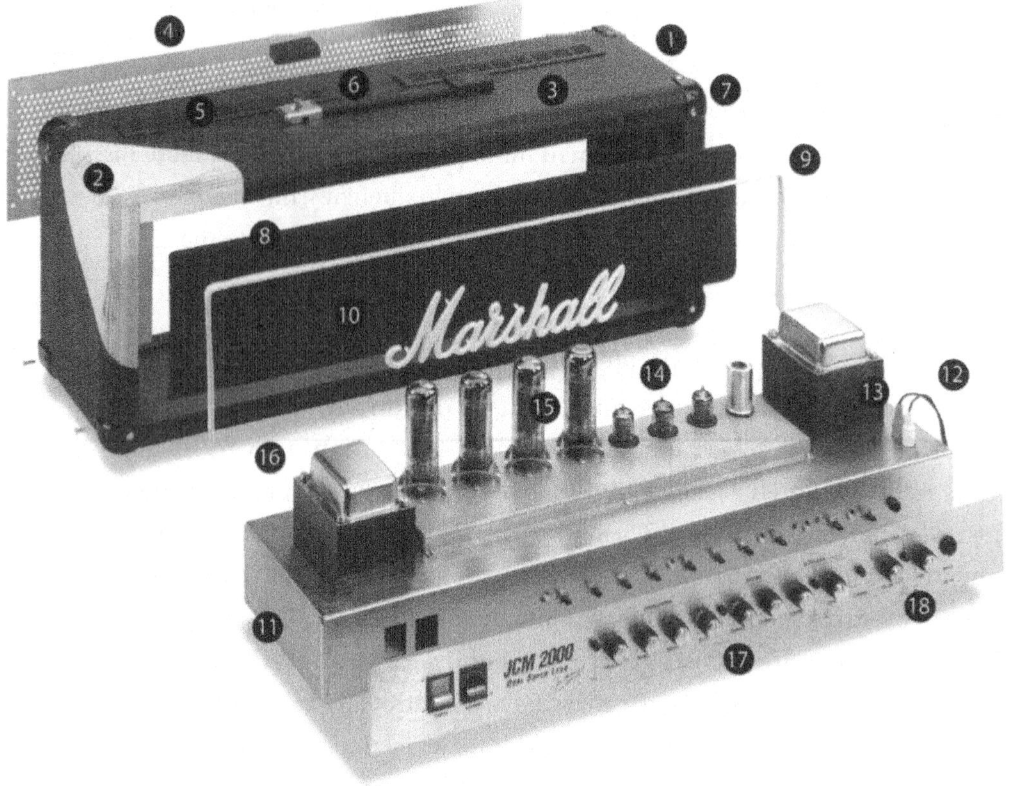

Elementary Amp Anatomy

Here we'll take a quick peek under the hood of a Marshall amplifier. Specifically, we're taking a short, guided tour of an "exploded" view of a 100-watt JCM2000 Dual Super Lead head—the DSL100. Though different amp models possess unique characteristics, plus specific components and specs, they are all similar in their basic electronic schemes. Jim has noted that the fundamentals of amp circuitry have really not changed much since the early 1900s, when the first tube amplifiers were used in early radios. While we're not going to get down to every last capacitor and resistor, we provide a good overview of the main parts of a typical tube guitar amp.

WARNING! For obvious safety reasons opening up an amplifier and poking around is not recommended, as the one thing all amps have in common is this—they contain extremely high voltages that can seriously injure or even kill you. Even when an amp isn't connected to the mains (that is, plugged in), it is still dangerous because it houses components that can store lethal charges for days on end. So, unless your name is Dudley Craven or Bruce Keir, we advise you to leave such prodding around to the experts. Warning over.

1. HEAD BOX FRAME Constructed of 15mm, high-grade, flawless (knot-free) birch ply, with fingerlocked (comb) joints, this frame is extremely robust. All edges have a 22mm radius. (Note: The top, left-hand front corner of the "exploded" frame is shown pre-radius.)

2. FINGERLOCK JOINT This type of joint adds greatly to the strength of the frame due to the interweaving of the wood and increased surface area being glued. In fact, it is often claimed that this type of corner joint is even stronger than the wood itself.

3. ELEPHANT GRAIN VINYL Supplied to Marshall by Brymor, this durable, cloth-backed covering has skinned countless Marshall heads, combos, and cabinets over the decades. Prior to the vinyl being applied by hand, the head cabinet is sprayed matte black. (See the Factory Tour at the end of this chapter for more details.)

4. BACK-PANEL GRILLE This sturdy, zinc-coated steel plate helps ensure the amp is properly ventilated while protecting the tubes and also protecting prying fingers from getting burned when the amp is on—those EL34s get mighty hot!

5. AIR VENT GRILLE Two top-mounted, heavy-duty plastic grilles aid in ensuring the amp is properly ventilated by allowing sufficient air flow. (Since hot air rises, these act as "escape ducts" for the tube-generated heat.)

6. STRAP HANDLE Steel strap handle sleeved in rubber with plastic covers over the metal end-caps.

7. CORNERS Constructed from heavy-duty ABS (acrylonitrile-butadiene-styrene) plastic and attached to the head box frame by three rivets, these help protect the corners from those inevitable bumps and bangs.

8. BAFFLE Made of 12mm MDF (medium-density fiberboard) and covered with the same grille cloth as used on Marshall's industry-standard 4x12 cabinets. The MDF is sprayed with flat black paint before the cloth is stretched over it. It's then fastened by being stapled to the rear (inside) of the radiused edge and along the edge of the other three sides of the baffle. The baffle is both cosmetic and protective.

9. PIPING Sturdy white plastic piping is attached to the upper and outer edges of the baffle, once again by staples. While being primarily cosmetic, the piping also helps ensure the baffle has a nice snug fit in the front of the head box.

10. LOGO One of the most familiar and famous fixtures of concert stages the world over, the 11" white script Marshall logo is fixed to the baffle via the clearly visible pins.

11. CHASSIS This houses the electronic "guts" of the amp. The chassis is manufactured at the Marshall factory from 16-gauge mild steel. Once the corner joints are butt-welded, it is passivated (an electroplating process that deposits a coating of zinc onto the steel) to provide lifelong resistance to corrosion.

12. REVERB CABLES RCA cables make an audio connection between the amp and the Accutronics spring reverb tank.

13. OUTPUT TRANSFORMER The output transformer acts as the "handshaking" link between the power amp and the speaker. It "transforms" the high-impedance signal of the tube output stage into the low-impedance signal speakers need to operate. Once again, made for Marshall by Dagnall. (Historic note: When Marshall developed the first 100-watt all-tuber at the request of Pete Townshend, there was no such thing as a 100-watt output transformer—so instead they paired two 50-watt transformers.)

14. PREAMP TUBES Four factory-tested premium 12AX7 tubes (called ECC83 valves in the UK) play a vital role in the DSL100 preamp, taking the weak and puny guitar signal and beefing it up, adding both gain and shape. The former is determined by both the Channel and Mode the user has selected on the DSL, plus the setting of the Gain control; the latter by the three preamp tone controls, Treble, Middle, and Bass. And why is the 12AX7 on the far right covered by a spring-loaded metal jacket? This jacket is actually called a screening can, and as its name suggests, its purpose is to screen the tube from unwanted, interfering electrical fields, such as those radiated by the nearby transformers. To achieve this screening, this sleeve is made from an electrically conductive material.

15. POWER AMP TUBES A quartet of high-quality matched EL34 tubes, working together in pairs, transform the relatively small preamp signal into a hulking brute capable of driving the speakers. Each pair is capable of producing 50 watts, hence two EL34s in a 50-watter and four in the DSL100.

16. MAINS TRANSFORMER/POWER TRANSFORMER This hefty device is used to convert the incoming mains (wall) voltage to the levels used by the DSL. As had been the case for many, many years, all the transformers (mains and output) used in 100-watt, all-tube Marshall amps are supplied by the English company Dagnall. (Until the mid '90s all Marshall all-tube 50-watters used transformers supplied by Drake. These are now also supplied by Dagnall. As a rule the label on a Dagnall transformer simply says DE Limited, for Dagnall Electronics.)

17. CONTROL PANEL Made of brushed-gold, anti-corrosive aluminum, the control panel is labeled and punched for each control, jack, and switch on the front of the amp. The panel has a self-adhesive back that secures to the front of the amp's chassis. Once the control panel is mounted, the jacks, pots, and switches are mounted on it.

18. FRONT-PANEL KNOBS Controls, knobs, pots—call them what you will; a number of styles were used in the early years, but they've gone generally unchanged since this gold-faced knob with a notched black body was first employed in 1965.

DSL100 Front Panel Tour

19. POWER SWITCH/STANDBY

Power Switch This dark red rocker switch is the amp's main on/off control. When the amp is on, a small neon bulb inside the switch glows so you can see at a glance whether the amp is powered up, even from a distance on a darkened stage. (Note: When the Power switch is on but the Standby switch is off, no sound will come from the amp.)

Standby Switch This black rocker switch controls HT (high-tension, or high) voltage to the tubes. When the Power switch is on and the Standby off, there is current flow to the tubes' heaters to allow them to reach the correct working temperatures before use, but there is no output to the speakers. To prolong the life of your tubes it's recommended that you leave the amp in Standby mode for approximately two minutes before switching the Standby to "on." Also, when powering down a tube amp, you should switch the Standby to "off" before turning off the Power switch.

Standby is particularly useful in live situations because it keeps the amp "ready to rock" before, after, and in between sets while keeping the tubes at operating temperature—without any sound being produced—while preserving the life of your precious valves. The switch is also useful for silent guitar changes onstage.

20. EQUALIZATION SECTION (left to right)

Deep Switch This universal switch works in the power section of the DSL. Engaging it adds a resonant bass boost to your sound, increasing low-end thud without making your tone sound woolly, thanks to the fact that its resonance is tuned to the resonant frequency of the cabinet it's driving—typically 80–120Hz for a Marshall 4x12.

Presence Control This universal control works in the power amp as opposed to working in the preamp, as the Bass, Middle, and Treble controls do. Specifically, presence is a function of a power amp containing a negative feedback circuit (which most all-tube Marshalls do—the DSL201 and

401 combos being recent exceptions given their lack of a Presence control). It adds high frequencies, giving the guitar's tone an in-your-face crispness and bite.

Tone Controls This trio of controls allows adjustment of the Treble, Middle, and Bass frequencies of both of the DSL100's channels. As these controls are passive as opposed to active, they attenuate (cut) frequencies already present in the signal—they don't add or boost frequencies.

In typical Marshall tradition, this 3-band tone network lies after the gain stages of the preamp (in the majority of Fenders, the tone network is before the preamp gain stages), allowing you to shape the tone of the distorted signal.

Tone Shift This switch reconfigures the DSL's tone network, adding another dimension to its passive tone shaping. When activated it scoops the mids, making it a particularly popular control with exponents of aggressive metal. For non-metal players, Tone Shift helps deepen the tone at low volumes.

21. REVERB CONTROLS One for each channel, these control the reverb level on Channel A (Classic Gain) and Channel B (Ultra Gain).

22. ULTRA GAIN/CHANNEL B SECTION

Volume Control Controls the overall level and also the balance of the Ultra Gain channel relative to the Classic Gain channel.

Lead 1/Lead 2 Mode Switch Selects the Ultra Gain channel's two modes: Lead 1 (switch out) or Lead 2 (switch in).

Gain Control This controls the preamp gain level (amount of preamp distortion) for the Ultra Gain channel.

23. CHANNEL SWITCH and LED INDICATORS Push switch that selects Channel A (out) or Channel B (in). When Channel B is selected, the LED to the left of the switch glows red; when Channel A is selected, the LED to the right glows green.

24. CLASSIC GAIN/CHANNEL A SECTION

Volume Control Controls the overall level and also the balance of the Classic Gain channel relative to the Ultra Gain channel.

Clean/Crunch Mode Switch Selects the Classic Gain channel's two modes: Clean (switch out) or Crunch (switch in).

Gain Control Controls the preamp gain level for the Classic Gain channel.

25. INPUT The ¼" jack input for your guitar cable.

The Marshall 1960A cabinet, the company's biggest-selling 4x12 and accepted worldwide as the "industry standard."

Hail Me a Cab

The Marshall sound had not come into its own until the first JTM45 was heard through a 4x12 cabinet Jim built in his garage workshop. Speaker cabinets are not complicated electronically, but the effects of their materials and construction, and of course the speakers used, are often underestimated. To better understand the construction and inner workings of a typical Marshall 1960 4x12 cabinet, let's take a closer look at the company's most popular cabinet, the 1960A.

1960A 4x12 Cab Anatomy

Weighing in at around 80 pounds (36.3 kg), like all Marshall 4x12 cabinets in the 1960 family, the angle-fronted, 300-watt 1960A is made of 15mm birch plywood—aside from its back panel, which is constructed using 12mm MDF (medium density fiber-board)—and built for durability and tone. To this end, as was the case with the head box, fingerlocked joints are used on all four corners of the cabinet's main frame—not only adding strength but enhancing resonance. With the exception of the initial cutting, which is carried out by state-of the-art machinery, the vast majority of the cabinet construction at Marshall is done by hand. (For more specifics, see the Factory Tour section that follows.)

1. ANGLED FRONT The world-famous Marshall slant, created because Jim felt a head sitting on a straight-fronted cabinet just didn't look "designed." The sides and the baffle of the 1960A cabinet feature an angled cut, a factor that not only has a cosmetic impact but a sonic one as well, since the angle tilts the top two 12" speakers slightly upward towards the cabinet top, where the amp head sits. In a full stack, the slanted cab is "stacked" on top of a straight cab. Although Marshall initiated the design, the company does not own exclusive rights on it; consequently, angled cabinets are a now familiar sight among many manufacturers' offerings.

2. SKID TRAYS A $9\frac{7}{8}$" x $2\frac{7}{8}$" piece of rubber with a plastic frame that's riveted to the top of the cabinet. As its name suggests, the skid tray's purpose is to hold the head securely in place on top of the cabinet, preventing the amp from literally getting vibrated off the cabinet by the mighty low end a stack or half-stack can produce.

3. FRET CLOTH (GRILLE CLOTH) This is tightly stretched across the front of the speaker baffle and attached to its four edges by tightly but neatly spaced staples. This is available in a variety of styles depending on the cabinet, including check (1960AX and BX), "EC" (1960TV), and the standard black shown.

4. LOGO That famous 11" white script plastic logo lurks for all to see. It is fixed to the baffle via six $\frac{1}{2}$" pins, which are part of the logo molding. (See the "exploded amp" photo, page 172). The logo on the 1960TV cabinet is 6" long with a gold face.

5. VINYL COVERING After the cabinet's birch frame has been constructed and hand-sanded, it's spray-painted matte black and the cloth-backed "elephant grain" vinyl is applied, also by hand.

6. PIPING Sturdy white plastic piping is stapled to the inner edges of the front opening of the cabinet and positioned so it is flush with the front face of the speaker baffle. Its function is purely cosmetic. Other piping is and has been used on cabinet variants; for example, gold in the case of the 1960TV.

7. NAME PLATE and NAME PLATE HOLDER A rectangular black plastic "frame" (plate holder) is fixed to the bottom left-hand corner of the cabinet via two $\frac{1}{2}$" wood screws. The $3\frac{1}{2}$ x $1\frac{1}{4}$ brushed-gold aluminum name plate is then fixed to the plate holder by its self-adhesive back. The plate on the 1960A and 1960B cabs states "1960 lead," the plate on the 1960AV and 1960BV states "vintage," and the one on the 1960AC and 1960BC says "classic." The 1960AX, 1960BX, and 1960TV don't sport a badge.

8. CORNERS Heavy-duty ABS plastic corners are riveted in place in order to provide protection from the inevitable rigors of the road.

9. CASTORS Standard on all full-sized Marshall 4x12s, these heavy-duty wheels can be unscrewed as desired. Removing the wheels and placing the cabinet directly on the floor or on top of another cabinet will yield different sounds. (In case you're wondering, a 1960A can safely be stacked on top of a straight-fronted 1960B cabinet without removing its wheels because the top of the 1960B houses four wheel wells to receive them.)

10. HANDLES Air-tight, recessed handles are riveted to the left and right sides of the cabinet for individual or two-man cartage.

11. BACK PANEL Made from 15mm chipboard, sprayed matte black and then covered with durable, cotton-backed "elephant grain" PVC vinyl. The back plate is secured to the cabinet frame with no fewer than 17 1¾"-inch wood screws—16 around the edge and one in the center that attaches to the cabinet post.

12. MONO/STEREO INPUT This is where the speaker cable from the amplifier is plugged into the cabinet. (Note: Speaker cable [unshielded] and instrument cable [shielded] are two very different beasts and should not be interchanged.) For maximum flexibility, the 1960A boasts a mono/stereo switching system which houses two ¼" input jacks and a centrally placed mono/stereo switch on a slightly recessed plate. The 1960A has had this switching facility since 1990; prior to then it had a single mono 16-ohm input.

Mono operation: When the input switch is set to mono, the left input (as you look from the back of the cabinet) provides a 4-ohm connection to all four speakers, while the right input provides a 16-ohm connection. When a head is being used, the 16-ohm input is the one used 99% of the time—especially in a full-stack situation.

Stereo operation: When the input switch is set to stereo, it splits the cabinet into two 8-ohm halves for use with a stereo head or rack system. The input marked "right" (actually on the left as you look from the back of the cabinet as, in this instance, "right" refers to the right stereo side of the cabinet as seen—and heard!—when facing the front of the cab) provides an 8-ohm connection to the right pair (top and bottom) of speakers. Likewise, the input marked "left" provides an 8-ohm connection to the left pair.

13. SPEAKER BAFFLE BOARD Made from 15mm birch ply, the front of the baffle is painted black so it can't be seen through the grille cloth under stage lights. In the case of the 1960A, or any angled cabinet, the top half of the baffle is angled as well. The four speakers are mounted to the back of the baffle by four speaker bolts, which screw into T-nuts pre-inserted into the baffle's front. The baffle is rear-loaded into the cabinet and secured by 16 2" wood screws.

14. CABINET POST This centrally placed horizontal post is secured to the baffle by two wood screws, and then the cabinet's back panel is firmly attached to it via a 1¾" wood screw. The purpose of this post is to prevent the back panel from vibrating in sympathy with certain low frequencies. In times past, this post wasn't present, but as rock became more and more aggressive and low-end-heavy, the post became essential. (Blame Kerry King & Co.)

15. SPEAKERS The 12" Celestion speakers are, of course, a mainstay since the first Marshall 4x12 cabinet. The speaker that's been used in the 1960A from 1986 to the present day is the 75-watt Celestion G12T-75. Prior to 1986, the 65-watt G12-65 (1979–83) and the 70-watt G12M-70 (1983–1986) were used. (Prior to being designated the 1960A in 1979, Marshall's angled 4x12 cab was simply known as the 1960. It started life as 60 watts with four 15-watt Celestions (1964/65), and then 80 watts with four 20-watters (1965–70) before becoming 100 watts thanks to a quartet of 25-watt Greenbacks (1970–79). Then, as we noted previously, it got bumped up to a relatively massive 260 watts and was renamed 1960A.)

The 1960 Family of 4x12 Cabinets

Marshall's 1960 family of 4x12s has no fewer than nine members. The reason for so many? Three different speaker-type options, angled and straight versions, vintage cosmetics on a couple, plus the "tall vintage" 1960TV. (Note: An angled 1960 cabinet has the suffix "A"; a straight one has the suffix "B," denoting "base.")

Marshall 1960 4x12 Cabinets

1960A 300-watt; mono (16 ohm or 4 ohm)/stereo (8 ohm + 8 ohm) angled 4x12 cabinet loaded with four Celestion G12T-75 75-watt speakers

1960B Straight-fronted version of 1960A

1960AV 280-watt, mono (16 ohm or 4 ohm)/stereo (8 ohms + 8 ohms) angled 4x12 cabinet loaded with four Marshall/Celestion G12 Vintage 70-watt speakers. (Note: This speaker is also known as the Vintage "30"—a misleading name that prompts many, including pro players and techs, to refer to the speaker as a 30-watter!)

1960BV Straight-fronted version of 1960AV

1960AC 100-watt, mono (16 ohm) angled 4x12 cabinet loaded with four Celestion G12M-25, 25-watt Greenback speakers

1960BC Straight-fronted version of 1960AC

All the above sport elephant-grain vinyl and black grille cloth.

1960AX Same as the AC except with smooth "levant" covering and checkered grille cloth

1960BX Straight-fronted version of 1960AX

1960TV Angled 100-watt, mono (16 ohm) cabinet loaded with Celestion Greenback speakers. Covered with "levant," it sports vintage-style "EC" grille cloth, and is 3" taller than a standard 4x12 (TV = "Tall, Vintage").

Sonically speaking . . .

- The difference between an angled and straight 4x12?

  Without getting overanalytical, an angled cabinet has more sonic "spread," or dispersion, and is typically brighter-sounding than its straight-fronted equivalent, which sounds more focused and has more low-end thump.
- The difference between G12T-75, G12, Vintage, and Greenback speakers?

  As with anything sonic, this is highly subjective. This said, in an "objective" nutshell:

G12T-75 A smooth, well-defined sound across the guitar's full sonic spectrum, with a tight bottom and clear top

G12 Vintage Warmer and darker-sounding than the G12T-75, with a rounder top and thicker mids

Greenback Very responsive, with more peaks in the mids and highs

FACTORY TOUR

It was June 1966 when Marshall Amplification first moved production out of West London and into the English countryside northwest of the city. Bletchley is one of three neighboring townships living off its factories and farms; Bletchley, Wolverton, and Stony Stratford joined under one name in January 23rd, 1967, to make Milton Keynes a manufacturing mecca, and Britain's newest city. It's about an hour's ride out of London, a pretty trip past fields of yellow and green and through a handful of rural towns where churches are still the tallest buildings.

The familiar white logo juts out like a bow from the Marshall headquarters mothership. Except for the overseas factories where MGs, acoustic amps, and pedals are manufactured, this is where it *all* happens. Jim Marshall lives a five-minute car ride away over the bucolic hills of Bletchley.

The high-ceiling reception area is distinguished and quiet, belying the cacophonous whir of production taking place on the other side of the wall. Glass cabinets lining two walls are full of international awards and honorary plaques, including Jim's prized Queen's Awards and pictures of him with everyone from Slash to Bob Hope. Straight on from the front doors, a flight of immaculate steps (they're roped off to remain in pristine condition for photo shoots) leads up to the unofficial "Marshall Museum," a sizable display of rare and landmark amps. It seems strange at first that a drum kit worthy of Spinal Tap takes up half the display, but it's a Premier kit—the brand Jim endorsed—given to Jim by friend and pupil Nicko McBrain of Iron Maiden. Jim's office is a few paces away, within shouting distance of the R&D department headed by Bruce Keir. Remaining administrative offices, IT, and other offices fill the front of the building facing Denbigh Road.

The front of the building may be where the company maintains its trade, but we're headed out back—to the *business* end of the Marshall factory.

Marshall owners may rightfully attach some mystique to their beloved amps, but if there is any magic, it's stripped away in the industrious din of the factory floor. The Marshall factory in Bletchley is massive and the logic of its layout at first difficult to discern. Once appreciated, though, the factory is evident as a model of efficiency with diligent workers, timely production, and minimal material waste.

Production is primarily divided into five departments: Engineering, Electronics, the Wood Mill, Covering, and Finishing (final assembly). The work of each department progresses independently while paced for a final merge in the Finishing area. With due respect to the dozens of factory personnel who haul wood, man computers, monitor shipping, test components, and sweep floors, the following tour represents the main stages of production.

CHASSIS SHAPING

>> Rolls of pre-coated steel feed the Dimeco machine at one end and come out the other as AVT chassis. The Dimeco is a £1 million, 20-plus-meter-long (65 feet) machine that punches, cuts, and shapes the steel per its computerized brain. Software is reprogrammed to output different chassis as required by production demands or new designs from R&D.

Steel is fed through this cassette on the Dimeco and punched.

>> The cost of developing higher-end amplifiers is evident from the earliest stages of production. The Amada punches chassis for tube lines (such as the JCM2000) from sheet steel that is loaded and unloaded by hand. The chassis are then welded and plated.

AVT chassis rolling off the Dimeco.

ELECTRONICS

>> Blank PCBs (printed circuit boards) made in southern Ireland arrive at Marshall by the gross. The boards are first loaded on the axial insertion machine.

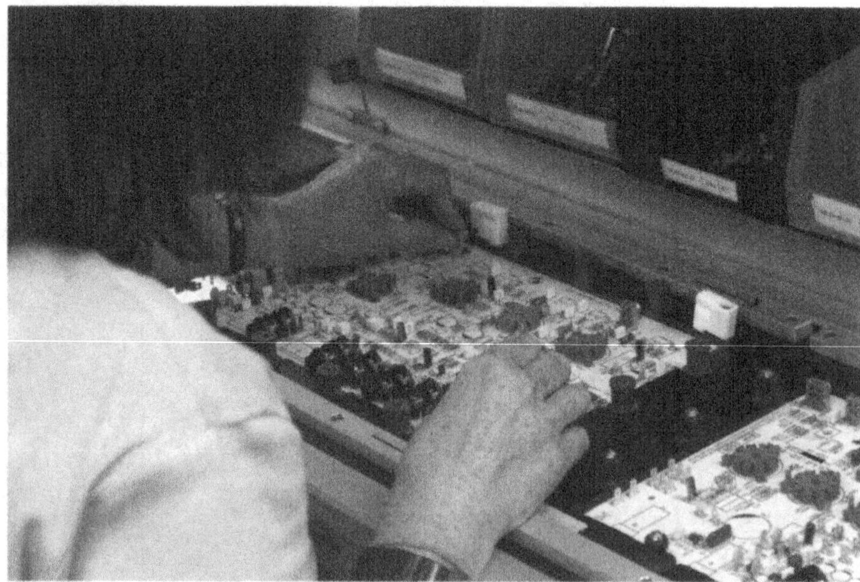

>> Some capacitors, resistors, and other components are too large to be fitted to the PCB by machine, and are loaded by hand.

>> In an impressive show, components are fused all at once to the PCB in a solder bath. The board skims over a wave of molten flow solder. (The board is machine-fed into the bath—not a job to do by hand.)

The bed of nails waiting for circuit board and . . .

>> This is the "bed of nails," which looks like a miniature iron maiden. The bed of nails tests the soldered points on a board. Bad solder points are an enormous hassle to locate and repair once an amp is fully constructed, so the bath and bed are crucial quality-assurance processes.

...descending on a circuit board for testing.

>> Meanwhile, larger components such as transformers, valve sockets, and tone-pot controls have been fitted to the chassis. The PCB is placed into the chassis and the components hand-wired to it.

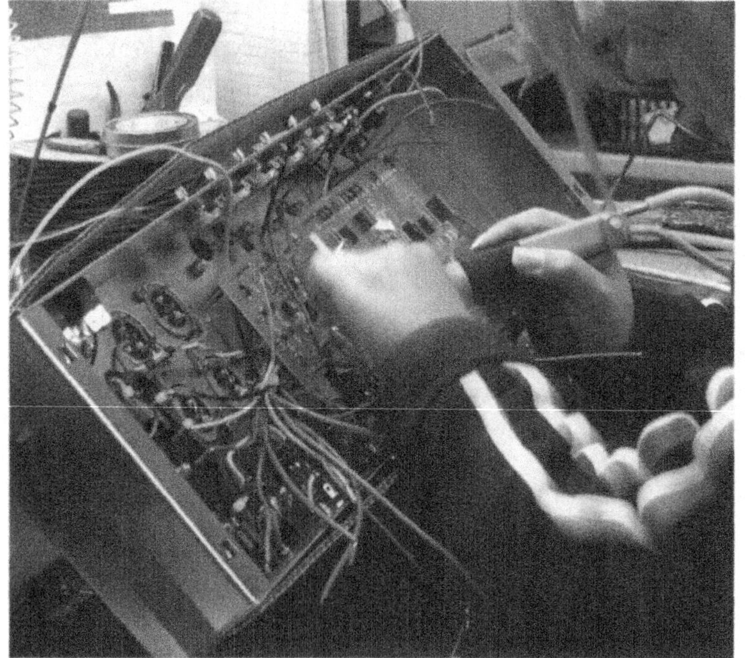

>> The chassis is ready to be installed into a head or combo.

Hand-wiring components to a circuit board.

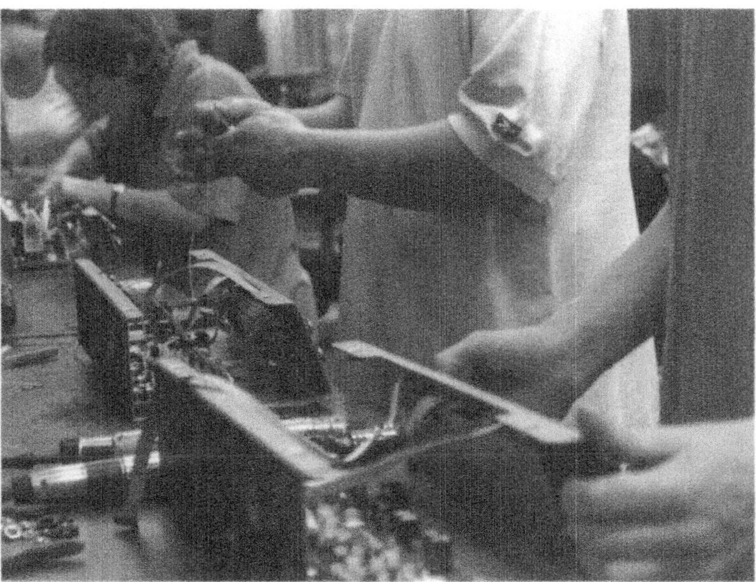

PCBs being installed in an AVT chassis.

The completed chassis for a tube head.

CABINET BUILDING

>> Birch plywood arrives at the factory's wood mill stacked in sheets, as do the sheets of chipboard used for AVTs. Cabinet components are cut on large routers.

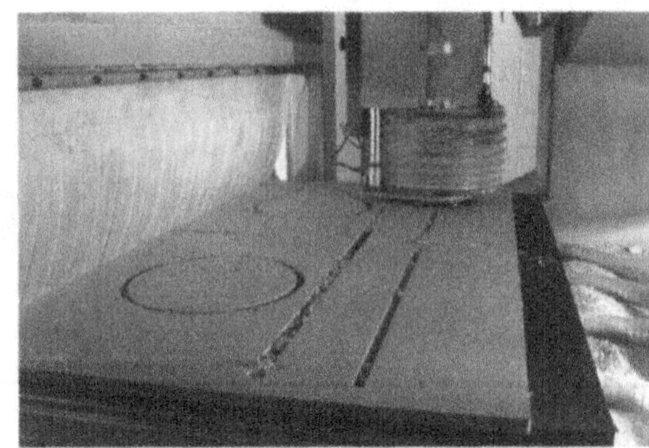

Two 1x12 shapes for an AVT are cut from a sheet of chipboard.

>> "Finger," or comb, joints are cut into the edges of birch sheets.

>> Finger joints ensure a tight fit between sides, make the cabinet less susceptible to damage, and allow the entire cabinet to resonate sympathetically to the sound from the speakers. After the components are glued, they go into the "carcass" press where the glue is cured using an RF generator. Then the cabinets go onto the battening benches where the fixing points for the baffle and back are attached. Then the edges and corners are rounded in a spindle moulder.

>> The cabinet frame is sanded by hand.

A stack of stacks-to-be. Note the angled fronts (these cabinets are on their side). Also see the bare-wood frames for heads on the right.

>> Each cabinet is hooked onto a conveyor to be heated (this helps the paint dry quickly and the adhesive to tack off so that the cabinets can be handled as soon as they reach the end of the conveyor) and sprayed.

>> Collectors go nuts for different-colored vinyl coverings; meanwhile, the colored rolls of material usually sit on the shelf unused. Marshall first used colored vinyl in 1970.

>> Classic black "leather" is applied at a covering bench. This is a tricky process requiring skilled hands to cut, tuck, and secure the vinyl.

>> Fret cloth is stapled to the edges of the baffle by an air-pressured gun. Depending on the line passing through production, a different style of fret cloth would hang on the spindle.

>> An enormous corner of the warehouse stocks Celestion speakers two floors high. On the floor, speakers are attached to the back of an installed baffle by hand.

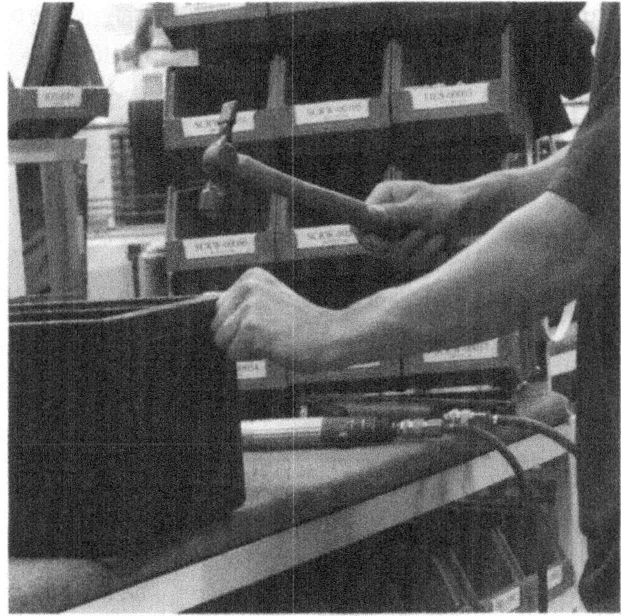

Corners are hand-riveted to a cabinet.

>> Affixing hardware (handles, corners, castors) is the final stage of cabinet construction.

>> Completed chassis are installed into head frames and combos. Then it's time for the final test. Every amp is checked the old-fashioned way: by plugging in a guitar.

Now *that's* mint condition. A new Mode Four head is tested at the end of the line.

>> The amps are packed using sturdy cardboard cartons and specially designed protective cushions. After getting a handful of complaints about damaged boxes, Marshall invested in a shrinkwrapper.

Packed amps are covered with plastic and briefly heated; this shrinks the plastic around the carton, enhancing the durability and performance of the packaging and the protection of the unit inside.

All factory photos courtesy of Marshall's Paul Hayhoe.

>>> The EMC Chamber <<<

Contrary to appearances, this is not a torture chamber for misbehaved employees. The truncated spikes that line the room's floors, walls, and ceiling are known in the business as anechoic lining. Made of sound-deadening acoustic foam—the room is so dead that you can lose your balance when you enter—they help provide a controllable test environment within the EMC (Electromagnetic Compatibility) chamber. The setting enables Marshall Amplifiers to be tested for potential electrical interference from other electronic devices.

The antenna pictured allows radio frequency (RF) waves to bombard a Marshall amp. The test is designed to simulate radio waves from devices such as cell phones, and is one of many required for today's European CE regulations.

Chapter 7

Jim Marshall's Top ~~10~~ 11 Amplifiers

It's been said before, but it's worth repeating: Tone is an elusive and subjective beast. What may be garbage to one player's ears is pure sonic gold to another's. Likewise, defining the "Marshall sound" is equally subjective. Not surprisingly, Jim Marshall's reference tone still emanates from the head that spawned his legend, the "first rock 'n' roll amp"—the JTM45. "To my ears, the complex and musical overdriven sound of the JTM45 is the essence of the 'Marshall sound' because that's where it all started in 1962. In the early days, our amps were built purely for rock 'n' roll, but these days they're capable of being used for literally any type of music—from the most modern heavy rock to even jazz and country. So, I'm sure if you were to ask a room full of guitarists to tell you what amp produces the 'Marshall sound,' they'd all give you a completely different answer."

"Jim makes a great point," agrees Marshall's US Product Manager, Nick Bowcott. "As the saying goes, 'Beauty is in the eye of the beholder.' Likewise, the Marshall sound is in the head and ears of the listener—or, arguably more important, in the hands of the player.

"One of the most important qualities a great Marshall—like a 2203 or DSL100 or MF350—possesses is *transparency*: Even though a Marshall amp has its own instantly recognizable sonic fingerprint, it still allows the player's all-important, unique voice to shine through. If you were to give five different players the same Les Paul plugged into the same 2203 and ask them all the play the exact same lick without changing anything on the amp or guitar, all five would sound completely different. Namely, like *themselves*."

In essence, Marshall amps have never strayed too far from the qualities that took the wind out of Pete Townshend and friends in 1962, but in 41 years of production the company has explored dozens upon dozens of variations on that theme. A few models, by Jim Marshall's own admission, have been clunkers. Others have been revisited time and time again as Marshall's R&D teams have sought to preserve tonal character while altering gain stages, output power, speaker configurations, EQ-shaping options, and cosmetics, adding channels, inserting effects loops, and more.

Herein, 11 milestone amplifiers of which Jim is particularly proud over Marshall's storied history.

JTM45

The tone and fundamental design of every Marshall amplifier can be traced back to "#1," the JTM45 head designed by Dudley Craven and constructed by Ken Bran in late 1962. Named after Jim and Terry Marshall (JTM), the amp was spec'd at 45 watts. In truth, though, it would actually only produce somewhere around 30 watts of "clean" (undistorted) power. (All Marshall amps that followed were rated by their "clean" output.) The JTM45 would kick out the jams at 45 watts when fully cranked and distorted to the max. It was originally fitted with American 5881 power valves, but later models were fitted with KT66 valves when the supply of 5881s became problematic.

1965 JTM45 head with gold "block" logo.

>>> The Return of #1 <<<

When the team of Marshall, Bran, and Craven tested their sixth prototype, they knew they'd developed an extraordinary amplifier. The amp that started it all—known affectionately as "#1"—is the most prized of Jim's career. But, as he tells here, it nearly slipped out of his hands on more than one occasion.

"The whole thing was, #1 was sold to a lad who'd come into the shop. He wanted a JTM45, but I warned that he'd have to wait a while because we'd already gotten 23 on order, and we could produce only one or two a week. So he asked if he could buy the prototype. I said, 'Well, okay; it should do you all right for a few years.' I didn't charge him that much because I thought, 'It's only a prototype.' His father came in and paid for it because the lad wanted to use it that weekend.

"Seven or eight weeks later, when we'd caught up with production of the 23, he came in again and said he'd rather have one of the new ones. So I gave him his money back, and the prototype came back into my possession. I put it in the cupboard under the stairs in the shop, and that's where I left it until we moved to Bletchley in 1966.

"When we were moving, I found it and thought, 'Shall I throw this on the skip with some of the other rubbish? But since I'd had it all that time, I decided to take it with me. In Bletchley, once again I put it under the stairs and left it there for years!

"I found it again in the late '70s. I looked at it and decided, 'I might just as well keep the damned thing, I've had it so long!' And I put it in my office. [English pop star] David Essex offered to buy it after I'd refused to sell him my car—I told him he could have the car but not the 'JMP 800' number plate, and that's what he really wanted, so he tried to buy #1 instead. I told him, 'Sorry, I've kept it all this time, I cannot do it!'

"Then, only a few years ago, Gary Moore offered me a blank check for it. I said, 'Sorry, Gary, I cannot part with it now. It's in the museum and I'd like to keep it there.'

"That's the story of how #1 came back. If that lad hadn't have wanted a new one, I might never have seen it again. He might have thrown it away!"

A primary difference—arguably, *the* primary difference—between the JTM45 and the Fender Bassman 5F6A on which it was based is the 12AX7 (a.k.a. ECC83) valves used in the first gain stage of the JTM's preamp section. "I always knew that the difference was going to be in the valves, or 'tubes,' as they're known in America," says Jim. "It was a matter of the harmonics produced when a valve is overdriven."

The 12AX7s went a long way toward delivering the rich, round overdrive the players in Jim's shop sought. Those tubes provided more gain and different loading characteristics than the first valve in the Bassman, a 12AY7 (a.k.a. ECC82), which offered far less gain (approximately half that of a 12AX7), better serving the country-western market Fender was chasing. While the JTM45 is unquestionably indebted to the Bassman 5F6A, the differences in tubes, transformers, feedback circuits, output impedance, loading and damping, power-amp input sensitivity, capacitors, makes and tolerances of components, chassis, speakers, and the cabinets used definitely set the Marshall apart.

Though it was the crunchiest amp anyone had played at the time, the JTM45 is not, by today's standards, an especially "gainy" amp—in fact, if anything, it would be considered a "low gain" amp. To achieve maximum overdrive from the JTM45, players have to max out the volume, thus overdriving the power-amp section. Marshall has steadily increased the amount of available gain on its amps over the past 41 years, and it's a bit ironic that the lasting charm of the JTM45 is not its ability to distort but to produce a tone that is warm, earthy, and bright—with the most shrill frequencies naturally rolling off. And from the start there was that phantom "feel" factor, in which the amp tone is so pervasive that the player senses a tangible reaction between his hands and the guitar strings.

The JTM45 came alive when combined with a 4x12 cab; the separate head/cab configuration helped define Marshall stylistically and further differentiated it from popular combos of the day like the Bassman and the Vox AC30. The cabs were fitted with 12" Celestions (as they are to this day) that employed alnico (aluminum/nickel/cobalt) magnets, and they also differed from the competition's combos by their fully closed backs, which controlled the direction of projected sound off the speaker's cone.

The amp that started it all is currently available as a reissue: the 2245 (JTM45), which, like the original, boasts a pair of 5881 power tubes, a GZ34 tube rectifier, and three 12AX7s in its preamp. To the delight of "angloamplophiles," in 1999 the JTM45 O/S—a Limited Edition, hand-wired reproduction of the famous and very rare off-set chassis JTM45—was made available. The reissue was released in a limited edition of 300 heads, each with 4x12 O/S cabinets fitted with reproductions of the original silver Celestion alnico speakers. (The "offset" designation came about because the chassis was positioned off-center right rather than being centered, supposedly to create a more comfortable balance when carried.)

> **Years originally produced:** 1962–1964

> **Distinguishing features:** The amp that started it all

> **Tube complement:** 3 x 12AX7, 1 x GZ34 rectifier, 2 x 5881 or KT66

> **Selected players:**[1] Big Jim Sullivan, Angus Young (AC/DC), Brian Poole & the Tremoloes, Gary Moore (reissue), John Frusciante (Red Hot Chili Peppers)

Model 1987, 50-Watt Lead

Marshall's 50-watt model number 1987 head (a.k.a. JTM50) was introduced in 1966, four years after the JTM45 debuted. Although it's a direct descendant of "#1," in that time the company had the benefit of advances in component technology, and were better schooled in how to work those components to a player's advantage.

The first 1987 was like a more aggressive JTM45, and it wasn't just about a 5-watt boost—all of that amp's most identifiable characteristics were upped a notch. The 1987 was brighter on top, bigger and tighter on the bottom, and the field of its over-driven midrange seemed to be more focused, tightening impact and increasing overall fullness. This was chiefly due to the change in power-amp valves: the old KT66s were tossed for EL34s due to the former's diminishing supply and increasing cost. Still widely favored today and considered by many to be "the Marshall power tube," the EL34s were more powerful and provided more discretely defined tonal characteristics, and were more affordable. What's not to like? (Two other design revisions shouldn't be overlooked: First, the GZ34 rectifier tube was replaced by a solid-state rectifier, and, second, transformer specs changed.)

[1]Lists include past and present players.

Marshall

50 WATT LEAD

The Marshall 50 watt amplifiers continue the hard driving Marshall phenomena. The 50 watt counterpart to the famous 100 watt Marshall produces the identical harmonic coloring.

Model 1987 is the "Standard" 50 watt model with two channels and two inputs per channel. The Master Volume counterpart to the standard is model number 2204 which is supplied with one channel and high and low sensitivity inputs. Preamp and master volume controls permit full operation at lower volumes.

The most popular speaker cabinet used with the 50 watt leads is the 1960A with four G12M Celestion speakers. Another popular speaker combination is the 1990 cabinet with eight 10" Celestions. The 10" speakers will render a brighter, crisper sound.

Amplifiers
Size: 29"W x 8¼"D x 10¾"H
Weight: 39 lbs.

Speakers
1960A Size: 29¾"W x 14"D x 29¼"H
Weight: 100 lbs.
1990 Size: 29¾"W x 14"D x 42"H
Weight: 125 lbs.

Amps supplied in standard black or fawn. Optional red, orange or purple available on special order.

Unicord, Inc.
a Gulf + Western Manufacturing Company
75 Frost Street, Westbury, New York 11590

For its first year the 1987's Plexiglas front panel was labeled "JTM 50" and "MKII," but in mid '67 those were dropped and either a simple "JTM" appeared on the left-hand side of the front panel where "MKII" used to be, or nothing at all. Then, in 1968, the "JTM" was also removed and replaced with "JMP" (Jim Marshall Products). As of early 1970 the amps were officially out of the Plexi age (the Plexiglas front and rear panels were replaced with gold anodized aluminum ones in mid '69) and began trending toward heavier gain and brighter mids and highs. In fact, the original 1987 had a pleasantly plump blues tone compared to the edgier, more saturated sounds of amps that followed. Those include a number of incarnations, including master-volume editions, a JCM800 version, and a handful of reissue attempts, the best of the bunch being the currently offered 1987XL, which is based on the 1966–1969 classic and also boasts a true bypass series effects loop.

A big shot in the arm for the amp comes directly from Jim: "For years the 1987 50-watt was my favorite sound. I especially liked it with an 8x10 cabinet—in fact, it *had* to be an 8x10 cabinet, to my ears. That's probably because if I were a guitarist, my style would be more toward a jazz feel—I'm an old musician, not a young musician! With 12" speakers the bottom end can get so heavy. In my book, the '87 with an 8x10 had a clearer sound. For a rock 'n' roll sound, obviously the JTM45 was my favorite, and the 2203 as well. But you could still get those sounds out of the 1987, and with the 8x10 cabinet you could also get a sweeter sound."

> **Years produced:** 1966–1981

> **Distinguishing features:** First use of EL34s

> **Tube complement:** 3 x 12AX7, 2 x EL34

> **Selected players:** Jeff Beck, Peter Frampton, Steve Marriott, Yngwie Malmsteen, Duane Allman, Mike McCready (Pearl Jam), Laurie Wisefield (Wishbone Ash, Tina Turner)

1959 100-Watt Super Lead Plexi

For many, the 1959 is the ultimate Marshall—add the nickname Plexi and amp lovers get weak in the knees. Jim credits Pete Townshend for inspiring the original 1959 100-watt amp, which allowed the guitarist to be heard over his bandmates' bass and drums—and to cover up whatever the audience might be saying while Pete was playing. The 1959's renown was secured a few years later when it was seen

LEAD, BASS & ORGAN AMPLIFIERS

MODEL 1959 100-WATT LEAD AMPLIFIER. This also serves to illustrate the general cabinet design of all the amplifiers listed on this page

CONTROL PANEL OF 200-WATT LEAD & BASS MODELS

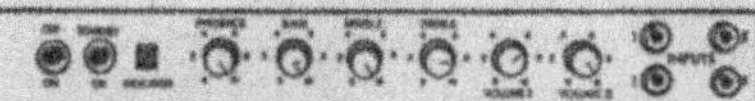

CONTROL PANEL OF 100-WATT LEAD & BASS MODELS

Models 1959, 1986, 1987, 1989, 1992, available with built-in Tremolo unit and remote control footswitch at small extra cost.

CONTROL PANEL OF 50-WATT LEAD, BASS & ORGAN MODELS

These Amplifiers have high impedance inputs and interchangeable output impedance. Voltage adjustment for use on 110/250 volts, 50/60 cycles A.C. At despatch they are set for 250 volts. All complete with mains lead, 5' (152·40 cms.) speaker lead and waterproof cover.

200 WATTS OUTPUT

LEAD MODEL 1967. Four inputs; separate volume controls for high treble inputs (channel 1) and normal inputs (channel 2). Presence, Bass, Middle and Treble tone controls common to both channels. ON/OFF switch and Standby switch. Cabinet dimensions: 10¾" (27·31 cms.), depth 11" (27·94 cms.), width 28" (73·66 cms.).

BASS MODEL 1978. Specification as above but with additional Bass lift.

100 WATTS OUTPUT

LEAD MODEL 1959. Four inputs; separate volume controls for high treble inputs (channel 1) and normal inputs (channel 2). Presence, Bass, Middle and Treble tone controls common to both channels. ON/OFF switch and Standby switch. Cabinet dimensions: height 10¾" (27·31 cms.), depth 8¼" (20·96 cms.), width 28¾" (73·01 cms.).

BASS MODEL 1992. Specification as above but with additional Bass lift.

50 WATTS OUTPUT

LEAD MODEL 1987. Four inputs; separate volume controls for high treble inputs (channel 1) and normal inputs (channel 2). Presence, Bass, Middle and Treble tone controls common to both channels. ON/OFF switch and Standby switch. Cabinet dimensions: height 10¾" (27·31 cms.), depth 8¼" (20·96 cms.), width 28¾" (73·01 cms.).

BASS MODEL 1986. Specification as above but with additional Bass lift.

ORGAN MODEL 1989. Specification as above but with overall Organ range lift.

The *PRESENCE* control provided on Marshall amplifiers is designed to give additional edge to the Treble tones.

2

onstage with the British Invasion's most famous guitarists . . . and lurking behind one James Marshall Hendrix, who, in 1967, remarked: "I really like my old Marshall tube amps, because when they're working properly there's nothing that can beat them, nothing in the whole world. It looks like two refrigerators hooked together. . . ." Another generation of players would stumble over themselves trying to achieve the legendary "brown sound" Edward Van Halen evoked from his 1959 a decade later.

The 1959 was first revisited in the '80s within the JCM800 line, and again in the early '90s, but never more accurately than when Marshall's R&D team went back to the drawing board in 2001. The following summer, the 1959 Super Lead Plexi was reintroduced to the world in the latest Marshall Vintage Series as the 1959SLP (SLP standing for—you guessed it—Super Lead Plexi). Facing the task of reproduction design was R&D head Bruce Keir.

"One of the problems we had to get around was that in the originals there were some subtle variations in the components that sometimes produced not-so-subtle variations in the sound. Also, there were differences in the quality of the components—these days you couldn't get components like that, even if you wanted to. That's another reason you can take two amps from the same era and get subtly different sounds."

Ultimately, Keir and design engineer Ian Robinson relied on their ears—plus the ears of experienced players—to identify the best-sounding vintage heads they could find from the celebrated 1967–69 Plexi era. The team then used those heads as design templates, mirroring their every quirk. The 1959SLP reissue's only overt departure from the originals is its inclusion of an effects loop. The design team indulged modern players with the feature, but also provided a true bypass for traditionalists: at the push of a button, the loop is completely disconnected from the amp's circuitry.

> **Years produced:** 1966–1981

> **Distinguishing features:** To many, the tonal holy grail

> **Tube complement:** 3 x 12AX7, 4 x EL34

> **Selected players:** Jimmy Page, Eric Clapton, Jimi Hendrix, Eddie Van Halen, Eric Johnson, Angus Young, Billy Joe (Green Day), Paul Kossoff (Free), Kirk Hammett

18-Watt Combos

First appearing in the summer of 1965, these little honeys offered Marshall's signature punch in a low-wattage combo. Putting a dent in the market previously dominated by models like Vox's AC15, the 18-watt combo was prized by studio owners and small-club musicians who valued a creamy tone but didn't need to hit the audience with G-force volume—after all, not everyone had to compete with a drummer like Keith Moon.

Not only was the wattage low, but the EL84 power-amp tubes in the 18-watt amps had relatively low voltage applied to their plates. With 300 volts, the EL84s heated up to deliver the tightly compacted Marshall tone as it was meant to be delivered: through the output section. Three 12AX7s in the preamp section and Celestion's early ceramic-magnet speakers contributed to the amp's sweetly compressed tone and sustain.

1958 18 WATT LEAD UNIT

CONTROL PANEL OF 18 WATT UNITS 1958, 1973 & 1974

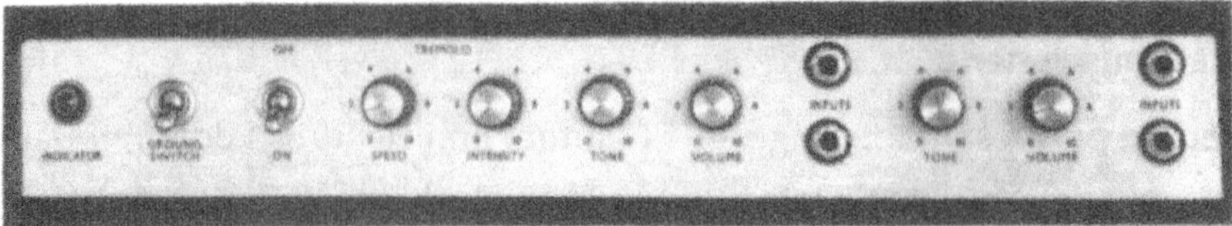

The 18-watt combos were available in 1x12 (model 1974), 2x12 (1973), and 2x10 (1958) configurations, few of which were shipped to the US. Today the 18-watt Marshall is a rare and coveted find, especially among pro- and home-studio owners who want to mic up an amp that's absolutely *floored* without blowing out their mic capsules or their eardrums.

Two years after the amp's initial release, the much-loved 20-watt model 1917 was introduced in 1967 (with other 20-watt models following in 1968). But the EL84 output tubes had 385 volts on the plates rather than 300 volts—boosting volume and headroom, but at the expense of that warm, compressed sound that distinguished the 18-watter.

The price of reissuing amps like these has to date been prohibitive for Marshall. If enough of us stand up and scream, no doubt they'll put them back on the production line in due time.

> **Years produced:** Mid 1965–1967

> **Distinguishing features:** low power on plates; low wattage; optional reverb—the first use of reverb in a Marshall

> **Tube complement:** 3 x 12AX7, EZ81 rectifier, 2 x EL84 (models with reverb also included an ECL86)

> **Selected players:** Gary Moore (check the cover of the album *Still Got the Blues*)

2203 Master Volume 100-Watt Head

Built in 1975 by R&D brain trust Steve Grindrod, the master-volume 100-watt 2203 head set a new design standard virtually every amp manufacturer would follow. It accomplished what previously had been possible only with 18- and 20-watt amps: desirable tube-generated overdrive at lower volumes.

Says Jim, "That amp came about because the guitarists at the time wanted the Marshall sound, but in some venues they had to turn the amplifier down. They couldn't run at full power."

The 100-watt 1959 that preceded the 2203 is venerable, but it required an overdriven power-amp section to unlock its potential—and at 100 watts, that means a *lot* of volume. Enter the master-volume (MV) idea. Thanks to the 2203's design, a Pre-Amp Volume control allowed the user to overdrive the preamp's tubes into distortion. This simple but effective scheme meant that the amp could be made to

The Master Volume Models

The Master Volume derivatives of the Marshall valve amplifiers enable the musician to obtain the Marshall sound at any volume level. This is achieved by providing two volume controls, one for the pre-amplifier and another-the Master Volume control-for the output volume. Presence control is also a feature, and the other controls provided are for Bass, Middle and Treble together with On/Off and Standby switches. There are high and low sensitivity inputs and the output impedance is switchable for 4, 8, or 16 Ohms to match the Marshall range of cabinets.

The Master Volume amplifiers are available in **100W (2203)** and **50W (2204)** versions.

sound distorted at any output-stage volume, controlled by—you guessed it—the Master Volume control. It goes without saying that pushing the output tubes hard in addition to cranking the Pre-Amp Volume optimized the amp's girth potential and delivered a chest-caving "woody" punch that was the 2203's celebrated sonic signature. But at lower volumes the MV design was still a winner. In short, MV guitarists had the best of all worlds: The amp did not have to be played at 147dB to achieve a satisfying overdrive—it revealed tube-driven harmonics at any volume. Plus there was a high threshold for producing a cleaner sound, and all of the power of a standard 100-watt amp was lying in wait, so at full throttle the amp could still blast like a 1959.

While the master-volume design was a quantum leap forward, the other half of the 2203's appeal was that it was stupidly simple: one channel, tone pots, and that invaluable knob marked Pre-Amp Volume. If you could find the power switch, you could operate it. The 2203 had a singular influence on subsequent Marshall lines, providing the blueprint for models including the enormously successful JCM800 line, which would prove to have a substantial legacy of its own.

> **Years produced:** 1975–1981

> **Distinguishing features:** The first master-volume Marshall amp

> **Tube complement:** 3 x 12AX7, 4 x EL34

> **Selected players:** Kirk Hammett (Metallica; studio), Judas Priest, and about any other late-'70s UK hard-rock act

The JCM800 line

It may seem a bit strange, even overly generous, to include an entire line of amplifiers in a list of superlatives, but the JCM800s are home base to an entire generation of Marshall players.

Jim had signed an international distribution deal with the Rose-Morris Agency back in 1966, when he knew the market for his amplifiers could well explode far beyond the UK. But with Rose-Morris's 55% markup on exports, Marshall's profits—and his ability to offer quality amplifiers at a reasonable price—were hogtied. When the contract expired in early 1981, Jim eagerly produced and released the JCM800 line. Famously, Jim named them after a glance at the license plate on his Jaguar, which contained his initials—JCM (James Charles Marshall)—and the seemingly inconsequential number, 800. But the latter proved to be a serendipitous match for the dawning '80s decade, which hard rock and the resulting series of amps would dominate. "I wanted a new name for the amps, but every idea we came up with was dreadful," recalls Jim with a wry grin. "And then one day I looked at the number plate on my car and immediately thought, 'That's it—that's what we'll use.' And it was staring me right in the face all along!"

Unleashed in March '81, the JCM800 line was initially merely a cosmetic redressing of the Master Volume and Super Lead models. And a bold new look it was, too: The small-script Marshall logo was replaced with a much bigger one, white piping framed the baffle (now covered with grille cloth instead of vinyl), and the control panel stretched the full width of the head. The new-look, new-priced amps were an immediate hit. Suddenly, novice players could afford to play the same (or something like the same) amps they'd seen their heroes use—albeit with a slightly different look. Classic Marshall models such as the 1987, 1959 Super Lead, and the master-volume 2203 and 2204 were repackaged for players who otherwise would never have been able to pony up enough cash for a Marshall stack. Combos were included as well, filling out the line even more.

Though the JCM800 line was initially somewhat akin to an affordable vintage-reissue series, some aficionados balked. Marshall had always developed loud, bright amplifiers, but they detected something a little too brash and even vaguely obnoxious in the tone of various JCM800 offerings. Adding to the "obnoxious" perception in the US was the fact that then-US distributor Unicord took it upon themselves to

Marshall

LEAD SET-UPS

1959/1982 A & B

2205/1960A

3210/1965 A & B

1959-1982A&B. The classic 100 watts Marshall stack comprising an amplifier, with one angled and one straight cabinet. Featured above is the 1959 Super Lead amplifier with 1982A and B cabinets. This is the set-up used by many leading bands to achieve a warm, driving rock sound.

Alternatively, a 2203 Master Volume amplifier would be used to create a more attacking heavy metal sound, or the new 2210 split channel amplifier can allow more versatility by being able to channel switch from a powerful clean to a raunchy overdriven sound.

The models mentioned above could be used with 1982A and B, or 1960A and B cabinets.

The Marshall stack is ideally suited to concert size venues — and many top bands can use up to seven or eight stacks at once to create that famous massive Marshall sound.

2205-1960A. The 50w. Marshall stack, comprising an amplifier with one 4 × 12 cabinet.

Featured above is the new 2205 Split Channel amplifier with one 1960A cabinet. This would provide a good clean sound with the added bonus of a controlled distortion sound at any level and would be ideal for club type venues.

The 2204 Master volume or the 1987 Super Lead amplifier, with a single cabinet, could be used for the standard rock type sound.

A single angled cabinet 1982A or 1960A would create an excellent stage sound with good projection.

However, where transportation is a prime consideration, the new 1936 2 × 12 cabinet can be used, with a 50 watt head, as shown on the Bass set-up page, where the 1986 is seen to be seated on the 1937 2 × 12 bass cabinet equivalent.

3210-1965A&B. The very latest addition to the formidable Marshall range is the 3210 lead amplifier with the 1965A and B 4 × 10 cabinets.

This highly portable 'mini-stack' is approximately three-quarters the size of the classic 4 × 12 and traditional valve amp set-up.

The 3210 has a new Mosfet power stage, producing a sound that is extremely versatile from clear country and jazz sounds on the clean channel, to warm sustain for blues and the hard overdriven sound for rock on the lead channel.

The matching cabinets for the 3210 are models 1965A and B, 4 × 10 140 watt 8 ohm cabinets. Each cabinet contains four Marshall-Celestion 35 watt speakers to give clarity, punch and definition, whilst retaining the sound quality at high volume. Full stacking facilities and side carrying handles are included.

JCM800 halfstack.

retube countless US JCM800s with 6550 tubes rather than EL34s, because the former were deemed more reliable. The 6550s have a much harder, more aggressive edge than EL34s and are much harder to overdrive. That makes them popular with many US metal players even today, but it upset lovers of the EL34 tone, many of whom didn't even know the change had been made.

Whether because of, or in spite of, such perceptions, players at every level gobbled up the JCM800 line. Modernizations like channel switching and effects loops made the amps even more attractive to amateurs, semi-pros, and eventually pro players—for example, the two-channel, 50-watt 2205 is *the* head behind groundbreaking guitar hero Tom Morello of Rage Against the Machine and Audioslave fame.

Kids grow up fast, and the single-channel, no-nonsense 100-watt head that 20 years ago ushered in a new age now has retro appeal. January 2002 saw the launch of the Limited Edition JCM800 2203ZW Zakk Wylde Signature Model, a 6550-loaded 2203 reissue, followed that summer by the 2203X, an EL34-powered 2203 reissue (complete with a "true-bypass" series effects loop, a feature the 2203ZW also had).

> **Years produced:** 1981–early 1990s (varies by line)

Note: In 1995 Marshall produced a limited run of 200 red JCM800 2203 heads (2203R) with matching red 1960A 4x12 cabs. In 1997, 200 virgin 2203 circuit boards were discovered—and used for limited amp run for the Guitar Center chain. Each head bore a plaque with the GC logo, Jim's signature, and the legend "1997 LIMITED EDITION JCM800, FINAL PRODUCTION RUN OF MODEL 2203." (The statement remained true until 2002's 2203ZW.)

> **Distinguishing features:** A bold new look; the amps that dominated the hard rock '80s era

> **Selected players:** Kerry King and Jeff Hanneman (Slayer, w/6550s), Zakk Wylde (w/6550s), Buddy Guy, Elliot Randall, Tom Morello (2205), Steve Cradock (Ocean Colour Scene), Leslie West, John Sykes (JCM800 1987), Brian Tatler (Diamond Head), Billy Corgan and James Iha (Smashing Pumpkins), plus Anthrax, Judas Priest, Iron Maiden, and about any other '80s hard rock/metal band

2555 Silver Jubilee

To commemorate two anniversaries—Jim's 50th year in music and the 25th birthday of his company—Marshall announced the Silver Jubilee series in 1987. The young man who was discovered as a singer at age 14 could not have dreamed the celebration that awaited him.

JCM 25/50 2550 50-watt head.

This year, Marshall is issuing a series of special, limited edition amplifiers to commemorate company founder Jim Marshall's 25 years as a successful amp manufacturer and 50 years in the music business.

A tribute to an exceptional career in music, the new Jubilee Edition amps offer a unique array of new sound and powering options, along with silver coverings, panels and rivets and a distinctive 25/50 Jubilee Series logo.

The series is available in several formats: full size 100-watt and 50-watt lead heads; a "studio-size" 50-watt lead head and 50-watt combos in 2 × 12" and 1 × 12" formats featuring Marshall Vintage speakers. Speaker cabinets include 2 × 12" and 4 × 12" A and B models (Angled and Straight).

As a special tie-in to the 25/50 theme, all Jubilee amps feature an output stage which functions as the classic Marshall circuit with an additional front panel switch that allows the circuit to be reconfigured from normal high power pentode operation to low power triode operation. This effectively halves the output power, providing 100 and 50 watts operation from the 100-watt models and 50 and 25 watts operation from 50-watt models. The final benefit for players is superior distortion tone and overall performance at low volume levels.

All Jubilee models feature quiet switching between lead and rhythm channels with a specially supercharged Lead mode. When you switch to the Lead channel, special overdrive and "re-voicing" circuitry provides an extreme range of distortion effects, including very long sustain with single coil pickups. The Lead Master control is also switched into operation, enabling the lead channel to be balanced with the "normal" rhythm channel while also providing increased gain into the master section so that solos can be brought out above the rhythm settings.

An input gain control modifies preamp gain for a wide variety of clean and distorted tones. It also includes a special "pull" switch that permits the rhythm channel to be changed from a high headroom, clean operating condition to soft clipping and heavy overdrive.

The amps' Master EQ section incorporates traditional Marshall treble, mid and bass controls featuring an updated passive design offering much more flexibility than any other passive system. A new Presence control also features increased range.

The Output Master controls the total output of the preamp section, giving the Lead channel the extra capability of being able to cascade the input gain and lead controls into the output master for more high-powered tonal variations. The Master Section includes effects send & return jacks at approximately −10 dB level, allowing both floor and rack effects to be patched in. For maximum flexibility, the effects loop is placed post lead-rhythm channels and pre- EQ and Master Volume.

Fo: ... ire information, contact: Korg USA, 89 Frost St., Westbury, NY 11590, or Korg USA, 7886 Deering Ave., Canoga Park, CA 91304

Based on the 2203 and 2204 master-volume heads, the Silver Jubilee series was like a great car: gleaming chrome on the bumpers and smart under the hood. The exterior was covered in silver-colored vinyl and complemented by a chrome control panel. A play on the 50/25 anniversaries was echoed in the Jubilee's design: on the 50-watt head (the 2550), a switch let you select between 50- and 25-watt modes. Following suit, the 100-watt heads (the 2555) were selectable between 100- and 50-watt operation. The selection was made via the front-panel Pentode/Triode switch, which cut the output power by half when in Triode mode. While providing a wink to the anniversaries it celebrated, this clever bit of engineering made the amp quite versatile. In addition to altering the amp's power output, switching to Triode mode subtly changed the tone and feel. (See page 98, The JCM900 Series.)

Shadow warrior: Slash parries with his 2555SL in the ad that unveiled Marshall's first signature amp.

Another of the Silver Jubilees' nifty features was the footswitchable Lead Master control, which effectively made them two-channel amps. When activated, the control beefed up the preamp's gain, enabling the user to switch between rhythm and lead tones. A push/pull Input Gain pot also added a subtly distorted "clip" to the amp's rhythm tone. A series effects loop and a DI output rounded off the features.

The Jubilees, which also included 1x12 and 2x12 combos (both 50/25 watts), were a big hit out of the gate, but their run was allegedly capped at 3,000 within the commemorative year. The limited release was another smart move: It guaranteed the series a place in the Marshall hall of fame, and after the anniversary, production resumed within the JCM800 line under the name Custom Series. The only concession was adopting the JCM's cosmetic scheme of black vinyl and brushed-gold panels.

Of the four Jubilee models, the 100/50-watt 2555 proved the most popular, with Slash of Guns n' Roses adopting it as his amp of choice. To celebrate this well-known marriage of amp and axeman, the first-ever Marshall signature amp, the 2555SL was issued as a limited edition in 1996.

Jim, we're looking forward to that 75/50 switch on the Golden Jubilees in 2012.

> **Years produced:** 1987–1989

> **Distinguishing features:** switchable between 100- and 50-watt operation

> **Tube complement:** 3 x 12AX7, 4 x EL34

> **Select players:** Slash, Steve Morse, John Frusciante, Geoff Whitehorn (Procol Harum), Richie Sambora (2555SL), Dave Baksh (Sum 41; 2555SL), Bill Frisell (2554 combo)

JMP-1 Preamp

Marshall has never been shy about exploring new markets, even after stumbling on keyboard amps, turntables, and a handful of bum combos that were poorly received in the Rose-Morris years. In 1992 the company took the bold step of releasing the JMP-1 preamp, a 1U rack unit that seemed strangely at odds with the "bigger is better" physicality that governed so many previous Marshall developments.

For players who want all the Marshall tones they can get under one roof, there is no rival to the JMP-1; this valve-driven unit offers hundreds of sounds from across Marshall's best-known lines. Live players love it for the options it makes available at the tap of a footswitch; studio musicians love its flexibility and the easy programmability it offers within a lightweight unit.

The JMP-1 bucks criticism of being less than genuine with its true tube heart: a pair of 12AX7s glow behind the unit's digital mind. The controls typically found on Marshall heads—volume, gain, presence, bass, middle, treble—exist here as buttons (with LEDs that glow when a button is selected) but are controlled by the guitarist's friend: a knob, in this case labeled Data. The JMP-1 further echoes the "real" amp world by housing four independently voiced channels: Clean1, Clean2, OD1, and OD2, each one selectable via its own LED button.

JMP-1 Valve MIDI Preamp.

Programming the JMP-1 is fairly simple: Select one of the four channels, then dial in your tone by selecting each of the parameters in turn and setting them via the Data control while watching the large red LED readout. In the style of multi-FX programming (something rack-savvy guitarists were already familiar with), the tone dialed in can be saved in a "patch" (100 patch spaces are available, numbered 0–99) and then easily recalled by either the front panel or MIDI. (The switching via the latter is effectively seamless, a rarity for such devices.) Not even the heavily loaded, three-channel 30th Anniversary Marshall and TSL heads can offer as much tonal variety and convenience.

The unit is effects-friendly thanks to its programmable Parallel/Series FX loop and MIDI-mapping facility, allowing the user to match a particular effect with any patch of his or her choice. Even though the dreaded MIDI acronym still strikes fear in many guitarists—even in this increasingly digital world—the fact the JMP-1 recently celebrated its 12th birthday indicates that a good number of 6-stringers have overcome this phobia.

Some want options, others want simplicity; the JMP-1 is for the former group. It sure doesn't look as cool as a full stack, but try getting 100 different heads into your car!

> **Years produced:** 1992–present

> **Distinguishing features:** Two tubes; four channels; 100 programmable memory locations; seamless MIDI patch switching

> **Tube complement:** 2 x 12AX7

> **Selected players:** Mike Mushok (Staind); Steph Carpenter (the Deftones); Dave Murray, Adrian Smith, and Janick Gers (Iron Maiden); Billy Gibbons; John 5 (Marilyn Manson); Vivian Campbell and Phil Collen (Def Leppard); Jerry Horton (Papa Roach); Kirk Hammett; Dave Mustaine: Ace Frehley; Al Jourgensen (Ministry); Richard Patrick (Filter)

JCM2000 DSL100

The JCM2000 line is the legacy of its JCM800 and JCM900 forebears, and arguably bests them both. At the top of the line, the 100-watt DSL100 is a sophisticated head with a simple front-panel interface that belies the amp's versatility.

Four 12AX7s and four EL34s provide the 100% pure tube signal path and the power that drives both classic and modern Marshall tones. There are two uniquely voiced channels in the DSL (Dual Super Lead)—Classic Gain and Ultra Gain—and both have two front-panel selectable modes: Clean/Crunch and Lead 1/Lead 2 respectively. Each channel has its own controls for Gain and Volume, plus a Reverb level control for the DSL's built-in spring reverb. The channels share these controls: tone controls for Bass, Middle, Treble, and Presence; a Tone Shift switch that scoops the mids, allowing lows and highs to dominate; and a Deep switch that gooses the bottom end by adding a resonant bass boost. There's a series effects loop on the rear

JCM2000 DSL100 100-watt head.

panel as well, with a Loop Level switch that matches the loop's level to either stompboxes (low, –10dB) or rackmount processors (high, +4dB).

The Classic channel's Clean mode lives up to its name with plenty of headroom, delivering polished tones across the frequency spectrum that are gorgeous and, for Marshall, uncharacteristically pristine. Max out the gain, though, and the amp evokes a cranked '59—suddenly Clean isn't so clean anymore. Punch into Crunch mode and you're in JCM800 territory but with higher gain possibilities. The Ultra Gain channel satisfies both soloists and high-gain rhythm crunchers. Lead 1 mode is a hotrodded JCM800 2203, spitting out a tight, responsive roar, and with the Gain set around 5 or 6, the tone can go from clean to raspy to full-on snarl as a player spins up the guitar's volume. Lead 2 is voiced for mega-gain, allowing for a sweet, wet distortion at the conservative end and scare-the-neighbors saturation at the other.

The DSL50 deserves an honorable footnote here as well. With two EL34s, the output stage overdrives sooner (that is, at a lower output volume) and, as is typical with Marshall 50-watt all-tubers, is warmer and less aggressive sounding. Players who need an extraordinary amount of volume while playing clean may require the DSL100, but with fewer output valves the DSL50 allows a guitarist to ride the EL34s to nirvana quicker. Remember that the archetypal Marshall sound, as heard on the first JTM45, was the result of overdriving the tubes in the power stage. While gain-stage distortion is convenient and has earned its place in amplifier history, there's no substitute for the organic, harmonically rich sound of a batch of power-amp tubes that are starting to cook.

> **Years produced:** 1997–present

> **Distinguishing features:** The perfect marriage of vintage and modern all-tube Marshall sounds

> **Tube complement:** 4 x12AX7, 4 x EL34

> **Selected players:** Gary Moore, Jeff Beck (DSL50), Richie Sambora, Allison Robertson (Donnas), Steve Morse, Quinn Allman (The Used)

MG Series

What are Jim's favorite solid-state Marshall amps? "Without a doubt our current MG line" is his instant response. "This range of solid-state amps was developed from our very successful Valvestate series of hybrid [tube preamp/ solid-state power amp] amps and have made it possible for a lot of youngsters to have a Marshall as their first amp, because they're a lot cheaper than the all-valve amps. Right now I've got what is, without doubt, the finest team of engineers in the world. This team is led by my technical director, Bruce Keir, and what Bruce has done with his lads [Ian Robinson and Laurent Veignal] over the past several years has just been fantastic. They are definitely the best and most consistent R&D department I've ever had. In fact, they amaze me at times."

MG100DFX 100-watt combo.

The MG lines may get kicked around by Marshall purists for being devoid of tubes, but their unparalleled popularity earns them a spot on Jim Marshall's Top 11. Designed at headquarters in Bletchley and produced overseas in Korea and India, the MG Series is priced so you can kick it down some stairs when you're ready for an upgrade. Some MGs are even packaged in a kit with an inexpensive guitar, so you can smash that, too.

Jim knew he was on to a new crowd with the success of Valvestate and AVT, so he took budget design one step further for the MG. Chipboard cabinets house solid-state circuitry, and the mark of the R&D department is on the amps' FDD (Frequency Dependent Damping) section, which acts on the power-stage circuitry. FDD goes quite some distance toward emulating the way a tube amp's output stage interacts with the speaker or speakers it's driving, with the result that the amplified guitar signal doesn't sound or feel quite so "transistor-y" when it hits the speakers. The team also aimed to please with a generous assortment of features: All MGs have an input for a CD player, a headphone jack, and a Contour control for sweeping the mids. Plus, those that boast the DFX suffix house built-in, easy-to-set digital effects.

MG10CD 10-watt combo.

The MG10CD, like the MG10MKII before it, is MG's biggest seller—and currently the single best-selling Marshall amp in production, in terms of units. It's a squat 'n' sturdy, no-frills, twin-channel, 10-watt, closed-back 1 x 6½ combo with built-in FDD and a CD input, making it ideal for practicing or warming up backstage. (Irish blues rocker Gary Moore practices with an MG10CD.)

The MG100HDFX 100-watt head also warrants a mention. Like the 8100 and G100RCD heads that spawned it, it's the most affordable 100-watt Marshall head currently available, and it also shifts serious volume—both decibel- and sales-wise. Its popularity comes from both its wallet-friendly price and its aggressive, high-gain punch—a trait that has earned the 8100, G100RCD, and MG100HDFX spots in the backlines of some gold- and platinum-plated metalheads.

> **Years produced:** 2002–present

> **Distinguishing features:** Good sound and looks at an affordable price

> **Tube complement:** None . . . zero . . . nada . . . zilch

> **Selected players (MG100HDFX):** Tommy Victor (Prong), Riggs (Rob Zombie), Wayne Static (Static-X); Gary Moore (MG10 for practice at home); Zakk Wylde (MG15MSII for practice)

Mode Four

At 350 watts the hybrid Mode Four MF350 head is an absolute behemoth that represents entirely new approaches in design, construction, and cosmetics for Marshall. At the same time, the amp upholds significant Marshall traditions: It's probably the loudest amp around—good luck finding an amp on which you can dial in more gain;

it builds on the proven success of hybrid valve/solid-state technology; and it looks like a million bucks onstage.

True to Jim's *modus operandi*, Mode Four is born of players' wishes. It's as if he carried the letter bag over to R&D and said, "Do what they want." What they wanted was an amp that mirrors the range of guitar tones heard from the currently ruling kings of rock and metal—a ton of headroom to deliver crystalline picked arpeggios; Marshall-worthy overdrive worthy of threatening riffs and aggressive chord passages; enough gain in reserve to dial rhythms and leads up to "stun" level; and a massive bottom end to ground it all and manage the low frequencies of detuned guitars.

The Mode Four distinguishes itself as a two-amps-in-one design. The head houses two preamps coupled to a 350-watt power stage that completely reconfigures itself depending on which of the preamps is selected. That's not two channels, that's not a two-way switch to regulate power; it's two separate and independent preamps—each driven by its own 12AX7—that feed a sophisticated morphing power amp. Other features include onboard digital reverb (due to the serious amount of low-end air the MF350 moves, a traditional spring affair was deemed unfeasible), with each amp having its own control; parallel/series effects loop; emulated DI outputs; tuner mute function; and footswitchable, adjustable Solo level control.

Head shots: Daron Malakian, Mike Mushok, Dave Baksh, Kerry King, Tripp Eisen, Sean Martin, and Terry Corso all profess their fealty to the formidable Mode Four.

The layout on its polished aluminum faceplate makes the MF350 easily approachable: Amp 1 is on the left, Amp 2 is on the right. Each has two modes (totaling four modes in all—get it?), with Clean and Crunch in Amp 1 and OD1 and OD2 in Amp 2. Amp 1, with nearly limitless headroom in Clean mode and a full-bodied overdrive in Crunch, is closely reminiscent of a JCM800 2203 front-ended by an overdrive pedal. When the Amp 2 side is selected, the power amp reconfigures itself to deliver the kind of deep, loose low-end punch favored by purveyors of baritone, 7-string, and detuned guitar—in fact, the MF350 delivers more bottom than any Marshall ever, especially when paired with one (or two) of its specially designed and voiced "bigger is better" MF 4x12 cabs. Plus Amp 2 delivers more distortion than any prior amp could muster; especially in OD2, it is super-saturated.

Tufnel went to 11, the JCM900 went to 20. Pick an exponent.

> **Years produced:** 2003–present

> **Distinguishing features:** "Two amps in one" hybrid design, 350 watts, new cosmetics. The MF line also includes four "XL" 4x12 cabinets: the MF280A, MF280B, MF400A, and MF400B.

> **Tube complement:** 2 x 12AX7—one in each preamp

> **Selected players:** Daron Malakian (System of a Down), Dave Baksh (Sum 41), John 5 (Marilyn Manson), Dave Navarro (Jane's Addiction), Sean Martin (Hatebreed), Matt Bachand (Shadows Fall), Tripp Eisen (Static-X)

See Chapter 5 for more on the Mode Four.

Chapter 8

Testify

"If you want to get a little bit rude and loud, you've got to have a Marshall. The Marshall sound is the balls. It's the big daddy, and it has that growl that no other amp has."

—Jeff Beck (*GP*)

Without an amp to plug into, a solidbody electric guitar is merely a hunk of wood with some strings attached. For well over 40 years, Marshall amplifiers have been the plug-in of choice for an ever-growing list of players in every style of music that requires an electric guitar.

In this chapter's collection of Marshallabilia you'll hear from some of the many players and personalities who have praised Mr. Marshall and his amps over the years. For your own tone quest, the chapter ends with detailed rig diagrams of six Marshall greats spanning the '60s to the '00s: Jimi Hendrix, Jeff Beck, Billy Gibbons of ZZ Top, Dave Murray of Iron Maiden, plus the only two players to have had their signatures sit alongside Jim's on the front panel of an amp—Slash and Zakk Wylde.

As you read the musicians' words and study the signal chains, keep in mind Jim Marshall's original mission when he had the lads in his shop put iron to solder: He wanted to do nothing more than help a handful of local guitarists bring their unique musical visions to life. Now in his ninth decade, Jim is pursuing that goal on a worldwide scale, and you can do nothing better to honor the man than to pursue a musical dream of your own.

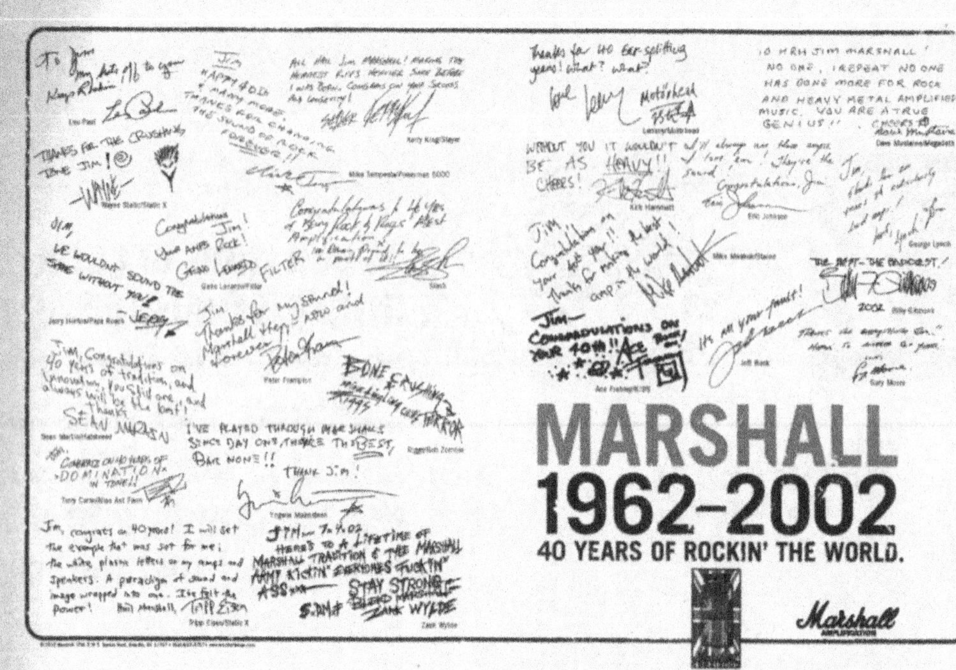

Warren Haynes

"When I was a kid, it seemed like the one common ingredient in every sound I fell in love with was some sort of Marshall amp. All sorts of different guitars and all sorts of different tones, but they all had that one creamy, common denominator. And it would always be the Marshall."

On his 1959SLPX reissue

"It just sounds like I want it to sound in my head, you know? When you go to play something and the amp responds and you don't have to manipulate it because the sound is already there—that's really a key for me. And with those amps, the sound is good as soon as you plug 'em in. You can tweak it and you can make it better, but the instant sound is always there." (NB)

Warren Haynes is a bottomless well of taste and technique. He breathed new life into the Allman Brothers Band when he joined in the '80s, and singlehandedly rescued the art of longform jamming both with the Allmans and with his own group, Gov't Mule.

Landmark recording: *An Evening with the Allman Brothers Band: First Set* (Epic, 1992)
Marshalls: 1959SLPX reissue, 1960BX and BV cabs

"I can make my Marshall go from a screaming loud tone to a beautiful clean, warm, bassy sound with a mere flick of a pickup switch."

—Paul Weller

“As players and writers our gear often serves us as a source of inspiration, and Marshalls have probably fueled more great guitar riffs than any other amplifier.”

—George Lynch (NB)

Mane event: Jim and Pauline Marshall present the first-place trophy to the winner of the Jim Marshall 40th Anniversary Handicap Hurdle Race, run at Towcester racecourse on Saturday, March 30, 2002. The Celestion company named the horse race in honor of Marshall's 40th year.

To: Nick Bowcott

Jim and I met at Guitar Center
in Hollywood. The police had roped off
the fans across the street on Sunset
Blvd. There was a mob of fans waiting.
I was asked to get on my knees, put my
hands into the cement like Jim. I got
a chuckle out of him when I mentioned
he reminded me of Jimmy Hoffa. We had
fun in the cement and later in a
saloon. We did talk about all our
musician friends who have accepted
our toys to play with. Thank you guys
and gals,

Jim you're a good friend, thanks
for helping make my guitars so loud.

Cheers

Quotes courtesy Marshall Amplification and its publications except the following:

GP Guitar Player magazine
GPM Guitar for the Practicing Musician
GS Guitar Shop
G Guitar
GW Guitar World
NB As told to Nick Bowcott

Special thanks to Nick Bowcott of Marshall Amplification for contacting the artists indicated.

"The Norse warrior image is way overused when describing the bearded guitarist, but when you see him with his back to the audience, riffing away while spreading his legs seemingly miles apart, you can only think of one phrase: Rock God." (*GP*)

Zakk Wylde

“There's a reason Jimi Hendrix used 'em, there's a reason Jimmy Page used 'em, there's a reason Eddie Van Halen used 'em, and there's a reason Randy Rhoads used 'em. 'Cause there can only be one—Marshall.”

On having a signature Marshall amp

“I'll drink to that! Obviously, without a doubt, it's a huge honor to have my name next to Jim Marshall's, because Jim and Les Paul are the forefathers of the whole thing.”

“What does a Marshall sound like? Strength, warmth, commitment, beauty and destruction . . . all wrapped up on a giant fuckin' wrecking ball.” (NB)

Discovered by Ozzy Osbourne as a teenager, Zakk Wylde is a self-described “meat-and-potatoes, bull-in a-fuckin'-china-shop” guitarist. Instantly recognizable, he can be heard on Ozzy albums from 1988 onward. In the mid '90s he busted out his own bruise-rock for solo outings, most recently including Black Label Society's DVD *Boozed, Bruised & Broken Boned,* which has won wide acclaim in guitar circles.

Landmark recording: Ozzy Osbourne's *No Rest for the Wicked* (Epic, 1988)
Marshalls: 2203ZW heads and old 2203s with 6550 power tubes; 1960B cabs with “EC” grille cloth and small gold logos, loaded with 200-watt EV 12" speakers

Five Towns College
Long Island, New York

Upon the recommendation of the Faculty and by virtue of the authority vested in them The Board of Trustees of the College has conferred upon

James Charles Marshall

the degree of

Doctor of Music
Honoris Causa

with all rights and privileges, immunities and honors thereunto belonging and in testimony thereof it grants this diploma bearing the seal of the College and signed by the appropriate Board and College officers.

Given this twenty-eighth day of January, two thousand and two.

Chairman of the Board — President of the College

For the Trustees of the College — Dean of the College

"It's funny how guys will say, 'Hey man, you oughta try this amp—it sounds just like a Marshall.' Well, why not just use a fuckin' Marshall?"

—Leslie West (*G*)

"The reason I'm drawn towards Marshall is simple: They are the best for what I do. They're heavy as hell and they have something that a lot of high-gain amps lack: actual tone! To put it simply, they rule. You couldn't ask for anything better."

—Sean Martin, Hatebreed

Landmark recording: *Nothing's Shocking* (Warner Bros., 1988)
Marshalls: JCM900 4100 head (distorted tone); Mode Four MF350 head (clean tone); Marshall 1960BV cabinets

Dave Navarro

"Marshall Amplification has been powering my sound for the better part of 15 years, and I find them to be the most durable, the most reliable, most concert-ready amplifiers of all. My [Mode Four] has enabled me to do away with half of what I used to use on the floor. You'll find your old distortion and boost pedals will make great gifts."

On his JCM900 4100s (circa 1996)

"I'm a fairly simple guy and I have a total lack of knowledge when it comes to musical equipment. You basically don't need to have intelligence to use the 4100, which is a good thing. What I look for in my gear is simplicity and range at the same time. I can get an amazing high-gain sound and a very clean sound at the flick of a switch. And, for what I do, that completely serves my purpose."

On what got him into Marshall

"Jimi Hendrix. That's what first attracted me to the amps when I was 11 or 12. I saw "Marshall" behind him, and that's all I needed to know."

From out of rock's darker corners comes the singular voice of Dave Navarro, who was first heard giving alternative rock a backbone on the live Jane's Addiction debut in 1987. His sonic imprint has marked recordings by a range of artists including Nine Inch Nails, Red Hot Chili Peppers, Alanis Morissette, and, most recently, a newly returned Jane's Addiction.

"I was the only kid in the area with a Marshall amp. I turned the sucker up to 10, and you wouldn't even hear our bass player. It was kind of good, too, because he couldn't play!"

—Eddie Van Halen on his high-school band, the Broken Combs (*GPM*)

Happy Birthday Jim – old Marshalls never die – they just blow your fucking head off!
Thanks for everything
love Lemmy

Many musicians know Jim Marshall as the man who created the finest amplifiers ever. Many charities also know his name because without any boasting, he has given millions of pounds helping children, the sick, and the needy. I raise my hat to my closest pal, Jim, who does so much good without seeking publicity.

Bert Weedon, OBE

Cream of the crop: Jim presents a 1962JAG Limited Edition to guitar diety Eric Clapton.

Lemmy

"Old Marshalls don't die, they blow your fucking head off."

"Marshalls are the best. No discussion. Sting like a butterfly, fly like a B-52, your choice. I just got some new ones, I bought the last lot in 1971. Any questions? Jim Marshall is my friend and I am his."

The legendary leader of Motörhead—the world's loudest band—Lemmy refuses to grow old gracefully. The back cover of his 2003 autobiography, *White Line Fever*, describes him in these reverent terms: "Medically speaking, Lemmy should be dead. After years of notorious excess, his blood would kill another human being. This is the story of the heaviest drinking, oversexed speedfreak in the business."

Landmark recording: Motörhead's *No Sleep 'til Hammersmith* (Bronze, 1981)
Marshalls: Super Bass 100-watt heads, Marshall 4x15 and 4x12 cabs

Billy F. Gibbons

"I can't tell you why, but I've tried 'em all and the Marshalls feel and sound like home."

"The fine Marshall line remains heavy as lead . . . solid as steel. The best."

The tres hombres in ZZ Top have been revving up their Texas blues for over 30 years. Billy Gibbons—friend to Stevie Ray Vaughan, praised by Jimi Hendrix—has been a proud Marshall man from the start: He cites his Les Paul/Marshall pairing on ZZ's debut "Pearly Gates" as his "cornerstone of tone."

Landmark recording: *ZZ Top's First Album* (Warner Bros., 1970)
Marshalls: JMP-1s with vintage Mullard 12Ax7s, Valvestate power amps, JCM900 heads, 1960AX and BX cabs (live) ; 1966 100-watt Plexi through two 10" Celestions (studio)

"If it was good enough for Jimi, then it's good enough for me!"

—Lenny Kravitz

"Nothing else is like a Marshall—you don't just hear the sound, you feel it."

—Gary Moore

Ace Frehley

"Marshall is the best rock 'n roll amp in the business. Nobody has topped them since they were first made in '62."

"I've A/B'd the JMP-1 against a regular Marshall with a Neumann U87 [mic] in front of it and I can't tell the difference. Before I started the reunion, I was doing some demos with my band, and Paul Orifino and I had a Marshall set up with a Neumann in front of it, and on the other channel I was going directly into the Marshall preamp. He said, 'Close your eyes,' and kept switching the faders while I was playing. Half the time I got it wrong. That's how close it was. It was mind-boggling!" *(GS)*

Space Ace launched a million young guitarists—his influence on an entire generation of players is undeniable. When Frehley parted ways with Kiss in 1981, he proved himself to be the most accomplished musician in the lineup and left a yawning gap the band was never able to adequately fill. Smoke continues to flow from his pickups in Frehley's Comet.

Landmark recording: *Kiss Alive!* (Casablanca, 1975)
Marshalls: Various models from the late '60s and '70s (early Kiss years); MV models (studio); Kiss' 1996 reunion tour: 441960BV cabs (20 on the floor, 24 suspended) and ten 2100SL-X heads were on display; as backup, the speaker-emulated outputs of JMP-1s ran to the board

My first recollection, and remember we're talking about two old duffers in their 80s here, was meeting Jim in 1954 in London. A friend of mine, Sam Norton, said, "Would you like to meet a few English drummers?" I said yes, and one of the guys that showed up was Jim Marshall. He was very interested in cymbals, and I remember he asked a bunch of questions that were much more intelligent than the average drummer would throw. We quickly became friends, and from that time on I would never get to London without hooking up with Max Abrams and Jim because those two guys were the icons of the English drum business back then.

Now, I know Jim is now the number one guy in guitar amplification, but as I'm continually telling you twangers, that is secondary to his primary function - which is playing drums! We've often talked about getting together after we retire, forming a quartet with Jim on drums, Gotthold Meyer, Bert Weedon on guitar, and myself on string bass, and then touring the world - the trouble is, I don't think either of us is going to retire any time soon. Jim may be 80 but I'll bet he could still really swing a group, even now.

Jim, it's a genuine pleasure to have you as a friend for 50 years - even though you insist on calling me "Dad" because I'm 15 days older than you! Myself and my wife have nothing but admiration for what you've done, going from performing on stage to building up what is, in my mind, is the prime amplification in the music world. You're also now a doctor but down deep you're a drummer and always will be.

Fondest regards, Your "Dad,"
Bob Zildjian
Chairman of the Board (even though I don't have one!), Sabian Cymbals

P.S. Jim, I know you're a connoisseur of fine booze, but even though I love you dearly, when it came to buying a #200 bottle of scotch for your recent visit I thought "What the hell" and settled for a #60 bottle instead - and that was #60 Canadian, too!

"I use the JMP-1 for its many sounds—from classic Marshall to modern. It just plain and simple kicks a lot of ass! It's the heartbeat of my rack."

—Stephen Carpenter, Deftones (NB)

Good company: Drummers Jim Marshall, Nicko McBrain, and Bob Zildjian, plus Procol Harum guitarist Geoff Whitehorn, Marshall's Nick Bowcott, and Bad Company bassist Jaz Lochrie, consort with glass in hand at a Frankfurt, Germany, affair.

Angus Young

"I've experimented with different makes of amp, but I eventually came to the conclusion that the Marshall 100-watt stack was the best way to go. I love 'em because they're great rock 'n' roll amps. They're roadworthy and they're noisy too, in a good way. I think if you're into rock music then that's what you should be using." (*GW*)

Landmark Recording: *Back In Black* (Atco, 1980)
Marshalls: JTM45 and 100-watt SLP (studio); JTM45, four 1959SLPS, eight straight-front 4x12 cabs with 25-watt Celestion Greenbacks (Ballbreaker Tour, 1995–1996)

Like no other band before or since, AC/DC represents the essence and strength of simplicity in rock. "Three chords and the truth" will always win out—as long as Angus Young is playing those three chords.

"That's the best kind of distortion—a humbucker into a Marshall, like Eddie Van Halen."

—John Frusciante (*GP*)

"I like to just be able to plug into an amp and the inherent sound is there, and then you just tweak it a little. That's why I've always played a Marshall."

—Peter Frampton (NB)

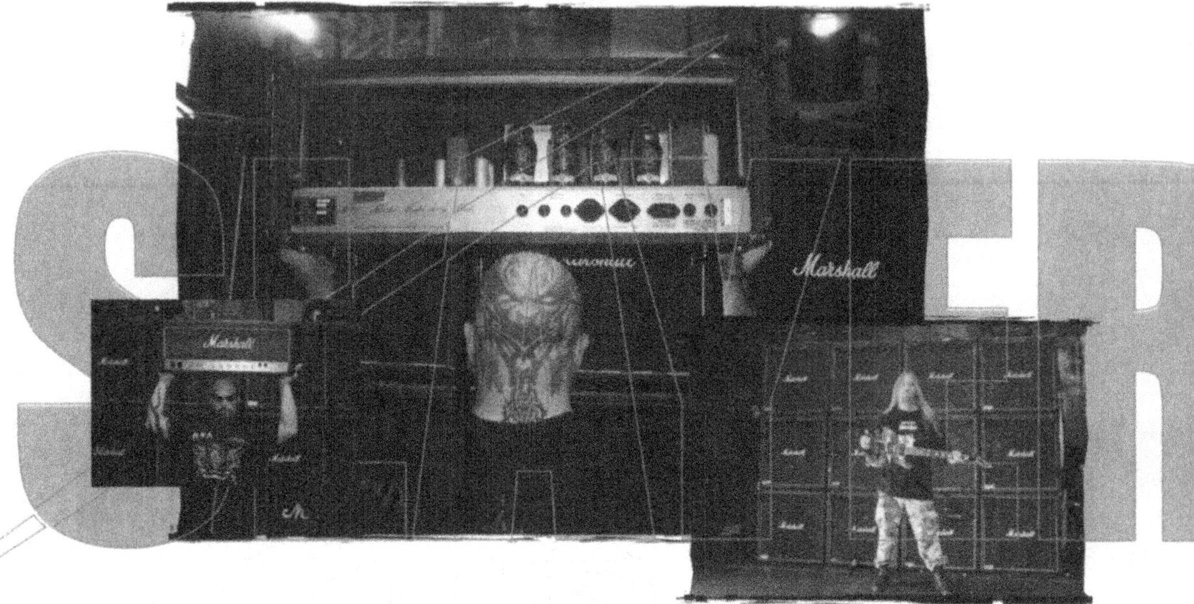

Kerry King

"I use Marshall because I demand the best, and nothing else comes close. Nobody touches it. I use Marshall. There's none better."

Why use Marshall?

"For one, Marshall had the name for heavy metal. For me personally, if I want to get into something I also want to get into what's going to get me there and, as far as I knew, that's what everybody who was worth a damn was playing."

On his JCM800 2203 head with 6550 power tubes

"I've got a bunch of killer-sounding 2203s, but that one is superhuman. Satan himself reached up and touched that head personally. It's a bastard child of Jim Marshall!" (NB)

Landmark recording: *Reign in Blood* (American, 1986)
Marshalls: (both) JCM800 2003s 1960B with cabs (24 onstage)

Jeff Hanneman

"I use Marshall because it is the most intense amp ever. I would not play anything else. If I had to play anything else, I'd set it on fire and destroy it."(NB)

Slayer is the undisputed master of the black art they created over 20 years ago. King and Hanneman have steadfastly refused to compromise or change the hell-bent direction of their bludgeoning rhythms and furious leads. "That's why our fans like us," says King, "so why would we even consider fucking with a machine that's obviously working just fine?"

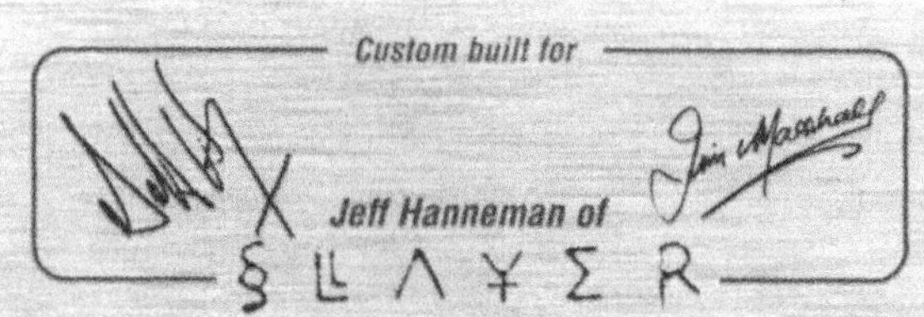

I first had the pleasure of meeting with Mr. Jim Marshall in 1978. At this time I was a director for a small independent drum manufacturing company called Staccato.
I had arranged to meet with Jim for lunch at a hotel in Milton Keynes to discuss a business proposition. We didn't end up agreeing on a future together but it was the beginning of what would end up being a wonderful friendship.
Over the next ten years or so I would search Jim out at the various trade shows that I would attend to say hello and pay my respects. Over these times we began to see a lot more of each other. Our friendship grew continuously and today I am very proud to be able to say that he is a very dear friend and he is very close to my heart.
Jim is a true gentleman. He is a gracious, kind, caring, and, most of all, honest man. I have never heard him say anything cruel, cursive, or unkind about anyone. I find that very commendable in this day and age.
I love you, Jim
Your friend always,
Nicko McBrain [drummer, Iron Maiden]

"People ask me all the time how I get my killer guitar sound—I tell 'em to go buy a Marshall."

—Wayne Static (Static X)

Like minds: Jim and Nicko appeared together in this Premier poster.

IRON MAIDEN

Dave Murray

"What's my secret weapon? Well, aside from sheer volume, I'd have to say Marshall amps in general. They are the secret weapon and there's no secret about it—historically, they've proved it! The amount of years Jim's been putting those babies together is wonderful." (NB)

Janick Gers

"They are simply the best, most solid-sounding, dependable, and toughest touring amps in the world."

Bassist Steve Harris

"Marshalls are the only cabs I have used for as long as I can remember."

Landmark recording: *Number of the Beast* (Capitol, 1982)
Marshalls: (Murray & Gers) JMP-1, JFX-1, 9200; 4x12 cabs—1960BVs (Murray, 1984's Gers)

Drummer Nicko McBrain

"Jim, you are one in a billion for the absolute brilliance—mid, treble, and bass. Life would be dull without you!"

Heavy metal, thy name is Iron Maiden. They weren't just part of the infamous New Wave of British Heavy Metal that stormed America in the early '80s and instigated a metal revolution—Maiden led the charge.

"I have enjoyed and relied on Marshall amps since 1989 for their thick and woody one-of-a-kind lead tone."

—Eric Johnson

"I introduced Marshalls to my backline in 1970. I've used them ever since and probably always will."

—Jimmy Page

DAVE MUSTAINE

Dave Mustaine

"When my tone sounds and feels right, something happens that makes me feel alive. That's why I use Marshalls. They inspire me to want to play and write."

"I remember the first time I ever played through a Marshall, I thought I'd died and gone to heaven! I was looking for that classic British guitar tone, plus I'd heard that Angus Young and Michael Schenker used 'em, and those were two of my favorite players that I respected the most when I first started out. As soon as I plugged into a Marshall, that's when I knew, 'Hey, you can make this magical or you can be some robotic GIT clone that just sits there and does scales all day.'"

Dave Mustaine is probably the only guitarist in the world who could forge a career strong enough to come out from under the shadow of being "the first guitarist in Metallica." Driven by his teeth-grinding rhythms—and leads to match any of his hired guns—his former band, Megadeth, garnered six Grammy nominations and sold in excess of 14 million albums worldwide.

Landmark recording: *Peace Sells . . . But Who's Buying?* (Capitol, 1982)
Marshalls: two JMP-1s, two EL34 100/100, four PB100s, eight 1960BV cabinets (live)

John 5 of Marilyn Manson

"Marshalls have such a distinct sound, you just can't deny it. And, of course, everyone who lives on this earth knows that Marshall is the greatest amp company in the world. It's easy to get a distorted tone from an amp, but from a Marshall it's just different. It's like driving a Rolls Royce. It's that very unique sound that you can only get from a Marshall. I would not do a session or a record or a jingle without them." (NB)

It takes a unique combination of aggression, chops, and stage personality to play alongside Marilyn Manson. But to judge John 5 solely by his current gig would be a considerable mistake. He can play a blurring, flickering blues and has been a first-call session player for everyone from Rob Halford to Salt-N-Pepa to k.d. lang.

Landmark recording: *The Golden Age of Grotesque* (Interscope, 2003)
Marshalls: Mode Four, EL34 100/100, '73 and '76 100-watt Super Leads; JMP-1; various 4x12 cabs

Mike Mushok of Staind

"From Eddie Van Halen to Hendrix to Jimmy Page, it always seemed no matter who I was watching play guitar there was always a stack of Marshalls behind them. Always. And you can't really argue with that, can you?! It was kind of like, 'You're gonna play guitar? Okay, then you've gotta go get a Marshall.'" (NB)

Mushok is one of a handful of modern metal players who manages to infuse aggressive changes and twisting tempos with soul. Limp Bizkit's Fred Durst helped Staind secure their label deal, and in a few short years they've won over legions of fans and critics.

Landmark recording: *Break the Cycle* (Elektra, 2001)
Marshalls: JMP-1, EL34100/100, 1960BV cabs (live); JCM800s; MF350; JMP-1, EL34100/100, 1960BV cabs (studio)

"While we've experimented with technology, I still haven't lost touch with the fact that a Les Paul through a Marshall sounds pretty good."

—Joe Perry, Aerosmith (*GM*)

Setups of the Marshall Stars

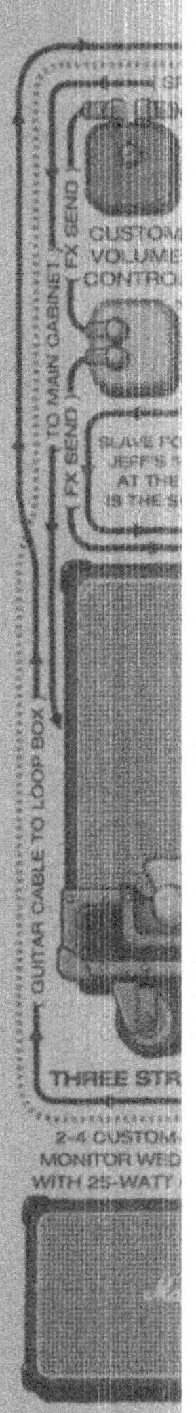

For most guitarists, chasing down great tone is an ongoing pursuit—not because it's impossible to grasp, but because what we want to hear evolves. The refrain about tone coming from the hands of the player rather than from the equipment is true enough, but worthy players of any style spend time with their gear, trying to make it sound in the world as it does in the imagination. Following are six diagrams detailing rigs that feature Marshall front and center. These rigs are the exact setups (current at press time except for Jimi Hendrix) of these great Marshall players, representing a range of tone, styles, and possibilities.

Illustrations created by Adam Cooper/guitargeek.com

Rig layout/research consultant PhD: Nick Bowcott

Thanks to the techs who provided invaluable information about each artist's equipment:

Slash: Adam Day

Zakk Wylde: Freddie Kowalo

Jeff Beck: Steve Prior

Dave Murray: Andy Ball

Billy Gibbons: Elwood Francis & Billy Hale

Jimi Hendrix: Roger Mayer (stompbox supremo) & Tom Lanik (North Star Audio)

Jimi Hendrix

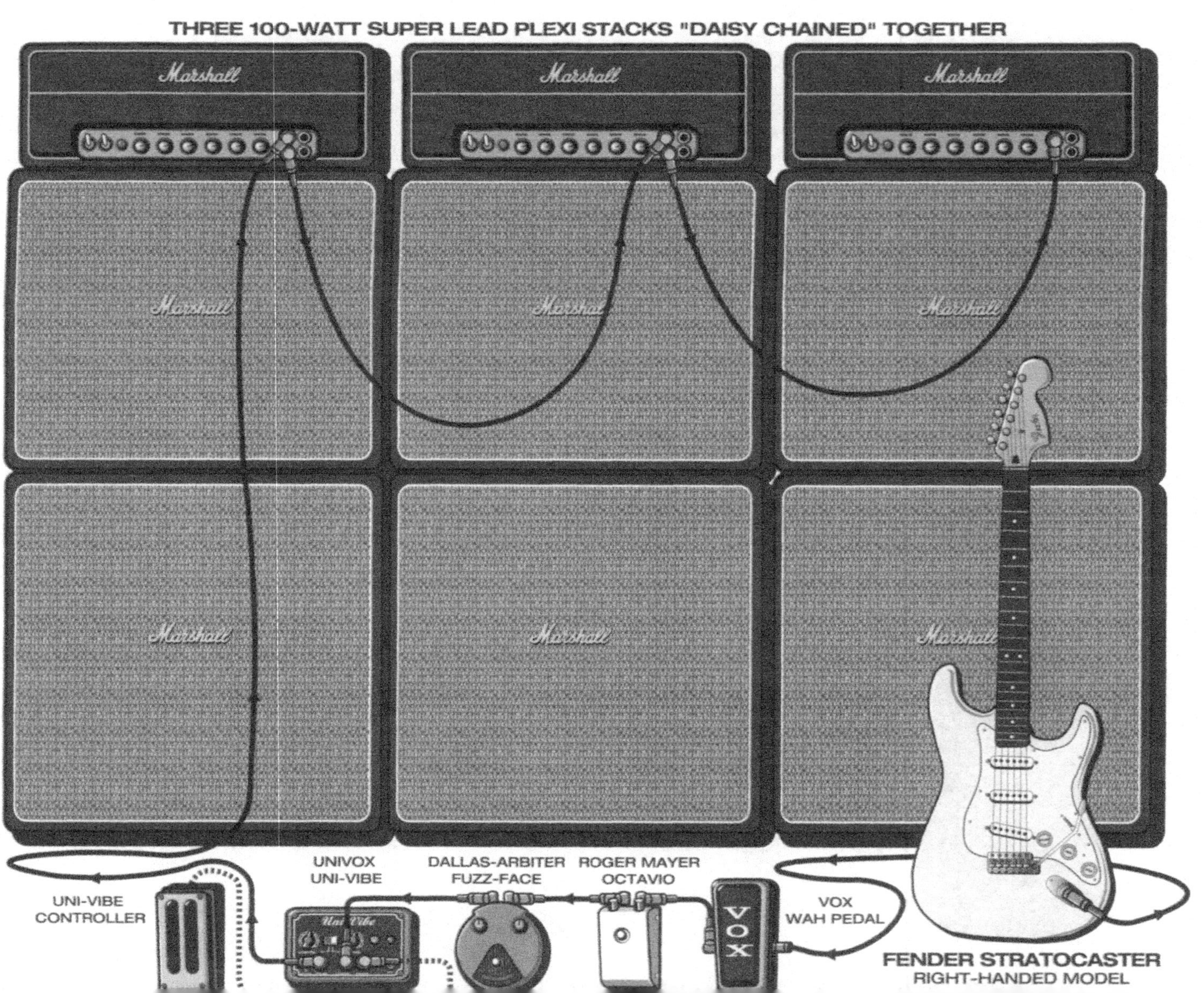

Jeff Beck

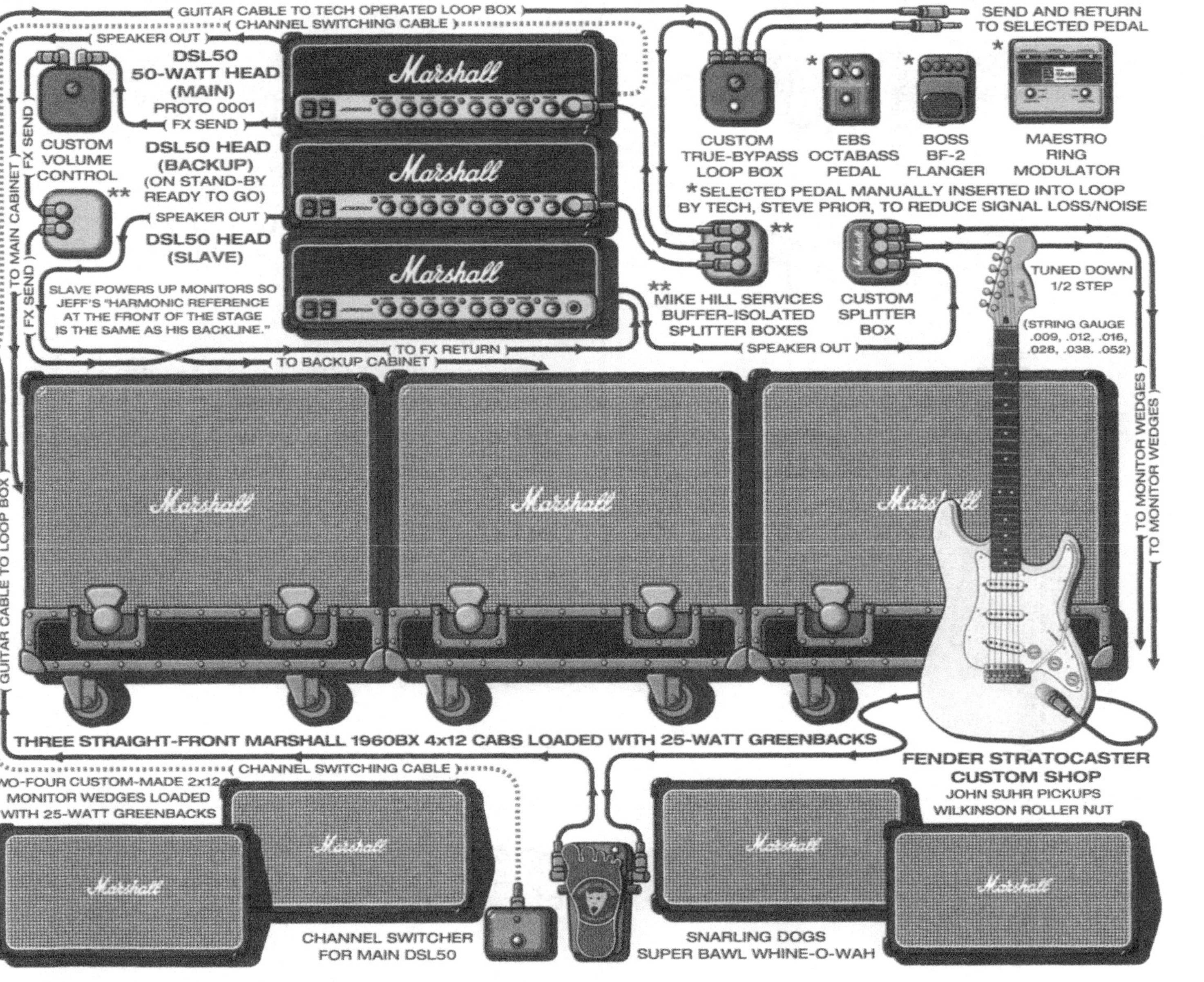

(GUITAR CABLE TO TECH OPERATED LOOP BOX)
(CHANNEL SWITCHING CABLE)
(SPEAKER OUT)
SEND AND RETURN TO SELECTED PEDAL
DSL50 50-WATT HEAD (MAIN) PROTO 0001
(FX SEND)
CUSTOM VOLUME CONTROL
DSL50 HEAD (BACKUP) (ON STAND-BY READY TO GO)
**
(SPEAKER OUT)
DSL50 HEAD (SLAVE)
SLAVE POWERS UP MONITORS SO JEFF'S "HARMONIC REFERENCE AT THE FRONT OF THE STAGE IS THE SAME AS HIS BACKLINE."
(FX SEND)
(TO MAIN CABINET)
(FX SEND)
(TO FX RETURN)
(TO BACKUP CABINET)
CUSTOM TRUE-BYPASS LOOP BOX
* EBS OCTABASS PEDAL
* BOSS BF-2 FLANGER
* MAESTRO RING MODULATOR
*SELECTED PEDAL MANUALLY INSERTED INTO LOOP BY TECH, STEVE PRIOR, TO REDUCE SIGNAL LOSS/NOISE
** MIKE HILL SERVICES BUFFER-ISOLATED SPLITTER BOXES
CUSTOM SPLITTER BOX
(SPEAKER OUT)
TUNED DOWN 1/2 STEP
(STRING GAUGE .009, .012, .016, .028, .038. .052)
(TO MONITOR WEDGES)
(TO MONITOR WEDGES)
(GUITAR CABLE TO LOOP BOX)
THREE STRAIGHT-FRONT MARSHALL 1960BX 4x12 CABS LOADED WITH 25-WATT GREENBACKS
FENDER STRATOCASTER CUSTOM SHOP
JOHN SUHR PICKUPS
WILKINSON ROLLER NUT
(CHANNEL SWITCHING CABLE)
TWO-FOUR CUSTOM-MADE 2x12 MONITOR WEDGES LOADED WITH 25-WATT GREENBACKS
CHANNEL SWITCHER FOR MAIN DSL50
SNARLING DOGS SUPER BAWL WHINE-O-WAH
Marshall

Billy Gibbons

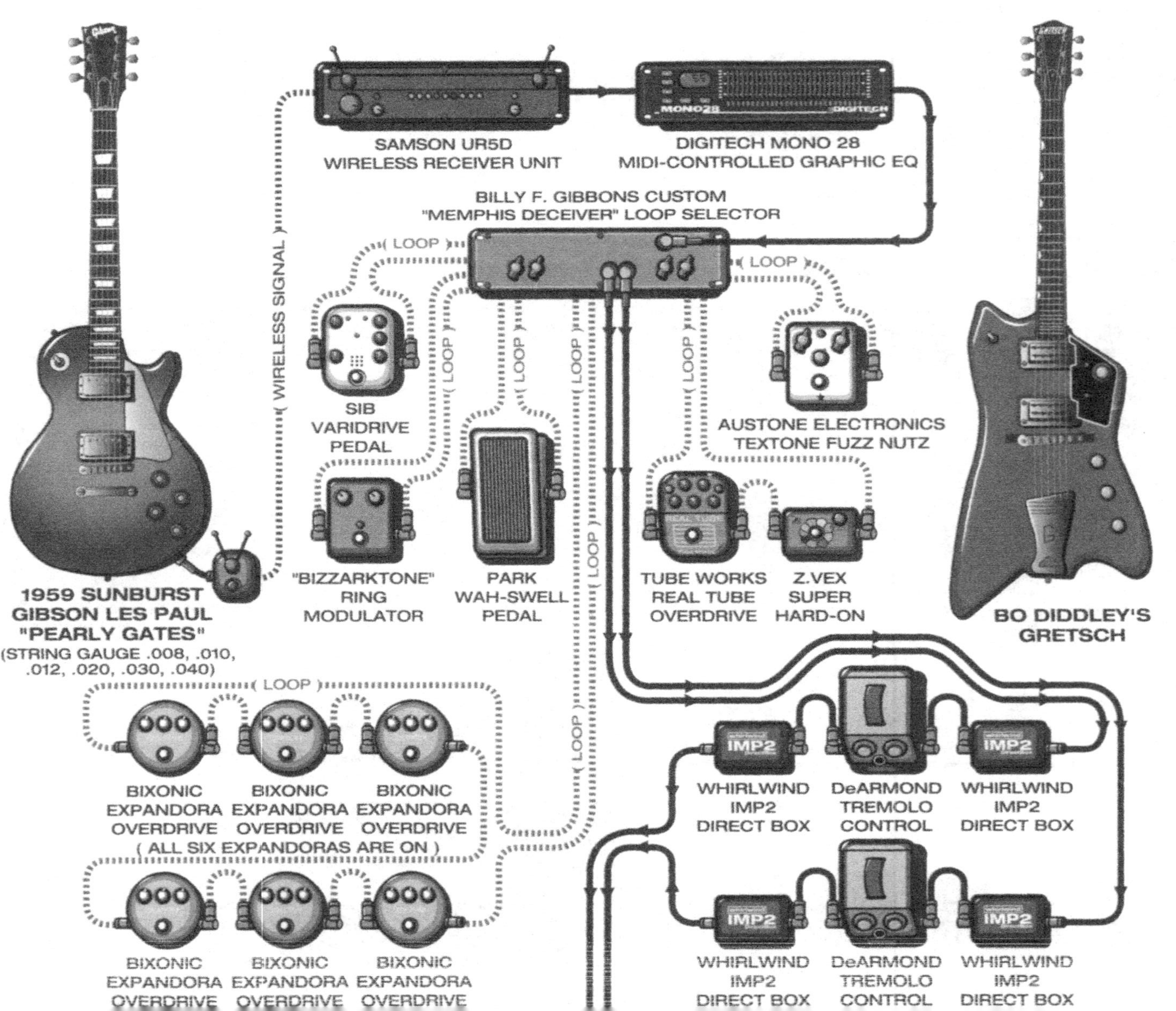

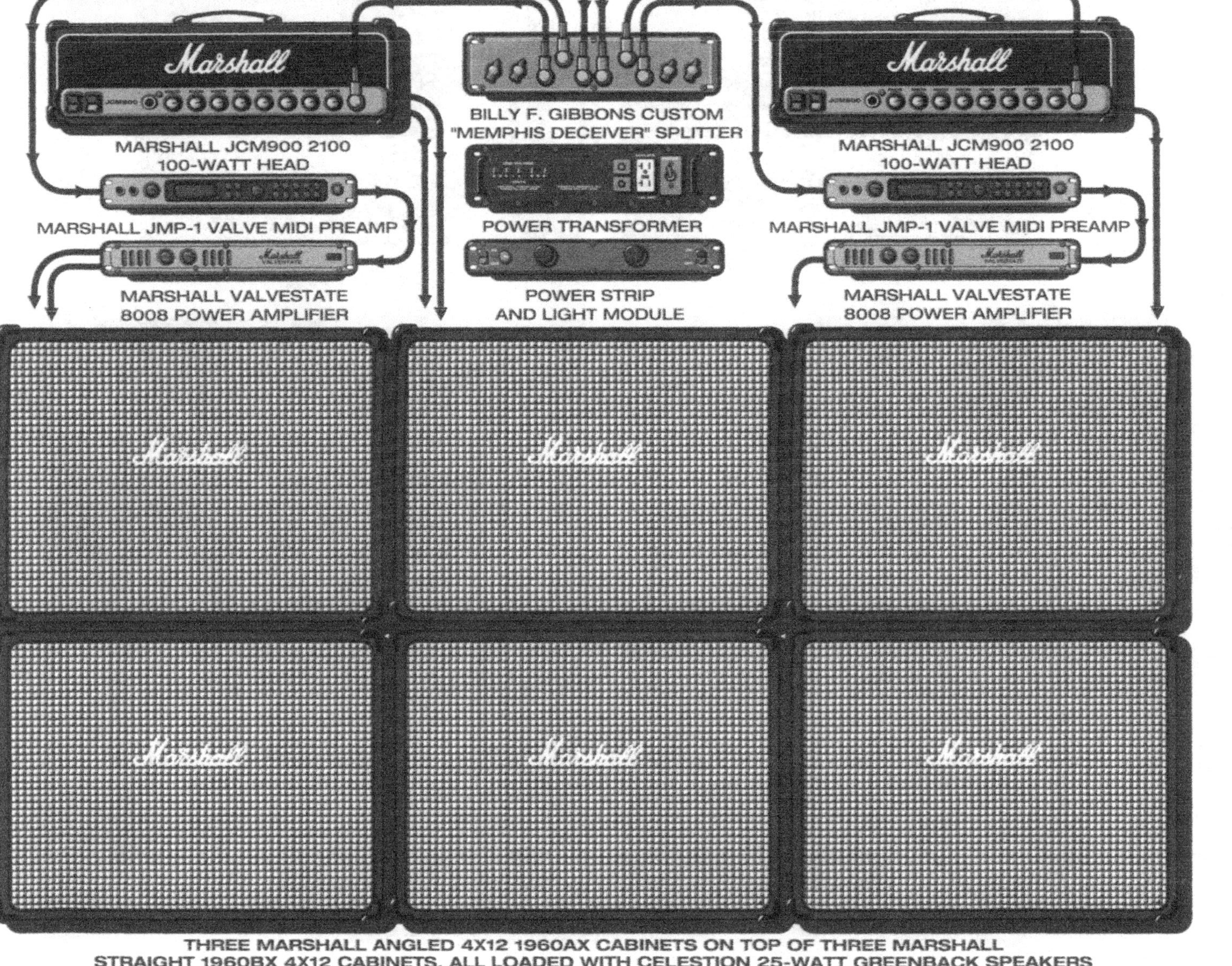

THREE MARSHALL ANGLED 4X12 1960AX CABINETS ON TOP OF THREE MARSHALL
STRAIGHT 1960BX 4X12 CABINETS, ALL LOADED WITH CELESTION 25-WATT GREENBACK SPEAKERS

Slash

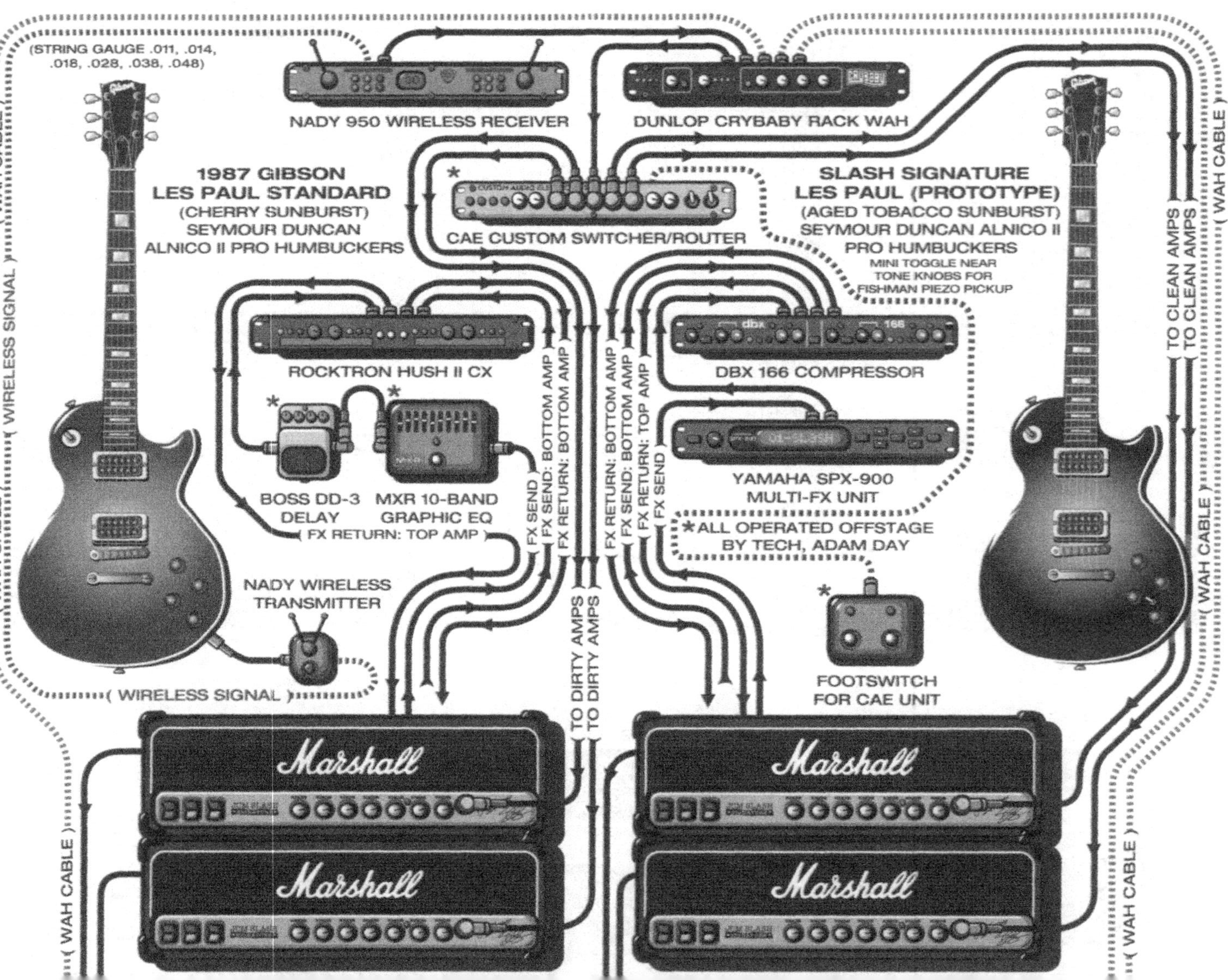
(STRING GAUGE .011, .014, .018, .028, .038, .048)
NADY 950 WIRELESS RECEIVER
DUNLOP CRYBABY RACK WAH
1987 GIBSON LES PAUL STANDARD
(CHERRY SUNBURST)
SEYMOUR DUNCAN ALNICO II PRO HUMBUCKERS
CAE CUSTOM SWITCHER/ROUTER
SLASH SIGNATURE LES PAUL (PROTOTYPE)
(AGED TOBACCO SUNBURST)
SEYMOUR DUNCAN ALNICO II PRO HUMBUCKERS
MINI TOGGLE NEAR TONE KNOBS FOR FISHMAN PIEZO PICKUP
ROCKTRON HUSH II CX
DBX 166 COMPRESSOR
BOSS DD-3 DELAY
MXR 10-BAND GRAPHIC EQ
(FX RETURN: TOP AMP)
FX SEND
FX SEND: BOTTOM AMP
FX RETURN: BOTTOM AMP
FX RETURN: TOP AMP
YAMAHA SPX-900 MULTI-FX UNIT
*ALL OPERATED OFFSTAGE BY TECH, ADAM DAY
NADY WIRELESS TRANSMITTER
(WIRELESS SIGNAL)
TO DIRTY AMPS
FOOTSWITCH FOR CAE UNIT
TO CLEAN AMPS
(WAH CABLE)
Marshall

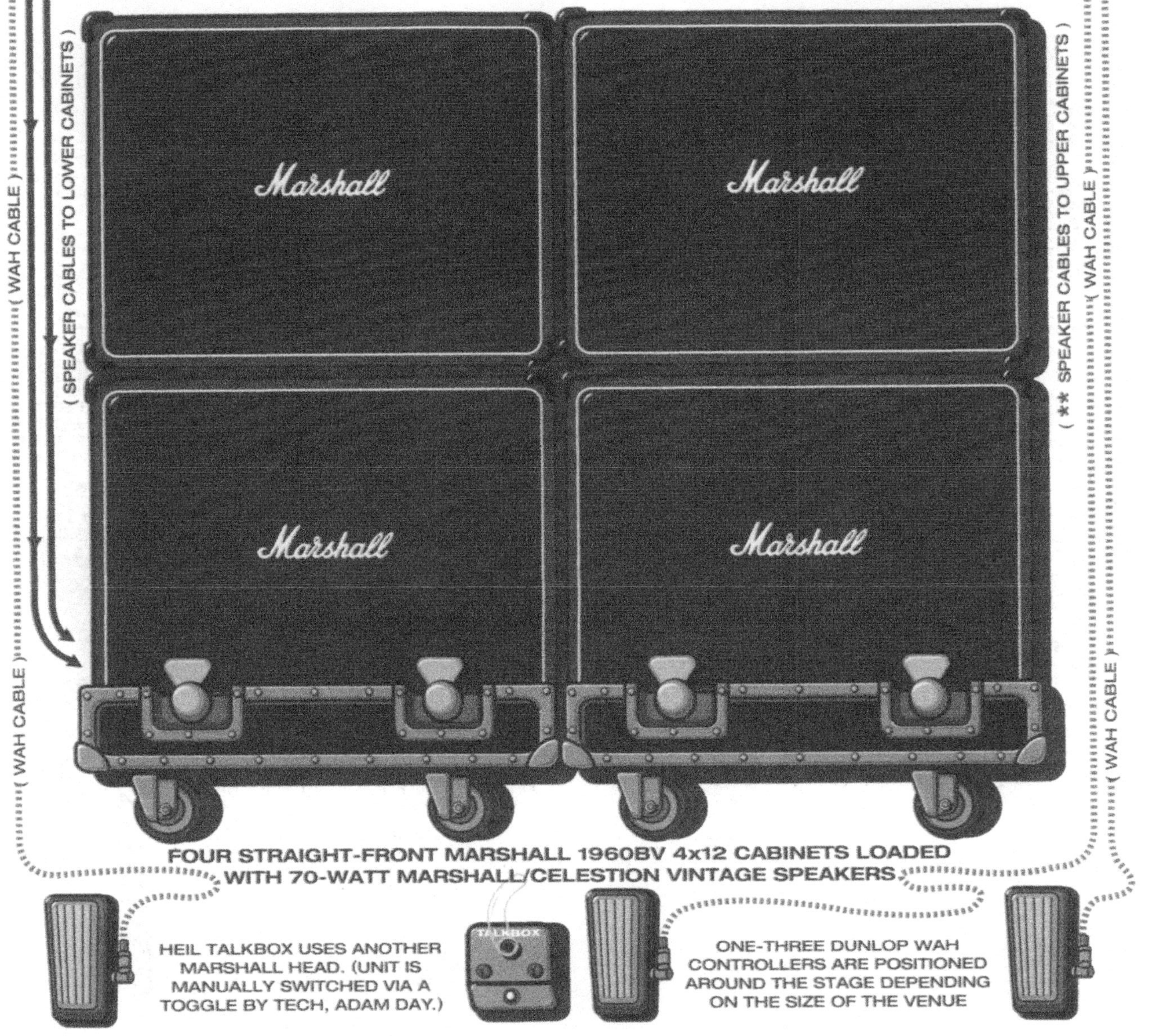

(WAH CABLE)
(WAH CABLE)
(SPEAKER CABLES TO LOWER CABINETS)
Marshall
Marshall
Marshall
Marshall
(** SPEAKER CABLES TO UPPER CABINETS)
(WAH CABLE)
(WAH CABLE)
FOUR STRAIGHT-FRONT MARSHALL 1960BV 4x12 CABINETS LOADED WITH 70-WATT MARSHALL/CELESTION VINTAGE SPEAKERS
HEIL TALKBOX USES ANOTHER MARSHALL HEAD. (UNIT IS MANUALLY SWITCHED VIA A TOGGLE BY TECH, ADAM DAY.)
TALKBOX
ONE-THREE DUNLOP WAH CONTROLLERS ARE POSITIONED AROUND THE STAGE DEPENDING ON THE SIZE OF THE VENUE

Zakk Wylde

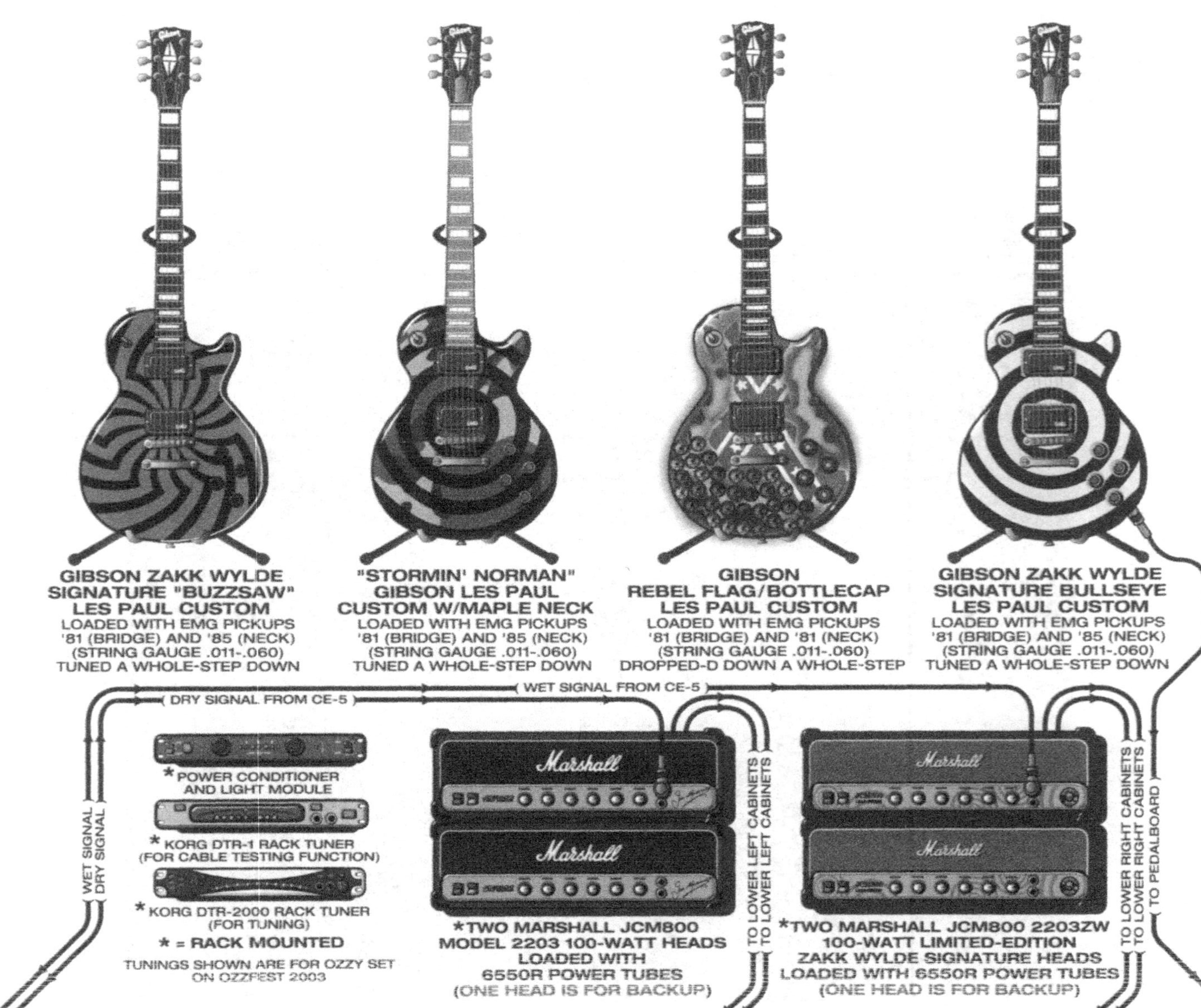

GIBSON ZAKK WYLDE SIGNATURE "BUZZSAW" LES PAUL CUSTOM
LOADED WITH EMG PICKUPS '81 (BRIDGE) AND '85 (NECK) (STRING GAUGE .011-.060) TUNED A WHOLE-STEP DOWN
"STORMIN' NORMAN" GIBSON LES PAUL CUSTOM W/MAPLE NECK
LOADED WITH EMG PICKUPS '81 (BRIDGE) AND '85 (NECK) (STRING GAUGE .011-.060) TUNED A WHOLE-STEP DOWN
GIBSON REBEL FLAG/BOTTLECAP LES PAUL CUSTOM
LOADED WITH EMG PICKUPS '81 (BRIDGE) AND '81 (NECK) (STRING GAUGE .011-.060) DROPPED-D DOWN A WHOLE-STEP
GIBSON ZAKK WYLDE SIGNATURE BULLSEYE LES PAUL CUSTOM
LOADED WITH EMG PICKUPS '81 (BRIDGE) AND '85 (NECK) (STRING GAUGE .011-.060) TUNED A WHOLE-STEP DOWN
WET SIGNAL FROM CE-5
DRY SIGNAL FROM CE-5
WET SIGNAL
DRY SIGNAL
*POWER CONDITIONER AND LIGHT MODULE
*KORG DTR-1 RACK TUNER (FOR CABLE TESTING FUNCTION)
*KORG DTR-2000 RACK TUNER (FOR TUNING)
* = RACK MOUNTED
TUNINGS SHOWN ARE FOR OZZY SET ON OZZFEST 2003
Marshall
Marshall
*TWO MARSHALL JCM800 MODEL 2203 100-WATT HEADS LOADED WITH 6550R POWER TUBES (ONE HEAD IS FOR BACKUP)
TO LOWER LEFT CABINETS
TO LOWER LEFT CABINETS
Marshall
Marshall
*TWO MARSHALL JCM800 2203ZW 100-WATT LIMITED-EDITION ZAKK WYLDE SIGNATURE HEADS LOADED WITH 6550R POWER TUBES (ONE HEAD IS FOR BACKUP)
TO LOWER RIGHT CABINETS
TO LOWER RIGHT CABINETS
TO PEDALBOARD

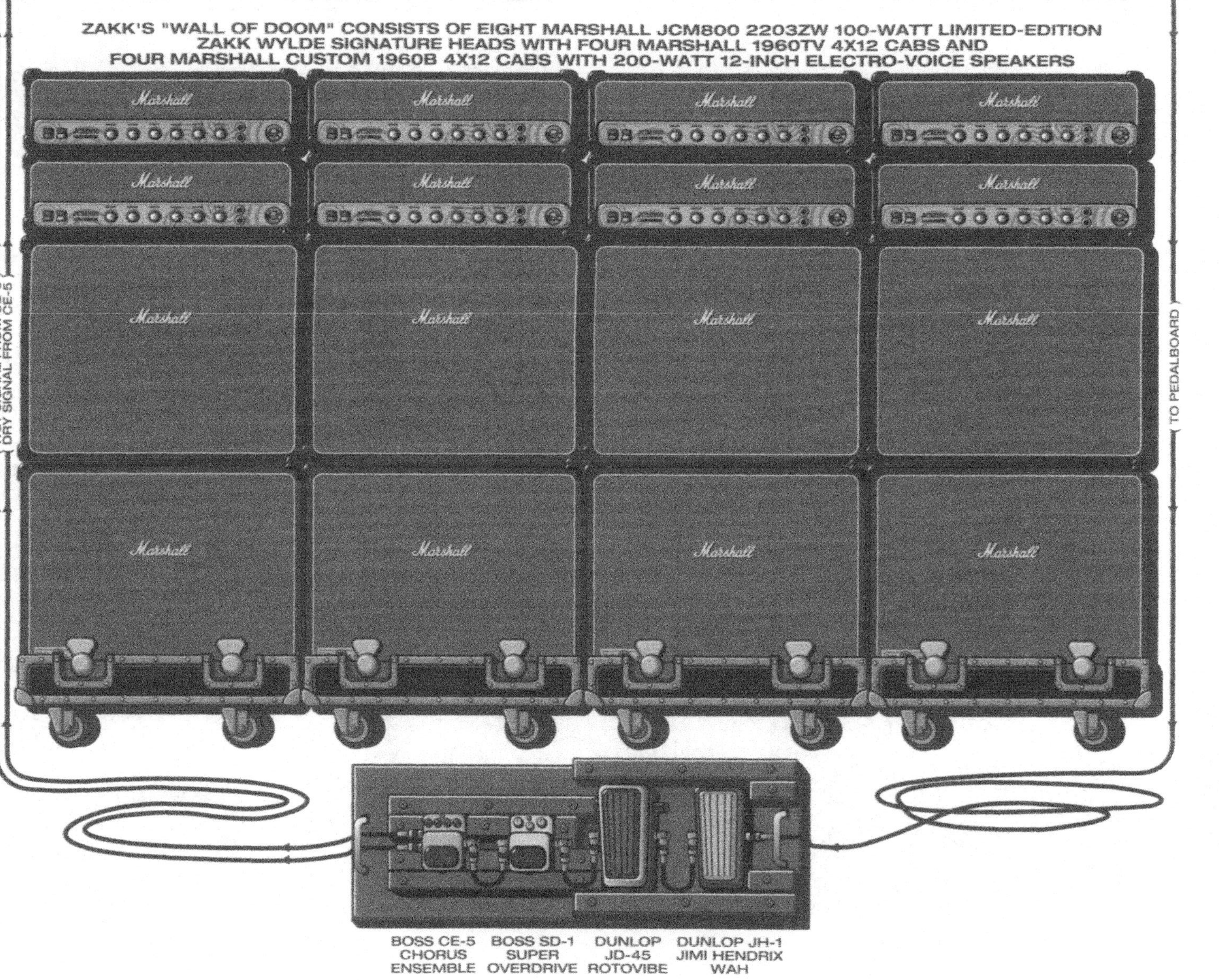
ZAKK'S "WALL OF DOOM" CONSISTS OF EIGHT MARSHALL JCM800 2203ZW 100-WATT LIMITED-EDITION
ZAKK WYLDE SIGNATURE HEADS WITH FOUR MARSHALL 1960TV 4X12 CABS AND
FOUR MARSHALL CUSTOM 1960B 4X12 CABS WITH 200-WATT 12-INCH ELECTRO-VOICE SPEAKERS
WET SIGNAL FROM CE-5
DRY SIGNAL FROM CE-5
TO PEDALBOARD
BOSS CE-5 CHORUS ENSEMBLE
BOSS SD-1 SUPER OVERDRIVE
DUNLOP JD-45 ROTOVIBE
DUNLOP JH-1 JIMI HENDRIX WAH

Dave Murray

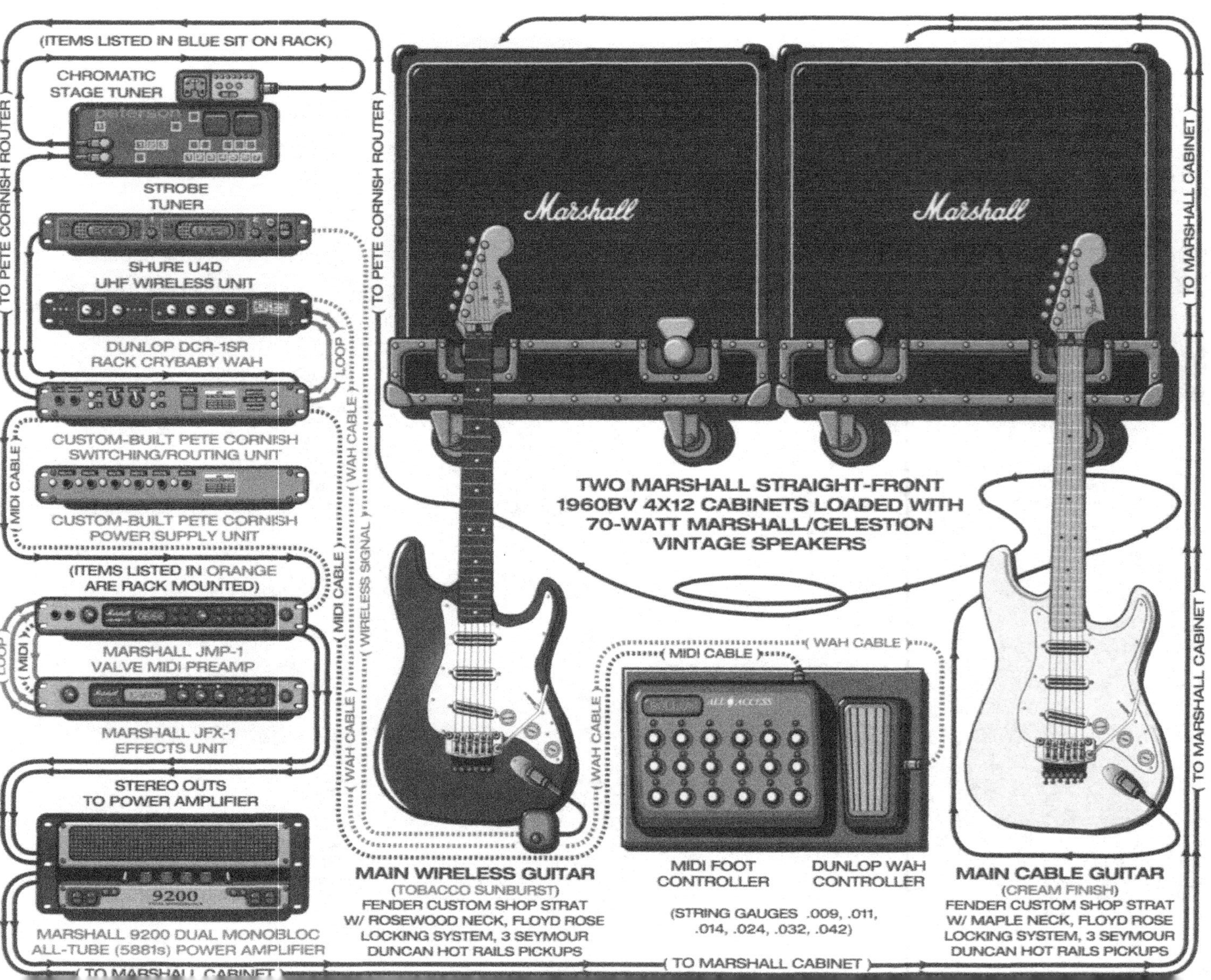

(ITEMS LISTED IN BLUE SIT ON RACK)
CHROMATIC STAGE TUNER
STROBE TUNER
SHURE U4D UHF WIRELESS UNIT
DUNLOP DCR-1SR RACK CRYBABY WAH
LOOP
CUSTOM-BUILT PETE CORNISH SWITCHING/ROUTING UNIT
MIDI CABLE
CUSTOM-BUILT PETE CORNISH POWER SUPPLY UNIT
(ITEMS LISTED IN ORANGE ARE RACK MOUNTED)
MARSHALL JMP-1 VALVE MIDI PREAMP
LOOP
MIDI
MARSHALL JFX-1 EFFECTS UNIT
STEREO OUTS TO POWER AMPLIFIER
MARSHALL 9200 DUAL MONOBLOC ALL-TUBE (5881s) POWER AMPLIFIER
TO PETE CORNISH ROUTER
TO PETE CORNISH ROUTER
WAH CABLE
MIDI CABLE
WIRELESS SIGNAL
WAH CABLE
TWO MARSHALL STRAIGHT-FRONT 1960BV 4X12 CABINETS LOADED WITH 70-WATT MARSHALL/CELESTION VINTAGE SPEAKERS
MIDI CABLE
WAH CABLE
WAH CABLE
MAIN WIRELESS GUITAR
(TOBACCO SUNBURST)
FENDER CUSTOM SHOP STRAT W/ ROSEWOOD NECK, FLOYD ROSE LOCKING SYSTEM, 3 SEYMOUR DUNCAN HOT RAILS PICKUPS
MIDI FOOT CONTROLLER
DUNLOP WAH CONTROLLER
(STRING GAUGES .009, .011, .014, .024, .032, .042)
MAIN CABLE GUITAR
(CREAM FINISH)
FENDER CUSTOM SHOP STRAT W/ MAPLE NECK, FLOYD ROSE LOCKING SYSTEM, 3 SEYMOUR DUNCAN HOT RAILS PICKUPS
TO MARSHALL CABINET
TO MARSHALL CABINET
TO MARSHALL CABINET
TO MARSHALL CABINET

Appendix

Dating by Serial Number

Unless your amplifier was built prior to 1969, identifying the date of manufacture should not be a difficult affair. For more than ten years Marshall serial numbers have contained dating information specific down to the week of manufacture. All through the '70s and '80s, serial numbers were month-specific. However, dating Marshall's earliest amps, including those of the heralded Plexi era, can be challenging.

The dating information that follows applies to the vast majority of production-model Marshall amplifiers. Some special-edition and limited-run amps present anomalies. Note that these dating systems apply only to amps and combos, not to speaker enclosures or other product lines.

1962–1964

The earliest Marshalls are the most difficult to date. An encyclopedic knowledge of early cosmetics—when various chassis styles, faceplates, logos, vinyls, and knobs were used—is necessary to narrow the possible date range to inside of a year. (In this respect, no reference is more helpful than Michael Doyle's *The History of Marshall.*)

There are no serial numbers at all on Marshall prototypes. The first production amps in 1962 and 1963 started at serial number 1001, with the number to be found on the back panel of the chassis. Some included a clear designation of model type by name (PA, Lead, Bass) as well.

In 1964 the first amp of the year carried the number 2001. Serial numbers followed sequentially, all led by the digit "2" for Marshall's second full year of production (2010 would indicate the 10th amplifier built in the second year).

1965–June 1969

The sparse dating scheme in place went AWOL in the Plexi years. With three separate subcontractors supplying Marshall's Plexi-panel chassis, no universal system governed serial numbering. Determining even a year of production is tricky; again, a knowledge of the history of the amps' cosmetics is helpful.

On the outside chance that the original speakers are still housed in a combo or speaker cabinet, they can be dated with reasonable accuracy by the codes of Celestion speakers. See the Celestion chart on page 250.

Model types were not designated on Marshall faceplates, but a code was instituted for identifying models. The code stood, with minor variations in 1969, for over two decades. See the codes in the next section to determine model type.

July 1969–September 1992

In mid '69 Marshall cemented its codes for models and adopted a formal letter code to designate production years. With a few exceptions, the newer model codes read as seen in the second column here.

Note: Inspection stickers, sometimes found on top of the chassis, will denote year, month, and even day of manufacture. But beware: It's rare to find genuine, undoctored stickers.

1965–June 1969 **Code**	July 1969–Sept. 1992 **Code**	**Denotes Model**
/A	A/	200-watt
SL/	SL/A	100-watt Super Lead
SB/	SB/A	100-watt Super Bass
SP/	SP/	Super PA
ST/	ST/A	100-watt Tremolo
S/	S/A	50-watt
T/	T/A	50-watt Tremolo
—	RI	Reissue

Code	Year	Code	Year
"—" indicates code letter was not used.			
A	1969–70	N	1981
B	—	O	—
C	1971	P	1982
D	1972	Q	—
E	1973	R	1983
F	1974	S	1984
G	1975	T	1985
H	1976	U	1986
I	—	V	1987
J	1977	W	1988
K	1978	X	1989
L	1979	Y	1990
M	1980	Z	1991–1992

From July 1969 to December 1983, these codes were combined with a serial number in this order: Model-Serial-Date

SL/A 12345 G: 100-watt Super Lead made in 1975

From January 1984 to October 1992, the serial and date positions were reversed: Model-Date-Serial

S/A T 12345: 50-watt made in 1985

December 1992–July 1997

At the end of 1992, Marshall amps changed to simple nine-digit serial codes. The year was represented in the first two digits; a sequential serial number followed in the next five digits; and the week of manufacture ended the code.

941234528: Amp #1234 was built in week 28 of 1994.

On some special-edition amps, or amps that were part of a package (denoted by "P"), the third character was a letter: 96P123420.

August 1997–Present

The current dating system is by far the most straightforward and informative. With amplifiers coming off the production line in four countries, the scheme even specifies factory of origin.

> **M-1999-31-1234-B:** Amp #1234 was built at Marshall's main factory in week 31 of 1999.

- The first letter denotes factory of origin:
  M = Marshall's main factory in Bletchley, Milton Keynes, England
  C = China
  K = Korea
  I = India
- The first four digits denote the year. (Note that from 1996 through 1998, some overseas manufacturers used a two-digit code instead.)
- The next two digits specify the week.
- The next four digits are the serial number.
- The letter at the end denotes voltage. Near the end of the production line, the bar code is automatically scanned and the power supply correctly set. The codes for voltage are as follows:
  A = 230v /50 Hz (UK)
  B = 120/60 (USA)
  C = 220/50 (Canada)
  D = 105/50/60 (Japan)
  E = 220/60 (Europe)
  F = 130/60 (Mexico)
  Z = no voltage (e.g., cabinets)

This detail of a plate from a 1962JAG shows it was manufactured in Bletchley during the second week of 2003.

Celestion Codes

Codes stamped on Celestion speakers can be helpful in dating early Marshall combos and extension speaker cabinets. Aside from the Celestion codes, Marshall cabs carried no dating clues until the practice of bar-coding products was introduced at Marshall in 1992. When it can be determined for a fact that a combo or cab houses its original speakers, Celestion codes reveal, within a reasonable margin, when an amp was produced.

The two-letter, two-digit codes are found either on the gasket (the metal ring around the mouth of the cone) or on the frame of Celestion speakers. Michael Doyle was the first to document Celestion's code for dating the speakers they produced from the mid 1950s (pre-Marshall) through the 1990s, and is owed a debt for the following information.

Months and years are both letter codes; a two-digit numeral denotes day of the month. In keeping with the written European style, the earlier Celestion codes logically appear in the order Day–Month–Year.

22 AH — 22 JANUARY 1963

The day of the month was switched to the end as of 1968:

CB 27 — MARCH 1969 27

The chart on page 250 represents only years of Celestion production relevant to Marshall (that is, 1962 onward). Note that Celestion, like Marshall after 1969, exempted the letters I and O to avoid confusion with the numbers one and zero.

Code	Month	(through 1967) Year	(1968 forward) Year
A	Jan		1968
B	Feb		1969
C	Mar		1970
D	Apr		1971
E	May		1972
F	Jun		1973
G	Jul	1962	1974
H	Aug	1963	1975
I	—	—	—
J	Sep	1964	1976
K	Oct	1965	1977
L	Nov	1966	1978
M	Dec	1967	1979
N			1980
O			—
P			1981
Q			1982
R			1983
S			1984
T			1985
U			1986
V			1987
W			1988
X			1989
Y			1990
Z			1991

About the Author

Rich Maloof is an editor, writer, musician, and former editor in chief of *Guitar* magazine whose work has appeared in numerous publications and Web sites. Co-author (with HP Newquist) of Backbeat Books' The Way They Play series, Maloof has also penned *Joe Satriani: Riff by Riff* and *The Alternate Tuning Reference Guide.* He has been playing guitar for more than 25 years. He lives in Brooklyn, NY.

Photo Credits

The photos in this book were provided courtesy of Marshall Amplification/Korg USA, with the exception of the following:

Nick Bowcott: pages 83, 129, and 232
Paul Hayhoe: pages 184–197
Rich Maloof: pages 16, 17, 19, 21, 31, 84, 85, 86, and 183
Gered Mankowitz/Starfile: page 50
Pictorial Press: page 55
©Norwood Price: page 70
Retna: page 58 (©Jorgen Angel) and 69 (©Neal Preston)
Ken Settle: page 67
Towcester: page 227 (Jim Marshall 40th Anniversary Handicap Hurdle Race)
Rich Watson, *The Music Trades*: page 231
Daron Young: page 6

Index

N

O

P

CPSIA information can be obtained
at www.ICGtesting.com
Printed in the USA
LVOW04*0616041217
558505LV00013BA/71/P

9 780879 308032

Chris,

Merry Christmas!

Love,

Donez & Mark

2017